FIRST CAME THE RUMBLE
FROM BLOCKS AWAY,

vibrating like thunder from an angry earth—
an impossible quake in sunny Miami. The
rumble became a roar and rattled eardrums as
the pointmen for a horde of Harley-Davidson
bikers heaved into view. Riding the hunks of
metal were burly guys wearing tattered jeans
and black leather jackets patched with skulls
and swastikas. Their massive arms bulged
with the combination of fat and muscle peculiar to beer-drinking fighters, and were tattooed with snakes, devils, and nasty images of
death. Behind them rode gangs of jackbooted
buddies, sometimes up to fifty at a time,
armed with chains, knives, and guns. Many
were vets who had learned how to kill in the
jungles of Vietnam and—with impressive rap
sheets for violence, drug-dealing, extortion,
and second-degree murder—could easily do
so now.

If you were driving, you'd better pull your
car onto a side street and pray they didn't follow. If you were standing on the sidewalk
you'd better disappear through a doorway.

WITHOUT A TRACE

THE DISAPPEARANCE OF AMY BILLIG—A MOTHER'S SEARCH FOR JUSTICE

GREG AUNAPU AND SUSAN BILLIG

AVON BOOKS
An Imprint of HarperCollinsPublishers

WITHOUT A TRACE is a journalistic account of the disappearance of Amy Billig in Coconut Grove, Florida, in 1974, and the investigation that followed. The events recounted in this book are true, although some of the names have been changed and identifying characteristics altered (where noted in the text) to safeguard the privacy of those individuals. The personalities, events, actions, and conversations portrayed in this book have been constructed using Susan Billig's contemporaneous personal notes, court documents, including trial transcripts, extensive interviews, letters, personal papers, research, and press accounts.

AVON BOOKS
An Imprint of HarperCollins*Publishers*
10 East 53rd Street
New York, New York 10022-5299

First Avon Books paperback printing: September 2001

Avon Trademark Reg. U.S. Pat. Off. and in Other Countries, Marca Registrada, Hecho en U.S.A.
HarperCollins ® is a trademark of HarperCollins Publishers Inc.

Printed in the U.S.A.

10 9 8 7 6 5 4 3 2 1

To Amy Billig

Acknowledgments

The authors wish to thank the many people who devoted their energy and compassion to the search for Amy over the years.

Thanks to law enforcement investigators around the country; detectives Ina Shepard and Jack Calvar of the Miami Police Department; Special Agent Harold Phipps of the FBI; and Miami-Dade Assistant State Attorneys Andy Hague (now Judge Hague) and Harold Rosen, whose efforts are detailed in these pages.

Thanks to the news organizations who kept the case in front of the public eye; the *Miami Herald* and its reporters, especially Edna Buchanan and Meg Laughlin, whose fine work over the years helped in the research of this book.

Susan Billig wishes to express her special appreciation to Judge Michael Samuels; Frank Rubino; Rex Ryland; and her family—especially her late husband, Ned; her son, Josh, and his wife, Michelle McGonigal—without whom she could not have endured.

Preface

As a freelance reporter for *Time* and *People* magazines
during the past decade, I have covered my share of
bizarre crimes and criminals. Yet, the strange disappearance of Amy Billig and the subsequent story of her
mother Susan's courageous search for her missing
daughter is one of the most compelling tales I've ever
heard—and one of the few stories that's ever made me
think, Somebody has to write a book about this!

Besides the high drama and unbelievable characters,
including one of the most twisted criminals I've ever
investigated, the case holds special interest to me because, unique from any other journalist who has reported on the case, I knew Amy. In 1973, when I first
met her, she was a vivacious, delightful sixteen, but,
alas, she was three years older than I was—decades
when you're that young.

My father had anchored our live-aboard schooner
off Key Biscayne, where we volunteered at the Dolphin Project, an organization which hoped to release
two captive dolphins back into the wild. Amy was also
a volunteer. She sang and played guitar and flute for

the dolphins, helped baby-sit them and feed them.

I used to live for those moments when she arrived because she was a genuine light, a charismatic, wonderful girl who seemed destined for great things. My memories might be the mere recollections of a boy with a crush on an "older woman" if so many other people, male and female, didn't remember Amy in the same way.

My mother and I then spent a year traveling in Central America. When we returned, Amy had disappeared. Her absence became a small void in the back of my mind which always gnawed at me. For her family, and for the village of Coconut Grove, where Amy had lived the best part of her life, the void was much greater—a wound that would stay unhealed until the mystery of her disappearance was solved.

In my mind, Sue and Amy's story is about much more than crime, mystery, and punishment. It's about courage, hope, and faith in the face of our darkest nightmares, taking place on the panoramic stage of the last quarter of our changing century.

I admire Sue Billig not just for her fortitude and courage, but simply for not losing faith in humanity and the universe. After the many permutations of evil that Sue has been subjected to, she is still the sweetest, most caring person I know. This book has been written with her complete support, and access to her personal diaries, audiotapes, and thoughts, much of which has never been divulged until now.

Greg Aunapu
Coconut Grove, Florida

1

March 5, 1974, was one of those pristine Florida days. The sky glowed with unknowable depths of blue, and sunlight dripped like honey through the branches of the grand old banyan trees that shaded the historic village of Coconut Grove. The Grove, a quaint neighborhood of boutiques, art galleries, and sidewalk cafés, was Miami's most popular hangout for tourists, artists, and musicians.

But 250 miles north, in Daytona Beach, Bike Week was scheduled to begin. All day long motorcycle clubs roared through town. Many had driven up from the Florida Keys, where they had followed the artery of A1A north across the mosaic waters and mangroves to the mainland. There, they had hooked up with Old Cutler Road, which ran past old coral rock estates and mango orchards—and finally through the heart of Coconut Grove.

First came their rumble from blocks away, vibrating like thunder from an angry earth—an impossible quake in sunny Miami. The rumble became a roar, rattling eardrums as the pointmen for a horde of Harley-

Davidson bikers heaved into view. Riding the hunks of metal were burly guys wearing tattered jeans and black leather jackets patched with skulls and swastikas. Their massive arms bulged with the combination of fat and muscle peculiar to beer-drinking fighters, and were tattooed with snakes, devils, and nasty images of death. Behind them rode gangs of jackbooted buddies, sometimes up to fifty at a time, armed with chains, knives, and guns. Many were vets who had learned to kill in the jungles of Vietnam, and, with impressive rap sheets for violence, drug dealing, extortion, and second degree murder, could easily do so now.

If you were driving, you'd better pull your car onto a side street and pray they didn't follow. If you were standing on the sidewalk, you'd better disappear through a doorway.

Paul Branch was nasty as they came. At six-two, he could hold his own in any barroom brawl. He had reddish hair, a short beard and mustache, fair skin, and tattoos running up both arms—half he couldn't remember getting. Some he had erased forever with battery acid, leaving scarred skin behind. He barreled along in the midst of a gang called the Pagans. A full-fledged member, his proper place was near the front of the second wave, but recently a few loudmouthed underlings had challenged him and his coveted position in the biker food chain. With his skin still showing a fresh jailhouse pallor, he rode under the lofty trees of Coconut Grove and wondered how he could add some green to the few grimy dollars in his pocket and maintain his power in the gang.

You had to be careful during Bike Week. If anything was going to happen, if anyone was going to pick a moment to stand up to you, cut you, take away your girl, your *face*, it would be there, all liquored up and full of shit. The pine forests around Daytona were littered with body parts. Yeah, Branch thought, it was time to do something drastic.

This particular day, with its blue skies, honey sun, and rumbling Harleys, should have been as innocuous as any, just an entry in the diaries of high school girls who had met a new guy, or a date on an old Miami newspaper found wrapped around glasses in an attic a few decades later, or someone's birthday. Instead, this day would be remembered forever by the Billig family.

Susan Billig recalls that it was a school day. "Just like any other day," she says. "Not the slightest ominous omen to warn us."

Her daughter Amy, seventeen, had stayed up late the previous evening at a friend's house to watch one of their group, a comedian, debut on a television show. She hadn't come home until three-twenty in the morning, which, understandably, provoked a small spat with her mother, who had been worried—especially since school started at eight A.M. Amy arrived late to breakfast and did not look too tired to begin a day at school. She had never been much of an early riser, anyway.

Amy preferred sunsets over sunrises, and often wrote poetry about that special time of day. She liked rain and rainbows, shade and trees and the freedom of birds, and the blue of that day's sky.

I am enjoying the most wondrous
  fresh, clean lovely rain
It brings out the earthy smell
  in the plants and trees.
I love it!
More! More!
The flowers are so thirsty these days,
  and the birds and possums.
Rain is especially pretty
  when the sun is shining and
The drops of water sparkle on the leaves
And blades of grass and petals of flowers.
Happy rain
Life rain
Feels so good on my skin.

                                        —Amy

She was five-five, 102 pounds, with luxurious dark hair and long, lanky legs. Her cherubic, oval face, combined with dark mischievous, almond eyes and an easy smile, caused dozens of whiplash cases on any given day. Amy planned to spend the summer in Manhattan—after she graduated from her private high-school—where she would visit a friend who played in the hit Broadway show *Hair*, and perhaps determine if she should attend drama school.

Amy already played the guitar and was a classically trained flutist. She loved Judy Collins and Joni Mitchell and had cultivated her own folksy sound. She played for friends and for the two dolphins, Florida and Liberty, at the Dolphin Project, where she volunteered as often as she could. The dolphins had once been part of a scientific research project and now were being taught to survive again in the wild. Amy could swear the dolphins listened and reacted to her when she sang. She'd miss the carefree sea creatures and the great group of people there once the dolphins were given their freedom.

> *Last night*
> *Dolphin Project*
> *Red sun going down into the ocean horizon*
> *While a beautiful full moon*
> *With a yellow haze around it*
> *Crept up into the night sky*
> *Guitar riffs*
> *Friends*
> *Mosquitoes everywhere*
> *Fine time*
>
> —*Amy*

Amy inherited her musical talent from her parents. The family—Ned and Sue, Amy, and younger brother Josh—had moved to Coconut Grove from New York to "get away from all the crime." In Manhattan, Ned, a WWII vet with a Purple Heart, was a well-known trumpet player who played in smoky Greenwich Village nightclubs. Sue was an accomplished singer who had met Ned on a gig. Sue's father had been a concert pianist.

Amy was Ned and Sue's "miracle child," who blessed the couple after ten years and five miscarriages. Josh followed a year later. On a trip through Coconut Grove in 1968, Sue remembers, "I just fell in love with the place. The art galleries, the cafés. The trees, the peace. I called Ned back in New York and said, 'Honey, we're moving here.' "

Ned and Sue easily created a niche for themselves in the Grove. Ned opened a popular art gallery, Dimensions; Sue made a good living in interior design; and they soon collected a large group of friends in a town where most people knew each other intimately.

Amy fell in love with the place, too. In a letter to a friend she wrote: *New York is so ugly. Let me show you some of the prettiness of Coconut Grove. Old stone houses and fruit trees and blue waters and sunsets that will blow you away.*

Still, Sue thinks that Amy, graced with an intelligence, wisdom, and maturity beyond her years, "always missed the city—the museums, the theater, and the intellectual stimulation of city people. She was really looking forward to attending university up there."

This was a strange time for our country balancing on the cusp of a new order: Society reverberated with echoes of disgrace after the Vietnam War; the Watergate scandal was making voters view their political leaders with a newly jaundiced eye; and Patty Hearst, heiress to one of the most American of families, had been kidnapped by revolutionaries. Yet despite such events that would reshape the way citizens perceived their country and the world, it was still a much more innocent and altruistic time.

Murders and rapes were rare in Miami, especially in artsy, upscale Coconut Grove, where the Billigs never locked their door, habitually left the keys to their '54

Bentley in the car, and kids parked their bikes in front of the house. The Arab oil embargo was front page news, provoking quotas and long lines at gas pumps, so people often tried to ride together. Amy, and many others, never thought twice about hitchhiking. It was not only an accepted mode of transportation, it was actually a way you met new people. Many Europeans were still sightseeing America that way. While Sue often begged Amy not to hitchhike, the teenager was convinced that your life was just a reflection of your own attitude. If she saw only good in people, nobody would harm her.

That morning, Amy ate lightly—just some toast with jam and a glass of orange juice—before hurrying off to school. Her horoscope said she should watch her finances. Ziggy was in traction in the hospital, and Charlie Brown was worried about his father's golf game.

"Love you," Sue called as her lively daughter exited, making up with her for their early morning tiff. "Love you, too," Amy replied, never one to hold the slightest grudge. She pranced down the walkway with her particular high-gaited, skipping step to catch the bus to school.

It was a lovely day. At noon Sue and a friend took off to their favorite nearby lagoon, Tahiti Beach, to enjoy the sun.

About ten minutes after Sue left the house, Amy arrived home—driven from school by a friend—ate half a container of yogurt and made plans to meet some friends for lunch in the Grove's Peacock Park—where people often gathered to play music, and the Krishnas served free food every Sunday.

Amy called her father at the Dimensions Art Gallery.

"Dad, can I borrow a couple dollars for lunch?" she asked. "I'm supposed to meet Kirk and Cathy in the park, but I don't have a cent!"

"Sure, no problem," Ned replied.

There was nothing unusual about the request. The gallery was only a mile away in the village center, an easy walk down shady but well-traveled streets. It was a trip that Amy had made hundreds of times.

But something unusual happened this day. At the crossroads of Main Highway and Poinciana Street, near where the family lived, Amy, already a little late for her lunch date, stuck out her thumb as she walked toward town. A group of construction workers building a house on the corner—whom Amy always greeted—remembered her walk by wearing a blue miniskirt and platform sandals.

The throaty rumble of Harleys swept through the sleepy village—Pagans and Outlaws, rival gangs—running five abreast across the center of the road on their long "chopper" style bikes, "old ladies" or "bitches" clinging to their backs.

The Outlaws wore black leather jackets sporting their "colors," called "Charlie," modeled after Marlon Brando's jacket in *The Wild One*. Stitched across the jackets were diamond-shaped patches commemorating their dead "brothers."

The Pagans' colors featured a Norse fire god with

the letters MC, which stood for Motorcycle Club, and patches with the letters PFFP, for "Pagans Forever, Forever Pagans."

During the day, several groups thundered through town, where they would meet at the Grove's Dinner Key Marina before blasting northward in a mighty brigade toward the hellish time known as Bike Week in Daytona.

The mid-seventies was the heyday for bikers, a decade before many groups were decimated by prosecutors wielding RICO (Racketeer Influenced and Corrupt Organizations) laws originally codified to conquer organized crime. The three main bike groups had divided the country like the Mafia had once done before them. The most famous, the Hell's Angels, were centered in California and the West Coast up to Alaska.

Florida was mostly Outlaw territory. But the Pagans, with a few clubhouses across the state—and undisputed control of Virginia, the Carolinas, Pennsylvania, and New Jersey—were tolerated in the Sunshine State, so that Outlaws, in turn, would be allowed unrestricted passage to their territories in Canada.

Altogether, the clubs were making millions of dollars. They rented themselves out as muscle to the Mafia, manufactured and sold "crystal meth," an amphetamine, and ran drugs and guns from one place to another. Women were owned, bought, and sold like objects, traded for credit cards or a bike, often forced into prostitution or to dance in strip clubs to earn money for the men.

Most bikers boasted long rap sheets. A new recruit spent a year as an underling, an "associate," before becoming a full-fledged member. To graduate, a major crime such as murder was often committed, which made it difficult for law enforcement to infiltrate the gangs.

Still, despite the drugs, alcohol, and crime, bikers were often highly intelligent. Though many were high school dropouts, others were sharp, educated men who just couldn't handle boring society. Big Jim Nolan, the Outlaws' president, had been valedictorian of his high school. Others were savvy, experienced Vietnam veterans who weren't about to take crap from some twit in a pin-striped suit. It was a wayward and appealing life for many people who couldn't fit into square society. In many ways, bikers were both feared and admired by regular guys for flouting authority. Even celebrities like Willie Nelson, the Grateful Dead's Jerry Garcia, and the Rolling Stones hung out with bikers. Gonzo journalist Hunter S. Thompson hooked up with the Hell's Angels in the mid-sixties and wrote a book about it before he started annoying them and they "stomped him good."

Today, many of the nine million weekend Harley enthusiasts, or Hog riders—chiropractors, surgeons, builders, waiters, psychologists, and thousands of others—are scoffed at by real bikers as "Rolex Riders" or "Weekend Warriors." The fakers shave their heads or grow long hair, sport mustaches, and don sweaty black leather clothes and chains to appear their menacing best when they roar through towns across America. In Coconut Grove they line up their pristine, $20,000 to $40,000 bikes curbside to be appreciated by the fawning masses as their daring, muffler-challenged owners sip cappuccinos at sidewalk cafés. But real bikers scoff at these guys. Outlaw bikers, traditionally considered only one percent of the total rider population, call themselves "One Percenters," and if you have that mark tattooed on your hand, *you damn well better be one*.

On that pristine March 5, Paul Branch and his friends roaring through the Grove were definitely not Rolex Riders.

Sue returned home in the late afternoon. She had left the house at twelve noon. According to Ned, Amy had called at twelve-ten, which meant she had only missed her daughter by a scant few minutes.

"She was supposed to come by to pick up a couple dollars," Ned said. "She must not have needed it."

Amy had earned confidence and freedom from her parents because she was responsible. She was allowed to stay out late and do what she chose because she always got her homework done, and always, always called home to check in. By evening Sue was nervous. No member of the family ever missed a meal without calling.

After Ned arrived home, the Billigs phoned a Miami police detective friend, Mike Gonzalez, at eight P.M. Gonzalez visited on his way home from work and questioned Josh about Amy. Was there any possibility the boy's sister could have run away?

"Never," sixteen-year-old Josh replied.

Sue agreed. "We're the kind of family that other kids run away to," she observed.

The family had always gotten along well. Amy,

seeming older than her years, often sat back and
watched the internal dynamics with amusement, as if
each person had been given roles to act out in this life.
In the next reincarnation, maybe everything would be
reversed.

> *Parents are funny sometimes*
> *they want to be my friends*
> *and we are—open and honest,*
> *but sometimes, I have to let*
> *them do their parent trip too,*
> *I guess*
> *it's only fair—but it's hard to explain*
> *to them, that basically we are*
> *only human beings*
> *not parents and children*
> *and being treated as such is where*
> *it's at.*
> *I am Amy and you are Ned and Sue and*
> *we can really get it on, if you just*
> *let it happen.*
>
> *   —Amy*

Gonzalez knew that more than ninety-nine percent
of children who are reported missing have only missed
a telephone call and show up again on their own. His
voice was calm. "She's probably just out with friends,"
he assured the frantic couple. "Don't panic. Call again
if Amy isn't home by morning.'
Sue spent all night worrying. She finally tracked
down Amy's friend Cathy on the phone. "Tell her I'm

mad at her," Cathy complained. "She stood us up for lunch, and she's got my shoes from last night to boot."

After spending a fretful, sleepless evening, Susan could take it no longer. At six A.M., she called Mike Gonzalez. "I am now panicking," Sue wept. "Amy is missing!"

Still, it was a more innocent time, and despite Gonzalez's friendship, the police considered Amy a low priority—probably a runaway. Sue assured them over and over again that Amy would never do such a thing. Her daughter wouldn't have run away because she didn't have to. She was a good girl who was looking forward to graduating high school in two weeks.

Even today Sue shudders at the trauma of those first days. "I can't imagine any personal disaster worse than having your child just simply disappear. No note, no body . . . just gone. Any time I see a family on the news going through something like this, it just tears my heart out. I was afraid. I felt she might be starving, sick, or hurt. . . . In that one moment when we realized she was gone, our lives changed forever."

Sue would stare into the night and conjure up Amy's face, see her daughter's smile, try to hear her voice, try to reach out with her mind to grope for Amy's presence somewhere out in the darkness and ask, "Where are you? Come home, sweetheart. Please, just come home safe!"

She spoke to the universe, offering Faustian bargains, anything and everything, just to see her daughter bounce through the front door with an embarrassed,

"Sorry I caused so much trouble" expression on her face.

The police made promises, but little more, assuring the Billigs that Amy would soon turn up.

Even the weather had changed its temperament. Gone was the glorious sun, giving way to depressing sheets of steady rain.

In desperation, Sue and Ned turned to friends, who scoured the neighborhood and posted signs with Amy's photograph on telephone poles. They beat the bushes—the Grove being heavily foliated—looking for an injured body. Nerves were frayed, as only one week earlier a woman had been hit by a car and found in the brush.

Josh hunted up and down the streets that he and Amy had walked together just days ago. "I was so scared, but I forced myself to look into every bush, praying I wouldn't find her," he says.

While a missing child would be front page news in almost any community now, it took nearly a week, until March 10, for the story to hit the local papers: the *Miami News* and the *Miami Herald*. The *Herald* buried the story on page six of the local section: GROVE 17-YEAR-OLD MAY BE KIDNAPPING VICTIM, POLICE SAY.

A benefit concert by popular Grove musicians raised $850, which seeded an expense fund started at the local Coconut Grove Bank. A $1,000 award was advertised in the local media. It doesn't sound like much money now, but at the time a brand new 1974 Mustang sold for $2,800.

Soon, tips began coming in. One caller insisted he

had seen Amy riding in a green Jeep. Another said he had seen her get into a white van. Green Jeeps were hunted all over the city. One poor guy, a friend of the family, owned such a vehicle in the Grove. Over fifty calls about him were made to police.

Sue and Ned contacted a private investigator, Frank Rubino, a former Secret Service agent, to aid in the search. The family pleaded with the FBI to get involved, but without real evidence that Amy had been kidnapped, and no formal request from local police to lend a hand, the agency could do little.

While Sue remained unconvinced that Amy had run away, she called friends across the country to keep a lookout for her in case she showed up somewhere.

Ned looked steady on the outside, calm and orderly, answering the phone with a voice now often steadied by alcohol. Inside he was Jell-O, praying every time the phone rang that it would bring happy news. Sue, a nervous wreck, stared out the window all night. When she would descend into some kind of unconsciousness, nightmares flung themselves at her. She told friends, "I keep seeing Amy outside in the rain, cold. She says, 'Mama, I need you!' "

On March 16 the phone rang. A friend, Toby, now staying at the house, took the call.

"Hello, Mr. Billig?" came a mature female voice.

"Who's calling, please?"

The person seemed unsure of her own identity. "Ah, this is . . . Susan Johnson."

"Susan, can I help you?"

"Yes, I saw Amy's mother in the Grove . . . with a poster . . ."

"Right," Toby said.

"Of course, Johnson isn't my real name, because I'm afraid. But I want to tell you what I know." The person sounded apologetic.

Toby had heard this type of call before. So many tips and false leads were coming in that the police had brought in a tape machine to record the messages. "Okay, fine," he said stoically, no change in his voice.

"A friend of mine went up to Daytona, where they had the motorcycle races last week. And a motorcycle gang was there. Now . . . they have her! They picked her up hitchhiking and she's being held against her will . . ."

"Are you sure about this?" Toby insisted.

The woman sounded tired, expended, as if she had been worrying about whether to make this call for a while. "I'm positive. I swear on my daughter's life," she replied.

"Okay, now what is the name of this gang?"

"The Outlaw motorcycle gang."

"All right now, listen, Susan, I know you're afraid . . ."

"Yeah . . ."

". . . but you're going to have to talk to someone besides me. Would you call this number back? You don't have to say who you are. There are no tracers or anything on the line."

"Okay."

"But are you a hundred percent positive of this?"

For the first time, this seemed like a real lead. The biker gangs that had swept through the Grove the day of Amy's disappearance were still fresh in everybody's mind.

"I'm a hundred percent positive."

"Do you know Amy?"

"No, I don't know her, but I know the person who told me and saw her with them. They are holding her against her will. They have another girl also."

Toby became agitated. It just sounded too real, much different than the other calls. The woman agreed to call back in an hour.

This time Ned answered the phone, picking up "Su-ann Johnson's" call. Ned had a low smoky voice with a New York accent.

"This is Amy's father," he assured the caller. "I'm Ned. And I'd really appreciate it if you'd do me one favor. You don't have to give your name. But there's a friend of ours who's handling this thing and he would like to hear it from you and find out what's going down so he can try to follow it up."

Johnson agreed.

Ned gave her Mike Gonzalez's phone number at the Miami police station. Ned assured her, "He's a friend who's been helping us—because he's a groovy friend." He explained that there was a $1,000 reward. "That's yours, too, and don't forget it."

Johnson's credibility rose a notch when her tired voice replied, "Really, I'm telling you the truth that I know is true. I don't care about the money. I just want you to have your daughter back."

Ned's voice softened. "Thank you, sweetheart . . ."

Gonzalez was optimistic when he phoned the house after he had spoken with the caller.

"This Susan Johnson did call me, as incredible as that may seem. She was worried that I would trace the call. But she wasn't able to tell me any more. Still, she sounds sincere, and like she believes it—in her present state of mind, anyway. While it's vague, she promises to go back to her friend and get some more information. They're supposed to be camped out around Titusville. . . ." Here the information became ominous. "The two girls are being held for white slavery . . . and he recognized the picture of Amy as being one of the girls."

Gonzalez relayed the information to the Titusville police, and the family crossed their collective fingers. The story had a ring of truth, and was corroborated by what the police knew about the Outlaws and their recent movements. They had blazed through the Grove, and they were known to kidnap and sell women. Amy would have been quite a prize.

The biker connection soon intensified as the couple received its first real evidence. A man named David Flemming called. He had found a camera with Amy's name on it at the Wildwood off-ramp of Florida's Turnpike. His mother actually lived in the Grove and had recognized the name on the camera. Wildwood was a small town on the turnpike just north of Orlando. Interestingly, it was on the prime route that a bike gang would take traveling north to any of the interior states from Daytona.

Flemming hand-delivered the evidence to the Billig house. No one could remember the last time they had seen the cheap plastic camera. It may have disappeared before Amy had for all they knew. There were four exposed photographs on the cartridge of slide film.

Had Amy flung it there as a clue? Had a kidnapper thrown it away as incriminating evidence? Stranger still, the camera was found on the southbound side of the road. If the bikers were headed north, which authorities noted, then why find the camera on the southbound side of the road?

Like so many events tied to this case, what happened next was an absurd comedy—which in turn led to more clues. No one with a car was available except one teenager from out of town, the brother of a friend. The only lab that could develop the slide film that afternoon was several miles away. On the way to the shop, the teenager was stopped by an officer for making an illegal left-hand turn. The boy, driving with an out-of-state license was arrested. He called Sue an hour later from jail.

Sue called a bail bondsman to spring the kid from jail. The bondsman, Joe Klein, listened to the story and informed Sue that he was a bondsman for the Outlaws. He vowed to get a couple of bikers to pay Sue a visit the next evening.

"They owe me," Klein said. "They'll come."

When Sue picked up the developed film the following afternoon, she broke open the envelope with shaking hands and prayed, "Oh, God, please give us a

clue!" Holding each slide up to the light was a crushing disappointment. Three slides were completely
overexposed. The fourth showed a wall with vines
growing up it. A white pickup truck was parked in the
background.

She began weeping and threw herself into Ned's
arms.

Dozens of people were coming in and out of the
house—friends, helpers, and media. So many, in fact,
that Sue forgot the bikers were scheduled to stop by the
following evening.

Sue opened the door and was shocked. Two bikers
were standing there, each well over six feet tall. One
was over 300 pounds. Her first words were, "My God,
you're huge!" Her heart jumped into overdrive, pounding in her chest.

The hefty biker shook his head. "Lady, if you think
we're big, you should see our friends. You gonna let us
in, or what?"

"Oh . . . y-yes, come in, please," Sue stuttered, her
mouth going dry. When she had imagined the bikers,
she thought back to handsome Marlon Brando and the
film *The Wild One*. "These guys made *The Wild One*
look like innocent babies," she remembers.

The two entered, looked disdainfully at the crowd,
and asked, "Got a private room?"

Sue ushered the bikers into the den, following them
on weak legs.

The two men wore crusty, oily old jeans with knees
showing through holes. When they turned around, she
saw big switchblades poking from their back pockets.

Over sweaty T-shirts sporting the Harley-Davidson logo they wore black jackets that read OUTLAWS across the back. Their feet were encased in muddy black boots with steel toes. Once a biker donned the biker jacket, it was never supposed to be washed again, so they got pretty nasty.

Sue asked if her friend, *Miami News* reporter Ann Friedman, could sit in on the conversation. "Fine with us," they agreed.

The bikers sat on a couch, making it squeak under their weight. One, with long tangled hair and wearing a huge Star of David, introduced himself in a New York accent as Sid Fast. The other wore a big gold cross and called himself "Greek."

Sue wanted to faint, thinking that bikers like these might have her daughter. She tried to loosen herself up with some small talk. "You have a New York accent," she said. "We have some friends named Fast in . . ." She named a town.

Sid brightened. "I know them. They're distant relatives of mine."

"No!"

"I'm not kiddin', lady," Sid said. "They're cousins. How 'bout that?"

Sue was amazed. "A Jewish Outlaw?"

Sid laughed. "What'll they think of next, hey? So tell us why we're here."

Sue told them about Amy and the call from Susan Johnson, explaining that her daughter had been abducted by Outlaws.

Sid shook his head and turned to his friend. "You hear of anybody taking a girl down here, Greek?"

"Whadda I look like, a narc?" Greek shot back in disgust. "Girls come and they go."

Sid shrugged and turned back to Sue. "Would Amy get on a bike?" he asked.

Sue sighed. "I don't know. I can't *see* her getting on one. But she *might*, if she thought she recognized one of her freaky friends from the Grove. She's very sweet and trusting. She always says mosquitoes don't bite her because they know she loves them. She would never think someone would harm her. She might go for a lark . . . for a ten minute ride . . . if the guy said he'd get her to her appointment on time. Do you think she could have gotten on the bike and then been taken forcibly?"

"Of course," Sid told her. "Bikers take chicks that way all the time. They tie 'em up to the bike . . . or hold them on the seat in front. You get some brothers to ride on the sides . . . no one would ever know."

"And this happens a lot?" Friedman asked.

"Listen, we get chicks in all sorts of ways. But usually they come of their own accord. Or they come to a party and get high . . . we keep 'em doped up and the whole gang bangs 'em. It's like an initiation. After they get hooked to the drugs and sex, they're pretty much ours forever."

Sue patted him on the knee. "Don't tell me any more. My daughter isn't a nun, but she's a real nice, sweet girl. I can't think of her like that."

The anguish and love in Sue's voice hit a chord with Sid. His eyes softened. "Listen, I feel for you, but I really haven't heard anything about a new girl. Tomorrow night, though, there's a big meeting up in Lauderdale. All the brothers will be there. You seem like a nice lady, and if you're friends of Joe's, that's enough for us. We'll give the message to Big Jim—he's the president. If Amy's in the Outlaw nation, we'll get her back for you."

"Oh, please," Sue said. "Please . . . There's a thousand dollars in it," she reminded them.

Sid rose heavily to his feet and passed gas. "We don't want the money," he said. "But some of the guys might."

Frank Rubino knocked on the door and entered. He wanted to get more details about how women were inducted into the group and turned into sex slaves, hookers, and strippers.

Sue went to fetch beer to get out of the room. But when she came back they talked about other things, such as Richard Nixon and his Watergate problems. Once during the conversation she even joked, "What does your mama think of you, a Jewish biker?"

"I make more money than my cousin, the doctor," Sid said, "I get better drugs and more pussy than any Jew outside of Bob Dylan. I'm sure she's quite proud. Now one thing we gotta get straight. You gotta keep the Man completely outta this."

Sue assured them, "I swear I won't prosecute. I don't like what you do, but it's not for me to judge. I just want my daughter back."

Sue followed the two men to the door. There was an old rusted van outside. Bikers didn't always ride bikes, apparently. "What if it's not the Outlaws?" Sue asked. "What if the Pagans took her?"

Sid grabbed Sue's shoulders with his big grease-smeared hands. "Sue," he said. "If it's humanly possible to get Amy back, we will. You got our word on it."

Sue felt so relieved she actually hugged the renegade and kissed him on the cheek. A few days ago she wouldn't have touched anyone like him. Now she was investing all her hope in Sid Fast.

The two men lumbered into the van. Greek climbed behind the wheel, turned the ignition, and steered the coughing van down the street, which sounded almost as loud as a Harley.

After they were gone, Sue turned to Frank. "This is like a bad movie," she said. "Who would believe it?" Then the enormity of it hit her. "They can't have Amy! They can't! Not men like those . . . not like those."

She remembered Sid saying, "Lady, you think we're bad? You should see our brothers."

Friedman's story about the possible Outlaw connection appeared in the newspaper the next morning. After that the phone never stopped. Each time it rang, Sue or Ned prayed it brought news of Amy. Over fifty calls came from psychics. "I see her near water," they would usually say. Rubino shook his head and explained, "They always say that. We're surrounded by water."

But the calls kept coming. "She's scared. She got on a bike voluntarily, but when she wanted to leave, they wouldn't let her," one caller said. "I think she's been taken West." Still another famed psychic claimed that for $5,000 he could definitely pinpoint where Amy was. Sue didn't believe a word of it. Opportunists were attracted to the case like parasites to an open wound.

The AP wire finally picked up the story, and old friends started calling from around the nation. Old ladies would call to give support and just break down crying. "I just want you to know, a group of us is praying for you."

Ned was always appreciative. "Thank you, sweetheart," he would say. "That's really, really groovy of you. Thanks so much for calling." His voice became more tired as time passed, but he was always sincere.

Sue couldn't eat and quickly dropped fifteen pounds. Friends were so worried they had a doctor come by and administer B-12 shots.

"You have to eat," Ned pleaded.

"Nothing stays down," she told him. "I just vomit it up. If only Sid would call back. I just see her being passed around from biker to biker, and it's driving me crazy."

Two days after Sid and Greek rode off in the van, Sue finally received the call she was waiting for.

"It's Joe Klein," the caller said.

Sue, who had been weeping for days, felt a surge of adrenaline hit her. "Tell me!"

"She's in Venice Beach, California," the bondsman said.

Sue was confused. "Are you sure? How'd she get out there?"

Joe's voice was hesitant. "Big Jim says she drove

out there with a biker, but now she's on her own. It's your ball from here."

The Billigs called Venice Beach police and Ned's sister, who lived nearby. Both scoured the small town, famous for its community of beach-camping run-aways, and it quickly became apparent that the Outlaws' information was bogus—perhaps even purposefully seasoned misinformation. Sue was in tears. What did that mean? The Outlaws had Amy but weren't giving her back? They didn't have Amy? They had already harmed her? She was dead? Could Friedman's news article have spooked them? What did it mean?

The Billigs' home was a large wooden cottage built in the shade of one of the Grove's most massive banyan trees, which had twisting roots growing from its limbs, trailing to the ground, where they would turn into addi-tional trunks. The house was furnished with antique wooden and white wicker furniture, ornately carved ar-moires and chests. The walls were decorated with orig-inal paintings from some of the famous artists whom the Billigs had known in Greenwich Village, such as David Levine, and Aaron Shikler, well-known for his portrait paintings of the Kennedys.

During a few minutes of calm amidst the normal pandemonium, Sue sat on the couch with an old family friend, Joe Adler—a local theater director—and con-fided what she hadn't even admitted to herself before. "Even if we found out she was dead ... I would mourn, and I would never be the same. But it would be finished. I would know. I've never said this before, but

I would know where she is. It's the thought that when it rains I think she's outside and it's raining on her. When it's cold I want to comfort her. She's lying somewhere and nobody is helping her. She's being hurt. . . . When the bikers told me what they did to girls—they call them trainees—I was horrified, and Sid saw it. I turned around and said, 'Sid I really can't take violence because I'm projecting my own daughter into this scene, and if you had a daughter you'd feel the same way I do.' So he didn't talk about it anymore."

Adler took Sue's hand. He was very worried about his friend, who had lost so many pounds but supported the weight of the world on her shoulders. Always a beautiful woman, Sue had aged years in the last weeks. "You have to start taking care of yourself, dear," he said. "If you lose your vitality, the whole damn thing's going to fall apart. I mean, you have to keep coming up with ideas. You have to get out of the house. You should definitely have come to Kathy's birthday last night."

Sue shook her head. "Would you leave the house if your daughter was kidnapped? Absolutely not." But as always, Sue was more concerned about other people than herself. "I didn't want to hurt anybody. I was afraid of even sending presents because I was afraid it would put a pall on the party. I have to think of my friends. They love me and are trying to help me. I don't want to hurt them."

Joe nodded. "Yeah, I understand."

Sue sniffled and held back another wave of tears.

She closed her eyes and let Amy's face come to her. Moments later she felt a sort of vibration coursing through her blood.

"Suddenly, you look a little better," Joe said. "There's color in your face."

Sue took a deep breath. "I don't know what it is. Every time I think I'm down for the count, I think of my child and suddenly there's a kind of energy that happens. I've operated all my life at an unbelievable energy. But this is something different."

Joe didn't want to respond. Maybe it was energy from God, he thought, giving Sue what she needed to keep moving on. Or maybe it was just desperation.

However, before any of this information could be digested, sifted, and contemplated . . . before the Outlaws could be brought in for questioning by authorities . . . came another fateful phone call.

2

On the strength of the Outlaw tip and the fact that the bikers had apparently crossed state lines, Sue spent a day downtown and convinced the FBI to look into the case. It was a grueling day of arguing her cause, made worse by lack of sleep. She was exhausted, but still answered the phone no matter what because she always had to be doing something, anything, to advance the investigation.

When the phone rang at nine A.M., it wasn't the first time it had rung that morning. Usually the calls were from northern friends who had just heard the news. Sometimes it was one of the myriad sympathetic women who called to say they were praying for the family. The most frustrating were well-intentioned callers with outrageous tips: Amy was working as a waitress in Jamaica; Amy was living on a sailboat anchored out in Biscayne Bay; or worst of all, she was turning tricks at a Miami hotel.

Sue was trying to get breakfast together for half a dozen people who had camped out at the house when the newest call came.

"Hello?" she answered, a little breathless, always hoping that this would be *the* call.

The voice on the line was male, young, businesslike, and courteous. "Hello, may I speak to Mrs. Billig, please?"

"Speaking."

The voice continued as calmly as if it were ordering a pizza. "Okay, now listen. We have some news about Amy. The Outlaws don't have her."

Sue dropped the washcloth she was holding and picked up the pen that was always by the phone. "Who is this, please?"

"Now, listen to me," the voice persisted. "She's fine. She's getting over a sore throat. Now, listen to me. We're going to have her speak to you at 2:45."

Sue was incredulous, her voice imbued with hope and fear. "At 2:45?"

"This isn't a joke. We don't want you thinking this is a joke. . . . We'll kill her if we have to." The voice became harder and more insistent. "This is *not* a joke. We will kill her—"

"Oh, please don't!" Sue cried.

"Our demands are threefold."

Sue took a breath and prepared to write down his instructions. "Okay, go ahead."

"First there's the money. We're going to need a *small* amount—$30,000."

Sue gasped. "That's small?"

"We're going to have her call you at 2:45. She'll speak to you then. This is to prove it isn't a joke. Now listen to me—don't tell the newspapers or we'll kill her."

"Of course not!"

"We hope you're cooperative. We'll have her speak to you at 2:45. She's fine," he emphasized. "Okay?"

Sue broke down crying. "Yessss . . . pleaasssee!"

"Okay," said the voice, completely matter-of-factly, as if the pizza transaction had been concluded. "Thank you very much."

He hung up.

Sue slammed down the phone and began wailing to anybody who could hear her. God, if possible. Her voice was full of mixed emotions: fear, dread, and hope. "Oh, for God's sake! Oh, for God's sake! I'm sorry. They're calling back at 2:45. They have Amy!"

She ran to the other line to call the phone company and try to get a "lock" on the call before a new caller dialed in. Unfortunately, the communication had originated from a pay phone. Sue went into overdrive. She called Frank Rubino. "Come right away," she said. "There's a ransom call." She phoned the FBI and the police. Finally it was something for the authorities to sink their teeth into. By the time 2:45 P.M. rolled around, the house was filled with cops and friends.

The minute came and went without a ring.

Ned took Sue's hand. "Just stay calm, sweetheart. Maybe their watch is slow."

The phone rang. Sue picked it up before it stopped.

"Hi," said a mature woman's voice. "Is this Mrs. Billig?"

"Yes!"

"Well, you don't know me, but I just wanted to call

and give you my support and tell you that my church—"

Sue's throat was almost too constricted to speak. "I'm sorry, but we have an emergency and have to keep the line free right now. I have to hang up."

This was long before Call Waiting.

Sue shook her head to indicate a negative to the crowd of people surrounding her and slammed the receiver down. Sweat poured down her forehead. "Can anybody else hear my heart beating?" she asked.

Ned smiled and squeezed her hand.

The phone rang.

Sue snatched it out of the cradle.

"Mrs. Billig?" came the calm, now familiar voice.

"Yes!" she said again. "Do you have my daughter?"

"Listen," said the voice.

In the background an agonized voice wailed, "Mama, Mama, please help me. . . ." It sounded like Amy.

Sue's heart melted. Amy! Blood rushed through her ears like a hurricane. "What . . . what do you want?" she sputtered.

The voice returned. "We want $30,000 in small bills. Put the money in a black briefcase and come to the lobby of the Fontainebleau at eleven A.M., Friday. Wear red, white, and blue clothes. Oh, and Mrs. Billig, come alone. Whatever you do, do not—I repeat, do *not*—call the police or we will kill her."

"Of course not," she said.

"We'll call you tomorrow morning to confirm the details and make sure you're getting the money. Thanks very much," he ended politely.

The call was quickly traced to a Miami Beach telephone booth, where detectives later tried to lift fingerprints. Playing back the taped conversation, everyone agreed the muffled, pleading voice that called "Mama" sounded like Amy.

"What do we do?" Sue asked. "How do we get $30,000?"

Rubino asked, "Know anybody at a bank?"

The Billigs did know somebody at a bank. A friend was president of a local institution. He agreed to allow police to mark $30,000 in small bills. Strangely enough, none of the Billigs' friends owned a black briefcase. They called stores all over the city. It was like something out of the *Twilight Zone*. Something as simple and ubiquitous as a black briefcase was nowhere to be found. Plenty of brown ones, though. In desperation, Sue spray-painted a brown briefcase black.

By nine A.M. the next morning she was holding a briefcase full of money. It was more than she'd ever seen at once before, and just thinking about it made her nervous. But it was nothing compared to what Amy's life was worth. Even if the kidnappers somehow got away with the cash, she would pay the money back.

The FBI wanted to wire the briefcase with a remote sensor and outfit Sue with a body mike in case she was taken somewhere. Unfortunately, the good old U.S. government, buying from the lowest bidder, did not have reliable equipment. Rubino, however, owned superior electronics, so he ended up doing the honors. The Billigs wiped out the Amy Billig Fund's $2,000, paying for extra surveillance, including a plane, boat, and frogmen, in case the kidnappers tried to escape by water. The famous resort was situated right on the beach.

The confirmation call came as promised.

"You have the money?"

"We're all set," Sue said nervously.

"Okay, everything's the same. Come tomorrow at eleven A.M. And remember, no cops. Follow our instructions to the letter or we will kill Amy."

Friends slept at the house that night as moral support. Sue tried to eat some plain toast and instantly threw it up. Even Amy's little mutt, Shawn, which she had rescued from the pound, seemed to know something was up. Instead of playing and jumping around as he normally did when company arrived, he moped. It was a long and sleepless night for Sue, and she didn't even have to close her eyes to have nightmares. She prayed that this would all be over tomorrow.

The next morning, Ned was so nervous he could barely walk. While Sue hadn't slept a wink that night, she exhorted herself to keep going. "Now's the time, Sue. If you've ever needed your last reserves, use them now!" She forced herself into the heightened energy level that had sustained her so far.

Sue hugged her husband and felt his body become liquid. "I could wipe you up with a sponge," she tried to joke. "What a couple, huh?" She looked down at her clothing. "I look like some kind of patriotic clown!"

As per instructions, she wore white pants, a blue-and-white-check shirt, and a red suede belt. She got into the passenger seat of their blue station wagon, with a woman detective, Ina Shepard, driving. Shepard, wearing dark slacks and a white blouse, was slim and pretty, with an oval face, short cropped hair and bangs, and would pose as Sue's neighbor.

Of course there was unusually heavy traffic, and they hit every stoplight on the way. Sue was ready to tear her hair out by the time they reached the Fontainebleau a few minutes late. They left the car with a doorman and walked nervously into the posh lobby.

The Fontainebleau had been built in the heyday of Miami Beach's popularity. It had several massive lobbies with ceilings nearly seventy-five feet high, decorated with gold leaf and hung with giant crystal chandeliers. The place boasted several bars and theaters that sat hundreds of people. Frank Sinatra was a regular act at the La Ronde room and maintained a suite where he entertained the Rat Pack members.

Even at the end of season the lobby was busy. A line of visitors was checking in, bellhops zipped around with luggage, hordes of conventioneers mingled, and kids wearing Mickey Mouse ears from Disney World played hide-and-seek around the chairs and sofas.

The two found an empty couch in the main salon and sat down. Sue's whitened knuckles gripped the briefcase handle so hard the black paint rubbed off on her fingers.

What an operation! she thought.

Ina sat down and held her other hand, the painted attaché case protected between them. Sue tried not to allow herself to look around. Over forty Miami and Miami Beach police officers had infiltrated the place wearing tourist clothes during the morning, and she didn't want to inadvertently recognize one of them and give the plan away. Outside, every exit was under surveillance. An FBI agent, drinking a Coke, observed from the lobby bar.

A young man approached. "He was freaky looking," Sue remembers "Creepy. He was wearing a green baseball cap with a visor and silver sunglasses. You couldn't see his eyes. But one thing I thought was good. He was just as nervous as I was. His hands were shaking!" She sucked in a breath. "Are you the man?" she asked.

The voice was nervous, higher and less controlled than it had been on the phone. "I thought I told you to come alone!" he declared.

The bustling atmosphere of the busy hotel faded away. Sue focused on this one boy as if he were the very center of the universe. She wanted to hate and memorize every smack of his thin lips—the only part of his face she could really see—which seemed magnified like a cartoon in slow motion. But she had cried so much over the last weeks that she had become an empty vessel, and empty vessels have no emotion to hate with. Still, Sue wasn't about to allow this scrawny pipsqueak to intimidate her. What could he be, a teenager? "If you'd done your homework," she scolded, "you would know we're from New York City

and I just learned to drive. I'm too nervous to drive today. This is my neighbor, Ina. She drove me."

"I'm more nervous than you," the boy admitted.
"Give me the money and Amy will be home by six
o'clock." He reached for the briefcase.

Sue clutched it like a treasure. "Oh, no," she said. "I
begged and borrowed from my family and friends for
this money. It's everything I have in the world, and I'm
not giving it to you until you give me some kind of firm
identification about my daughter."

The kid gulped. "What do you mean? You heard her
on the phone."

"Tell me something about her."

"She's . . . she's got long brown hair," the boy said.

"Everybody knows that," Sue told him. "If you have
Amy, you'd know more. What's she wearing? What
kind of jewelry did she have on? Give me something
concrete!"

"Listen, I don't have her myself," the boy said. "If
there's going to be a problem, I'm going to have to call
somebody."

"You said you had her," Sue said.

The boy shook his head, looking around nervously.
"I'm only in on this for like two grand. I'm just picking
up the money. I'll have to make a call."

"Then get the information," Sue demanded, stabbing
a finger at his chest. "Let's go find a phone."

The boy was shaken by her temerity and took a few
steps back. He looked around, seemingly mollified that
no police were descending on him, and conceded,
"Okay, let's go make a call."

Despite the air-conditioning, sweat steamed down Sue's forehead. She could feel it dripping down her neck and into her bra where the microphone was. They followed the young guy to a phone booth in the lobby. "Call them!" she commanded.

The guy dialed the phone. Ina knew that a detective with binoculars would be jotting down the numbers, so she pulled Sue to the side to make sure the view would not be obstructed.

The boy listened in the receiver and shrugged. "Busy," he said.

An officer had indeed seen the numbers. He handed them to another cop who casually brought them outside to a waiting car. They rushed off to get the address.

The boy dialed again. Again he shook his head. Still busy. "Listen, I'm going to go meet with these guys nearby. You wait where you were and I'll get the information you need. I'll be right back." He strolled away, and they watched him punch the elevator button and disappear into the car with some Hawaiian-shirted tourists. One or more may have been cops; Sue didn't know.

"Oh, God, Ina," Sue said, "I hope they have her."

Sue and Ina headed back to the couch. "Sssh, don't say anything," Ina whispered. "We don't know if they have accomplices watching us."

It was the longest ten minutes Sue had ever endured. Time had never ticked so slowly. Not when she'd brought the kids to the doctor for a high fever. Not even when she'd sat waiting to find out if her mother's cancer operation had been successful the year before. Nothing in her life had prepared her for this.

Finally, he returned. His voice had lost all traces of calmness. "She's got long brown hair, is about five-five, is wearing a blue denim miniskirt, and has platform sandals."

"All that information is in the flyers we handed out!" Sue exploded. "What kind of ring is she wearing? Does she have a scar?"

"Like I said, I'm just the messenger. Give me the money, and Amy will be back home this evening. Otherwise they'll kill her."

Sue looked at Ina. Ina gave her a short shake of the head. Sue steeled herself.

"Then we keep the money until you get the information," Sue said, amazed at her courage. She knew that once the money was gone, her leverage was gone.

"Come with me," he said, then pointed at Ina. "You stay here."

Sue stood her ground. "Oh, no. I'm not going by myself."

The boy grunted in frustration, then turned and headed for the elevators. They boarded without other passengers. The kid hit the button for the fifth floor. As the doors closed, Ina wiped her forehead, exposing five fingers to Detective Orlando Martinez, who appeared to be a patron waiting for someone in the lobby.

The kid was more observant than they thought.

"I saw that! You flashed that guy the number five."

"You're paranoid," Ina said. "Can't I wipe my forehead?"

The dark sunglasses gave no response. "You're too much," the boy said, apparently satisfied.

The elevator stopped on the fifth floor. As they exited, another boy in a hat and sunglasses, the spitting image of the first, but wearing different colors, was waiting for them.

"Give me the money," he said. Same voice.

Brothers. Sue thought. Where the hell did they get Amy? Did she know them?

"It's easy," Sue said. "I told your friend here. You give us details about Amy, you can have the money, and I'll bless the ground you walk on."

"There's been a change of plans," the brother said.

At that point the second elevator stopped on the floor. Ina knew Martinez was probably in it, and she was fed up with the boys. She drew a revolver from her purse. "Police officer," she shouted. "You're under arrest. Get down on the floor." Martinez arrived in the other elevator, instantly assessed the situation and drew his weapon.

"Damn right there's been a change of plans," Ina said. "You're going to jail." She looked at Sue, sorrow in her eyes, realizing that Amy wasn't waiting in a nearby room. "I'm sorry, Sue," she said. "I think it's just a cruel prank."

The Glasser twins, Larry and Charles, were sixteen years old and had never met Amy, who attended a different high school. They were from a well-off family and lived with their divorced mother. Neighbors described the twins as "good kids," and their school records were spotless. They were very close-mouthed at the time, and never explained what had sparked their foolish actions or what plans they had for the money. They were released into their mother's care, and in court showed absolutely not a shred of remorse for their actions. They sat in the defendants' chairs looking smug and smiling, insisting that their crime was simply "a prank."

The calls made from the lobby were traced to the phone number of a friend who had no knowledge of the crime. The two teenagers had masterminded the masquerade by themselves.

The one good thing about the incident was that it brought Amy's disappearance into the national spotlight, and it was soon front page news around the nation. At the trial, Sue met the twins' mother, Maryon, for the first time. The two hugged and cried, simultaneously saying to each other, "I'm sorry." Dozens of news teams interviewed Sue about the twins and what she thought about them receiving no jail time.

Sue told them variations of the same thing. "I feel sorry for their mother. I don't feel anything about the kids. As soon as I found out they did not have my child, they vanished from my mind. I don't wish them any ill. All I want to do is find Amy."

Sue did confront the twins about one thing, though. Just to make absolutely sure, she asked, "What about Amy's voice?"

Larry Glasser shrugged. "It was me . . . just me. That's why we told you she had a cold."

Sue could only grit her teeth, close her eyes and sigh.

Several years later freelance writer Mark MacNamara happened to befriend one of the Glassers, Charles—known as "Chuck"—and in 1985 wrote a story about the boy, then in his twenties, for the *Miami Herald*. By then Chuck was a photographer working for the *Fort Lauderdale Sun-Sentinel*, living in an Ocean Drive weekly rental on Miami Beach. *He was a pushy kid, caustic and clever, with a good camera eye. But he also tended to be brash and insulting*, MacNamara wrote.

Michael Stock, now forty-three and host of a popular folk-music show on Miami's public radio station, was a member of the same Boy Scout troop as the Glasser twins. He remembers that Chuck, "a scrawny guy," seemed to try to make up for his small stature with an abrasive personality. "He was always cursing and vulgar," Stock says. "But they were both real smart alecks. One day Larry was spitting in our sterilized water as a prank; the next thing I knew they were on the front page of the *Miami Herald*!"

Shortly after their court case the brothers returned to camp accompanied by their parole officer, where Stock recalls that "Chuck admitted they had done something wrong, but didn't understand why it was such a big deal. He said, 'It's just like breaking a window. You have to pay for your crime.' The concept of extortion probably never entered their heads. They just thought about it as a prank," the radio personality observed.

Apparently, Chuck's fascination with pranks was not diminished by his terrible caper with the Billigs, either. McNamara wrote that Chuck once "went into the ladies room of the Cardozo with a fire extinguisher and sprayed women in the stalls."

But Glasser, who apparently could not understand

why he was shunned and had trouble making friends, never publicly apologized for his actions, telling Mac-Namara, "Why won't they forget? I was a kid. I was incredibly stupid. It's over. I paid for it. Everybody's got some dirt."

In the late 1980s, Sue Billig was dining with a friend at the Cardozo Hotel's café. Glasser tried to speak with her. She shooed him away. "I have nothing to say to you," she told him calmly, but firmly. Glasser wrote Sue a note on the back of a menu and dropped it on her table before he left.

Again, there was no remorse.

Mrs. Dillig,

Why can't you understand that what I did was just the act of a stupid kid? Why does it have to plague me for the rest of my life?

Sue could only shake her head. Some people would never learn.

While she bore the Glasers no specific ill will, their idiocy had affected the lives of dozens of people, caused the Billigs emotional turmoil, and cost thousands of dollars. Worse, as the years passed, one thing became certain. The three wasted days spent on the Glasser red herring was valuable time lost when authorities should have been tracking other leads. In that time, with the pressure off, Amy's true abductors could have spirited her anywhere.

And the Billigs were back at square one.

Today Sue shakes her head, remembering the event.

"When people ask me how I survived those times, I say, 'I just did what I had to.' I felt like I had walked barefoot through Hell. But I wasn't going to give up. There had to be something concrete somewhere. I just felt in my heart if Amy were dead, I would know it. This wasn't a time for me to slow down, it was a time for me to speed up."

3

"How can I describe what we were going through?" Sue Billig asks today in wonder. "It was chaos. One day the house would be full of people looking for ways to be of help. And, although I loved them all, it made everything so chaotic that I couldn't think straight. I would go crazy just trying to make breakfast for everyone. Then, the next day, the house would be empty, and I would have to call someone just so I didn't feel so alone."

Ned was a caring and fun father, certainly a great husband, but it is clear that his jazzy personality was not suited to this type of continuing crisis. He adored Amy, and was completely supportive in every effort to find his daughter, but he had to run the gallery. So it was Sue who was gradually transformed from a groovy Grovite, whose greatest worries were deciding which beach to go to that day, to a general who commanded the search plans.

Ned later told Edna Buchanan, the *Miami Herald*'s Pulitzer prize-winning police reporter, that he demurred to Sue's authority because of her "incredible ability to keep notes and records and stay on top of things. She has a better ability to deal with some of the very strange people we've had to deal with along the way. I don't think I could have controlled myself as well. I knew Sue was going into some situations that were somewhat perilous. I trust her judgment."

It can be emotionally draining for journalists to interview the parents of young suicides or murder victims, but we realize that as difficult and miserable a task as it is, what we do often allows the grieving family a way to vent their anguish in front of the public, and thereby begin whatever cathartic healing process they can achieve. At least, that's how we rationalize the brash job of invading and revealing someone's private nightmare.

While many parents weep, it's amazing how many are able to accept their loss with a brave, stoic calm and continue with their lives, even though they will never be the same again. Many will always prepare an empty place setting at the dinner table, keep the victim's bedroom complete and clean, and hold memorials on birthdays. But day-to-day they continue the same routine, go to work, cook dinner, knowing their child would want them to go on.

Sue, on the other hand, had no such closure, and was galvanized into action. She couldn't enjoy a dinner out, couldn't allow herself comforts, or even a good night's sleep while Amy was missing. How could she, knowing her daughter might be hungry, beaten, or worse? She suffered a love-hate relationship with the phone. It could never be left unattended, as any strange and distant voice might provide the critical clue. Yet, most calls and leads proved worthless.

The pile of tattered twenty-five-year-old notebooks tell the story in Sue's hastily scrawled handwriting, done with whatever writing implement was handy, from thick black markers to blue ballpoint to fading pencil.

> *March 27, 12:30: Anonymous—Man crying for God to give me strength. She is a beautiful girl and he is praying for me.*

Or one of the many psychics giving an earnest reading. This one a black female reverend:

> *You will find out something in seven days, seven hours. Amy's nauseous, sick feeling. She's got a sore feeling in her neck. It's hot. She is being held against the wall. Her feet are tied. But she's alive! I feel like she's further north. Maybe Texas. Or Okeechobee. There's something about a ring. Someone who gave her a ring may know more about what happened.*

Calls like these were well-meaning but ultimately unhelpful. They were salves that soothed the burn of despair for a short while, only to allow a greater and more aggressive pain to take hold.

That date of March 27 was important, too. It was one day after the Billigs' twenty-seventh wedding anniversary. It was, unfortunately, not a joyous day.

Sue remembers: "Amy was always very conscientious of birthdays, anniversaries, and holidays. She made people cards and gifts or called them. We stayed at home by the phone because we felt that nothing in the world could stop Amy from calling us if she could." Sue sighs. "The enormity of her absence, the completeness of it, really hit home that day, because she never called."

Amy's friends from the Adelphi School held a gathering in Coconut Grove's bayside Peacock Park, where they raised over $1,500 for the Amy Fund. Ned attended the function with Josh—who donated every cent in his savings account—absorbing the condolences uneasily, while Sue stayed at home jumping at every jingle of the phone.

But waiting was too passive, so Sue became ever more galvanized to bring her daughter home. She printed up thousands of flyers and convinced airline pilots and flight attendants to distribute them in cities across the country. She stopped traffic at the intersection of Poinciana and Main Highway, where Amy was last seen, and passed out flyers to drivers who might be taking the same route they had driven on the fateful day that Amy disappeared.

As much as Sue knew, as any mother knows, that she loved her children, the intensity and boundlessness of her love for Amy had only been guessed at before this. Had she realized it when Amy was just five and almost died of appendicitis? Or at age six when Amy had fought a 106 degree fever and dropped into a coma?

"No," Sue says. "Those things you handle. But when

your child is missing, then you get up and shout, 'No! This doesn't happen to real people!' "

During this time, Josh, a formerly rambunctious and outgoing youth, retreated into his own head, became ever more quiet, and started to hate going to school. "A lot of kids would say real mean things," he says now. " 'Hey, I've got your sister tied up in my room!' Things like that."

Sue was so focused on finding Amy that she now wonders, "How much pain did I cause Josh by putting our lives on hold? Did he think we loved Amy more than we loved him because of the time we were spending looking for her? Did we stop communicating because I was trying to protect him from the ugliness by being so private with my feelings?"

Josh, now a stonemason with a family of his own, admits that as a child he must have felt neglected, "And I guess the entire situation depressed me for years, although I didn't realize it at the time. Yet I don't think about it now like I didn't get a fair shake or something. Every family goes through their own pain, even though you might not see it on the outside. Self-pity is a weakness. I don't blame them or anybody for not having a normal life. Life isn't easy for anyone."

An award-winning photograph of Sue taken back then shows her carrying a sign among cars, with her jaw as taut as a protestor's. Such photos burned themselves into people's memory, though Sue's true nature is one of sweetness and caring. But she was aggressive at the time, feeling betrayed by law enforcement, trying to get the message out to the world that an innocent girl was missing. "I wanted helicopters in the sky, I wanted a nationwide search, but all the police would say was she was probably a runaway. I knew she hadn't run away. They acted very nonchalant about the whole thing. I begged them to come to the house and take Amy's fingerprints from her room. They always promised, but you could tell they weren't serious about this investigation, because they always put it off."

Within weeks of Amy's disappearance, one particular telephone call generated a sense of dread. Sue wrote down the words in her notebook, as she had with so many unidentified callers before this, though it is not one of the early recorded conversations.

The first communication in what eventually became a marathon series was pretty simple. "Your daughter's dead," stated the steady southern male voice. Complete calm, no evil in his voice, as if he was reciting an item on a grocery list.

Sue's heart felt like something was crushing it. "Dead? How do you know?" she asked in sudden despair.

But the man didn't answer. There were a couple of half breaths, the stifled beginning of an utterance, but instead of continuing, he just hung up. His words left Sue shaking for hours. How could she have guessed at the future anguish this new voice would cause her over the years, or surmise that this was, in fact, her first contact with one of the most twisted stalkers that America has ever known?

He wasn't the only fiend, either. In March there was yet another extortion attempt. A deep-voiced male told her to bring $2,000 to an inner city telephone booth where she would be given further information.

"If you want to see her alive again," the voice intoned, "bring the money!"

Again, hope and dread. Bring the money to an address where even the police were scared to go, let alone taxi drivers! But Sue would do anything for Amy.

"Give me some information about her. Ask her who got married at our house."

"Just bring the money," the voice commanded.

Police eventually traced this latest attempt to a mentally deficient man with no connection to the missing girl.

Sue was heartbroken to find out the latest lead was a lemon. She declined to press charges, later saying, "He was a sick boy. All these kids are somebody else's children. I don't believe in an eye for an eye, a tooth for a tooth."

How does a family keep itself together while the world around them keeps shredding, when the slightest clue, like the latest phone call, turns your stomach upside down but makes your heart soar in the hope that this ordeal would soon be over? Whoever first described such emotions as a "roller-coaster ride" has yet to be surpassed. You're up and down, and rushing wildly out of control, hoping to God that this little basket of safety you're sitting in doesn't careen off tracks that you can only hope are really there. Ned told reporter Edna Buchanan: "I was a manic depressive, I think, for a period. Sitting and waiting is the worst kind of thing to do." Only counseling sessions with a nearby rabbi may have kept them from going mad.

Months of this tense limbo went by as they searched for biker contacts who might have seen Amy. A friend led them to a Baltimore lawyer, Bobby Franks, whose college friend represented the Pagans. He in turn contacted "Satan," president of the Pagans, who promised he would use his authority to find out the truth.

Franks seemed sympathetic to the Billigs' cause, but had warned them not to become too optimistic. "When bikers get girls, they become their property," he told them. "They bang them up, trade them for credit cards. . . ."

"I've heard it all," Sue retorted. "Just let everyone know we're not the 'heat,' and we won't ask questions. We just want Amy. That's all we care about. We'll buy her back if we have to."

In April, after several bad leads, Franks finally received a call from a Satan. "You know that business we were talking about down South?"

"Is she alive?" Sue asked.

"Yes. The Outlaws left Fort Lauderdale with her."

The informant said the Outlaws were heading north, hightailing it out of South Florida in the wake of several headline-making territorial clashes with the Pagans and the Hell's Angels. Even a handful of peaceful concerts—"love-ins," as they were commonly called, attended mostly by nonviolent hippies—had been broken up for no apparent reason by drunken bikers wielding chains. Authorities speculated that the clubs were battling ever more aggressively for greater shares of the drug market. At the peak of the war, the bloated bodies of three Hell's Angels were found floating in a secluded rock quarry in far west Broward County. Now the Outlaws were "getting out of Dodge" before the police could round them up for questioning.

After a month of agonizing dead ends, where the days slipped by in a frenzy of phone calls and false sightings, the Billigs' hopes were refueled on June 5. That evening at seven-thirty, under a dreary, overcast summer sky, they received a visit from an undercover Treasury informant, Casey Lange. [We believe Lange is now in the Witness Protection Program, so we have changed her name.]

Lange was tiny, only about five feet, with small bones and pixyish brown hair. "She was probably in her thirties, but looked like she was fifteen," Sue remembers. The quasi-agent was energetic and very positive about finding Amy.

Sitting on the edge of the sofa, holding hands, the Billigs listened to terrible words that were in a sense more beautiful than a Beethoven symphony.

Lange said, "I've been involved in a long-term investigation of the Outlaw gang, and I'm certain I saw Amy at a place called the Oasis Bar in Fort Lauderdale a few weeks ago."

Sue gripped Ned's hand as they both gasped. "You saw her? You're sure it was her?" Sue asked.

Casey nodded. "I wouldn't have come to you unless I was very sure. You have to have a very good ability to identify people in my line of work."

"But—But . . . if you saw her, why didn't you grab her?" Sue wanted to know.

Lange shook her head. "I wanted to, but it was too dangerous. She was in there with some pretty heavy-duty bikers. If I'd tried to get her out, it might have blown my cover and gotten us both killed. She looked really out of it . . . drugged, I guess. Then there was a big fight and the owner and his son had to run them all off with shotguns. It was a pretty tense situation. But they were on their way to Kissimmee, where they have a clubhouse."

Kissimmee is just outside of Orlando, a blue-collar town filled with cheap hotels and cheaper roadside attractions, festooned with more ugly highway signage per square inch than the per capita income. It was where people who couldn't afford the cheapest Orlando hotels stayed when they brought their families to Disney World.

"Listen," Casey said, "I'll see what I can do to help find her. I feel really bad, but you have to understand . . ."

About that time, the biker Sid Fast called with information that the Pagans were holding Amy and "another girl." Until then, the focus of the investigation had always been the Outlaws, and this was the first time the Pagans came up as a possible lead. Susan Johnson, the original caller, had also mentioned "another girl." Fast came up with a name, "Look for a guy named 'Animal,'" Sid said, "from the Ohio chapter. That's all I can give you right now. If I ask too many questions I could get labeled a snitch."

Sue went into high gear, calling the Orlando police to be on the lookout for Amy and trying to find out information about Animal.

"Lady," an Orlando police captain told Sue, "we got some real friction here with the bikers, and it's pretty dangerous. I don't suggest you come up here unless you're sure your daughter's here."

Frank Rubino, the private detective—today a well-known criminal defense attorney based in Miami—was trying to find out the address to the Outlaw and/or Pagan clubhouses. If they weren't going to get much help from the Orlando police, who at the time were more afraid of the bikers than the bikers were of them, they would try to get somebody to infiltrate the gang, find Amy and "grab her." Money was tight, so they would only go up when they knew exactly where they were headed.

Sue began numbering the days that Amy had been gone in her notebook: *June 10—98 days*.

The entry went on to detail a biker incident that in retrospect would stand out as a flashpoint in the ongoing war that was becoming ever more violent. An Orlando Pagan—a police lieutenant's son, it turned out—had escaped from the Outlaws after he and two comrades had been kidnapped by the rival gang. His two friends had been shot dead, but the lieutenant's son had gotten away and was now being held in protective custody by authorities.

As soon as their prisoner had escaped, knowing the murders would be revealed, the Outlaws hastily left Central Florida in their exhaust. Now all hell was about to break loose in this sleepy Florida town where

Disney was still a lengthy ride through orange groves that flanked most of the surrounding countryside on which megamalls, office complexes, and town homes had yet to be built.

Casey Lange, making good on her word to help out, and Kim Smith, a fledgling private detective, traveled up to Orlando to interview the escaped Pagan, but the police refused to let them speak to the terrified prisoner. On June 13, Kim called the Billigs and told them he had gotten friendly with some biker women at the Copper Penny lounge in Kissimmee, and gone back to a biker's apartment. There wasn't much information yet, but he was hopeful.

Orlando detective Mike Calamia said a clerk in a Majik Market near the Outlaw clubhouse could describe a customer who might have been Amy.

At that point, such information was enough for Sue. She couldn't take sitting at home by the phone any longer. Nobody wanted to find Amy as much as she did. To everyone else, Amy was just a picture of another pretty girl who had been filed as a missing person. Did Detective Calamia stay awake at night with his stomach churning? Did he or the other detectives fall into fitful sleep, only to dream of Amy being beaten and abandoned, left for dead in a ditch by the side of the road? No, all they heard was the voice of her mother harping in their ear, questioning their efforts. No matter how good-hearted they might be, to them Amy was another case that could be put off until after lunch, or tomorrow, because their son had a Little League game tonight. But Sue, finding Amy was her life. What she lacked in detective experience, in law enforcement authority, and in strength, she more than made up for with sheer willpower to find her daughter.

Funds in the Amy account were dangerously low, but they would be enough to fly up to Orlando. She phoned Calamia. "I'm coming up there," she told the detective. "I'll meet you tomorrow morning and you can take me to the Majik Market."

The Outlaw apartment was located on Ferncreek Drive in Kissimmee, in a poor area that was a mixture of termite-ridden Florida "cracker" clapboard houses and stained concrete-block houses with weed-filled yards. Orange pickers and maids for the hotels might live there.

Calamia, an effusive dark-haired man who unconsciously hummed underneath his breath, drove Sue out to the area. Sue clutched Amy's picture in sweaty, shaking fingers as they pulled up to a small, square, cement two-story duplex surrounded by dirt, sandspurs, and rusting motorcycle parts. "This is the clubhouse," Calamia said. Sue wanted to go directly to the store where Amy had been seen.

Down the block was the Majik Market, a convenience store with grimy Formica floors and Budweiser stacked in the aisles. You could buy any one of twenty brands of cheap beer there, but only one kind of coffee. There were a dozen titles of dirty magazines, even more kinds of rolling papers behind the counter, but only American cheese and three kinds of Campbell's soup on the shelves.

The woman behind the counter was in her fifties,

looked burned out, with strawlike hair and crow's-feet around her bloodshot eyes. *The Beverly Hillbillies* blared from a small, faded black-and-white television behind the counter. As soon as Calamia entered, the woman tensed and stood up from a plastic chair.

Her name was Sue Lynne, and she instantly sympathized with Sue's cause. "I have a daughter a couple years older," she said in a tired voice tinged with a hard southern accent. "I can't imagine what I'd do if she disappeared."

Sue handed over pictures of Amy: a profile shot and one of her sitting in a chair with sunlight washing over her. That's the way Sue always pictured Amy when she could—almost angelic looking. Happy.

"That's her," Sue Lynne said. "I'm sure of it. Came in every Sunday morning and bought crackers and Campbell's vegetable soup."

"Amy's a vegetarian!" Sue volunteered eagerly. "What else can you tell me? Did she ever say anything? Did she look all right?"

"The last time I saw her she mentioned that she felt sick," Sue Lynne recalled gravely. "She thought she might be pregnant. She didn't have much money, so heck, I gave her the crackers. I'm the owner, so I can do that," she quickly told the policeman.

Sue wrote down the information in a notebook, as did Calamia. He asked, "Who might the girl have come in with?"

Sue Lynne closed her eyes and tried to remember. "Seems to me she usually came with this big biker they called 'Creature.' Had a black Harley—he's tall and husky, with real bushy hair. Looks like a creature! Got tattoos, of course. I think he's the head man around here. Sure acts like it. Sometimes there was a blue van, I think. I think Amy—if that's who she is—said someone was trying to take her away. . . . I think I may have heard them talking about her dancing in clubs. But she told me good-bye. They left last Monday."

Sue's heart plunged. She already knew from the police that the clubhouse had been vacated after the Pagan escaped. But still, hearing those words put a value on the short amount of time involved. Sue Lynne had actually spoken to Amy, heard her voice, looked her in the eye—something Sue longed to do—and such a short time ago.

And to hear she was sick? Possibly pregnant? Definitely scared and uncared for. Maybe even beaten. Why would she even stay with bikers if she could possibly talk to someone like Sue Lynne and say, "Call the police—I'm a hostage?"

But then, Amy was supposedly drugged up. Maybe she didn't even know who she was anymore.

Billig steadied herself, gripping the policeman's arm. "I'm going to give you my number," she told Sue Lynne. "If you see Amy or anyone she was with, or hear anything, please call," she pleaded, a catch in her voice. "As a mother you must know how I feel." She explained there was a reward as well.

Sue Lynne nodded her head with regret. "I just wish I knew last week, honey. I wish I had known."

The two-story biker clubhouse down the street was an architectural eyesore with jalousie windows that sported aluminum grating across the interior to ward off any thief dumb enough to try to rip off a biker gang.

Calamia parked at the curb, and the two skirted the rusted motorcycle and car parts with weeds growing up through them. Left long enough, the place would become some kind of archaeological site where future scientists would be able to deduce details about the culture from the trash they left behind.

The apartment had been vacated in a rush. An ugly brownish-orange shag rug was stained with beer and other liquids, burned by cigarettes and joints and littered with old pizza boxes, beer cans, and drug paraphernalia. A phone cord was ripped out of the wall, and the phone bills themselves were scattered like fallen leaves across the floor. The smell of spilled beer, alcohol, and stale urine made breathing the air seem like sucking dirt into your lungs. There was some crusty material leaking out of a used condom in a corner.

A tear came to Sue's eye. She was a meticulous housekeeper, and couldn't stand the thought of Amy living like this. The nicknames of these bikers suddenly seemed more appropriate.

"Now I see why they call themselves things like 'Creature,' " she told Calamia.

She steeled herself against the disgusting mess and found a bedroom with a bare, stained mattress on the floor with heaps of old cigarette butts overflowing from plates commandeered as ashtrays around it. A couple of large palmetto bugs scurried away from a half-eaten cheese sandwich. There was an old beaten, chipped, and burned vanity with a cracked mirror and a woman's hairbrush.

The hair was the same color brown as Amy's. Sue picked the brush up carefully by the bristles, not wanting to smear a fingerprint, and sniffed—did it smell like Amy's shampoo? No. Only the odor of smoke. But maybe the police could match the hair sample. Could it be some kind of message from Amy? Why else would a girl leave her hairbrush in any kind of haste?

She secured the brush in a plastic bag and dropped it into her handbag. In the living room, Calamia was picking up various marijuana roaches and hash pipes and dropping them into evidence bags. "She was here," Sue told him with conviction. "I know it. I can feel her." She sifted through the telephone bills. "Maybe we can trace some of these calls," she continued. "Find out where they were headed, or find someone they know."

Calamia sighed. "I looked. The phone was registered to some alias. . . . The renter is an alias, and the bills are in different names. You take the phone bills, Mrs. Billig. If we ever get that far into the investigation, we'll get copies from the phone company. I really hope you find your daughter, Mrs. Billig, but the Outlaws have clearly gone, and they're someone else's problem now."

Back in Miami, she brought the brush into the police lab along with a hair sample from a brush left by Amy at home. Results showed that the two specimens were "consistent with a match." They lifted clear fingerprints off the item as well. "Now can I get someone to fingerprint Amy's room?" Sue asked Mike Gonzalez.

Finally, three months after Amy's disappearance, a technician, Al Heath, arrived to dust for Amy's prints. His daughter was actually a former schoolmate of Amy's, so he took great care to do the best possible work.

But he had bad news for Sue. "I don't know what to say," he told her. "But prints don't last long in the tropics. Humidity is my worst enemy. There's not a single clear print here!" The most he could determine was that "her prints run to ovals," a technical observation about the general shape of Amy's fingerprints.

Sue wanted to bang on his chest and yell, "Why didn't you come sooner? I pleaded with the police to send someone," but she held it in. She knew, and he knew, and there was nothing anyone could do now. She was not a blamer, never had been and never would be. But still, how could anyone not want to howl in frustration!

This would prove an even greater failure in the future, as Amy's fingerprints could have been filed with police all over the country and, later, in a central data bank, to be compared with arrestees and victims around the country.

"That was one of the most blatant failures of the investigation from the very beginning," Sue says now. "But it would be one of many."

Still, she was feeling optimistic. Maybe there was no fingerprint, but the hair was a decent match, combined with the identification by Sue Lynne at the convenience store. The police lab felt that if they "had

Amy's blood type, it would be a positive match." It was enough for a mother.

She also had the biker's phone bills. There was one number in Hollywood, Florida, that had been called multiple times. Long calls. Long calls were usually important. Who would the Outlaws in Orlando want to talk to so much?

Sue had done what local authorities could not. She had found Big Jim Nolan—president of the Florida chapter of the Outlaws. If anyone would know about a kidnappee, it would be him.

If he would talk.

The number wasn't in Big Jim's name, of course. Nothing would be. Sue dialed the Broward number in trepidation. A gruff voice answered, "Yeah?" She heard the sound of dogs barking and people arguing in the background, though it might have been a television.

"You don't know me," Sue blurted out. "I'm a mother looking for my daughter."

There was a snort of derisive laughter. "Lady, you called the wrong fucking number."

"I'm looking for Big Jim Nolan," she said.

Silence.

Then, "Who the fuck did you say you were?"

"My name is Susan Billig. My daughter disappeared a few months ago, and I've heard she's with bikers. Outlaws. They said she was in Fort Lauderdale, and then up in Orlando."

"Oh, yeah," the man said, "I heard about you. Well, lady, if she's with us, she's a biker chick now. Don't try to find her."

"Please," Sue cajoled, "let me talk to you, show you her picture. I swear, all I want to know is if she's truly alive. If she wants to stay a 'biker chick,' her father and I can handle that. We just want to know she's all right."

Big Jim was hesitant, but finally agreed to meet her—alone. She didn't dare tell Ned where she was going, so made an excuse to go out for a while, then rode a long, hot, nervous twenty-five-mile bus trip to Hollywood. She sat in her sticky plastic seat, watching passengers get on and off the bus: mothers with screaming children, the elderly, the poor, and the barely sane—each with their own story, their hopes and dashed dreams, their failures and disappointments. No one who could ride any other way would ever pick a sweaty, huffing, chugging Dade County bus. A bus full of hard luck stories. And hers, perhaps not even the saddest of them. But she brightened up. If Amy were in the Outlaw nation, Big Jim was the one who could find her.

She arrived at the bus stop and got off. Of course, Nolan wasn't waiting. She sat in the hot sun and sweated on the bus bench until a rusting, dented van sputtered around the corner. Through the dusty windshield, she could see a long-haired man driving. The van came to a brake-squealing stop in front of her. The unshaven man leaned out. "You looking for Big Jim?"

"I'm Sue," she said, hoping her terror wasn't too evident.

"Well, I'm Big Jim," the man told her. "Get in, lady."

A few months before, Sue barely knew a man like this existed. She certainly would never have spoken to him, let alone get into a van with him. If Ned knew what she was up to, he would have had a conniption.

"You coming or not?" Jim said, putting the vehicle back into drive.

Sue pulled the door open with a yank. The smell of broiling plastic, stale beer, cigarette smoke, and wet dogs wafted out—the biker perfume she had come to know.

The house was yet another modest cement-block structure in a neighborhood of middle class homes. All the other yards were semipruned, semiraked, with a mango tree or some yellowing palms for shade. No one would be picked for a turf-builder commercial, but the ratio of sod to weeds was respectable. Except for the Outlaw residence. Here, the carcasses of aging cars vied for room with gritty black Harleys. Scruffy mutts lolled among the dog crap that was not exactly providing fertilizer for the rocky lawn.

"Home sweet home," Big Jim joked when he saw the look on her face. "Don't worry, you won't catch anything."

When the biker got out of the van, she could tell why he had been nicknamed Big Jim. He was a massive man, as tall as a basketball player, with large arms festooned with tattoos. He should have been called King Kong. "Watch out for the dogshit," Jim cautioned.

The blinds were shut, making the inside of the house dark as a cave. The air smelled more of marijuana than cigarettes. Tacked to the wall, Sue remembers vaguely, was a poster of a giant tattooed biker striding through a canyon, with a caption reading, *Though I walk through the Valley of Death I will fear no evil, because I'm the meanest son of a bitch in the Valley*. A Jim Morrison song blared on a tinny radio, while two biker women, wearing sweaty black T-shirts, soiled jeans, and scuffed boots, sprawled on a couch and passed a joint between them. A biker came out of a door, with a flushing toilet in the background.

Sue's little voice was yelling at her to leave, but her willpower reigned. The idea of Amy living like this was unbelievable, untenable. If she was, she had definitely been brainwashed.

"Can I get you a beer?" Jim offered.

Sue's throat was dry and swollen, but she didn't want to touch anything. "I'm fine," she croaked, fishing in her purse for Amy's picture. She held it out to Jim. "This is my daughter."

Jim snatched the photo and fell heavily into a cracked recliner. He snapped his fingers at a woman who passed him the joint. He took a deep toke. "And a beer," he commanded. The woman jumped off the couch and scuttled for the kitchen. You could see she hadn't been fast enough sometime in the past, and had probably been punished for it.

Jim studied the photograph of Amy under a dim light and let out a low whistle. "No one's gonna want to give her back," he said.

"Please," she said. "I don't want to make trouble for anyone. I don't want to put anybody in jail. I just want my daughter back."

Jim handed the picture to the other biker, who had

meandered over. Another large, mean-looking guy with scars and tattoos. "Never seen her," the biker said.

"Me either," Jim admitted. "But you know, we don't see everyone all the time. I get reports. We talk on the phone, but we rarely all get together at one time."

Sue told him about Creature and the Orlando trip, the identification from the Majik Market. Jim asked several questions, all coming back to: "What are you going to do if your daughter doesn't want to come back?"

There was something highly intelligent in Big Jim's enunciation.

"I told you, that's her choice. But you must know how I feel. I can tell you're an educated man," Sue concluded, purposefully trying to appeal to his vanity.

Big Jim laughed. "Hell, lady, what do you think bikers are? We're too smart to take shit from anybody in some nine-to-five job. I was valedictorian of my class! Now, have a beer, lady. While I make a few calls."

Sue sipped from a cold can while Jim got on the phone. He seemed to be talking in code with guys about how many "shirts" had been sold, or how much "heat" was around. Little by little he would get around to the subject at hand. "Tell Creature to call me if you see him. He's headed to Tennessee," he said during the final call. He turned to Sue. "If your daughter is in the Outlaw nation, we'll find her," he said.

"I've heard that before," Sue said doubtfully.

"Oh, yeah? Well, you never heard it from me." Big Jim responded.

Sue looked at this giant, filthy, tattooed Sasquatch

and realized that he was president of a nation within a nation, every bit as powerful in his own way as a great Mafia boss. He had the power of life and death over his tribe, and beware anyone who lied, cheated, or stole from him. A bit of calm washed over her, and she patted his large, callused, greasy hand. "I believe in you," she said.

Big Jim's eyes locked with hers, and she could feel some softness, some communication, between them. His would be an act of mercy, not because he was kind-hearted or sympathetic, if those emotions could still be found in his heart. No, he would do it because he had the power. Simply because he could.

4

This crisis provoked a strange paradox by bringing out the nobility in the most brutal of people and turning otherwise normal characters into vultures. The Glasser twins' "prank" and the other false extortion attempts are prime examples of the amazing depths that some people can sink to in order to prey on their fellow human beings. But as vile as they were, these acts were arguably perpetrated by the immature, people whose moral compass had not yet been formed. But how do you explain the following?

In October of 1974, two former Dade County narcotics agents, Bobby Barr and Carlos Rojas, contacted the Billigs through a lawyer. "We really know these bikers," they told Sue over the phone. "We will find her."

"Oh, thank you," Sue said, deeply grateful.

"We will need $3,000," the man continued.

A lump formed in Sue's throat. "We're selling everything we own, but we just don't have much money left," she confided.

"See how much you can dig up," the man told her.

Sue and Ned spent a couple of days raising the cash. The couple had already sold their 1954 Bentley, which was well-known around town, and that money had already been spent. The Help Find Amy Billig account was down to a few dollars. The gallery had pretty much already been cleaned out of its valuable stock, but a few customers bought some lesser known artists at cut rate prices to help them out. Susan sold some jewelry. They scraped together $1,500 and, accompanied by Father Hingston, a local minister, met the ex-policemen at a Denny's.

The two men, with dark Latin looks that had helped their undercover careers in Miami, were dressed professionally in suits and ties and exuded an air of authority.

"All we can put together is $1,500," Sue said. "But believe me, if you find her, we'll make it worth your while. There's the $2,000 in an escrow account at the Coconut Grove Bank, and we'll hold a benefit if we have too. Anything. You won't be sorry."

One man looked at the other and nodded, then reached across the table for the envelope of cash. He didn't count it before putting it in his jacket pocket. He patted Sue's hand. "Don't worry, Mrs. Billig, this is the best investment you ever made. We'll call you every day from wherever we are." He smiled.

"Call collect from anywhere," Sue said in a hopeful tone. "It'll make me feel good knowing you're out there."

"We will," the detective assured her.

They ate their sandwiches, drank their coffees, and

Sue paid the check. The group of five left the restaurant together and said their good-byes in the parking lot.

While driving their silver station wagon home, they came across a lovely young teenager hitchhiking under the shade of a banyan tree, just blocks from where Amy had last been seen.

Something roared in Susan's head. "Stop, Ned. Stop!"

Ned pulled the car over to the side of the road and Sue jumped onto the sidewalk. The young blonde, wearing Birkenstocks, a tie-dyed T-shirt knotted at the midriff, and blue-jean hip-huggers, skipped toward the car in glee. "Thanks for stopping!" she called out.

"What, are you crazy?" Sue scolded. "Do you know how dangerous hitchhiking is?"

The girl halted. "This isn't a ride?"

Sue sighed. "My daughter was picked up a few blocks from here, just months ago, and we've never seen her again. Haven't you seen the signs we put up? I used to hitch all the time, but it's too dangerous now."

The girl crinkled her blue eyes and flashed a smile. "I don't get in a car if there's a bad vibe."

"My daughter said the same thing, honey," Sue reprimanded. "You just have to be wrong once! We'll take you into town, but you have to promise me you won't do this anymore. You can't. Don't put your parents through what we've been through."

On the short ride into town, Sue told the girl Amy's story and could see it gradually sinking into the young woman's naive head. By the time they left their passenger in Coconut Grove, the young woman had been evangelized. "Okay, Mrs. Billig," she said. "I swear I won't hitch anymore. I swear."

"And tell your friends, girls and boys—it doesn't matter," Sue said. "It's a different world we're living in now."

And it was. The Broadway musical *Hair* was still a success. The Fifth Dimension version of the great new age optimistic song, "Age of Aquarius," was a radio hit. Even five years later, the feeling of Woodstock still reverberated in the air. Peace and understanding would rule the world. But as the Watergate investigation inched forward and gas shortages became common-place, cruel reality was slowly impinging on this age of innocence.

The ex-officers were just more evidence of the changing world, showing the true nature of the Age of Aquarius being ushered in.

Night after night, Sue and Ned made sure someone was always by the phone. The detectives had taken their money, spoken their promises, and kissed Sue good-bye on the cheek. Sue had invested more than her money. She had invested her priceless trust in the basic goodness of man, a human trait that she wouldn't dis-believe. It kept her sane, hoping that even if Amy had been kidnapped—a terrible act—that she was still alive unharmed, because there would be no reason to kill her.

"God, have I learned about human nature," she says now.

Night after night they waited for the detectives to adhere to their promise: "We'll call you every day from wherever we are."

They took the money the Billigs scraped together. Money that could have gone to useful purposes. But they never called. "A month later I finally tracked them down," Sue recalls. "They said they'd searched all over Central Florida, all the way up to Atlanta and Tennessee, before the 'expense money ran out.'"

They never called collect because, Sue says, "I don't think they ever left town."

Vultures.

This was an achingly difficult time for the Billigs. The trail had cooled. Calls to Big Jim Nolan were producing little. "I'm on it," he told her. But he had bigger things on his mind.

A lot bigger things.

Authorities were beginning to crack down on the brotherhood. The Hell's Angels bodies found at the rock quarry had caused an outcry. At a recent concert in a public park, the Outlaws had started whipping hippies with chains again. The public's love fest with the biker image was eroding. Arrests were being made. One biker got time for kidnapping, another for drug charges. Soon prosecutors might get someone to "flip" on his buddies.

Sid Fast called. His deep New York accent sounded sincere. "Big Jim wanted me to give you some info. Seems Creature sold Amy before he left for Tennessee."

Sue wished she could order Fast to explain just how a woman could be bought, sold, traded, and treated like an animal or a slave. The idea turned her stomach inside out. But that kind of anger wouldn't get her any-where, and it certainly wouldn't help Amy. "Sold her? To who!" she asked, her voice shaking.

"I don't know. Someone who isn't an Outlaw. They were taking her to New York. We'll see what else we can find out. But if she isn't with Outlaws anymore, it's going to be a lot harder."

If this was a put off, Sue wanted him to feel bad. "I trust you," she told him with a shaky voice. "I know you're a good man and you'll do your best."

That made him think. "Yeah, that's what my mother always said."

But the calls petered out. Big Jim's big promises were abruptly back burnered when he was arrested for threatening a police officer at a bar. It was really just a reason for authorities to keep him from skipping town. But afterward, finding Amy wasn't his top priority, if it ever had been. Prosecutors had something else up their sleeve, too. Soon Big Jim was indicted for the Hell's Angels rock-pit murders.

Sue and Ned stayed in therapy to control the depression. Sue would have a glass of wine or two, but was never a big drinker. It was more difficult for Ned, perhaps because of his supportive rather than front-line role in the search. He had loved his little girl, and this wasn't the future he'd seen for her or their family.

The big question was: Why didn't Amy call? In all this time, hadn't there been a second when she was left alone near a phone?

The couple's therapist advised them that Amy "might be subject to the Stockholm syndrome. You know, like Patty Hearst." The syndrome was ground-breaking news at the time, categorized in 1973 after four hostages were taken by robbers during a failed bank heist in Stockholm, Sweden. When authorities tried to rescue them six days later, the captives resisted. Later they refused to testify against the criminals and helped them raise money for their legal defense. One hostage even became engaged to one of her former captors during his prison sentence.

About the same time Amy had disappeared, the heiress Patty Hearst had been kidnapped by the Symbionese Liberation Army and become a fellow revolutionary who helped them knock over banks.

The same syndrome was rampant in the biker culture. While many women gravitated to the life for their own reasons, others were basically kidnapped, indoctrinated, and brainwashed so thoroughly that they stayed for life, even when they could have escaped.

The more time that went by, the bolder Sue became. In the first days, she had cried endlessly. But by the time of the Orlando trip, she had become indomitable. Like mothers who had lifted wrecked cars off of their children, finding unknowable depths of strength and courage, she had entered the intimidating biker lair at Big Jim Nolan's without anybody knowing where she'd gone. In the future she would do worse.

One incident from that period is branded forever into her memory.

"Some friends of ours from New York had come down to lend moral support. After dinner, the guys were doing something in the other room, and my girlfriend and I were sitting on the couch reminiscing about Amy. Suddenly I heard a girl screaming outside, 'Help me. Help!' To me it was Amy. My friend froze, but I jumped up and rushed outside into the darkness. Bushes were rustling across the street, and the girl was screaming. I dashed across the street, where there were two figures fighting. One was a girl, with blood smeared across her face."

The other person was a man twice Sue's size, but she didn't hesitate. She threw her tiny, 100-pound body between the victim and assailant and thrust him aside. "Get out of here!" she yelled, and the man scuttled away.

"It's all right," Sue said, hustling the terrified teenager into her house. "Ned, call the police."

"I was babysitting," the girl explained as Sue wiped the blood from her nose. "I can't believe it, that was my old boyfriend. He's mad because I'm seeing some-one else. He's a very violent guy, and I think he would have hurt me."

It was only after the police had arrived and taken the girl home that Sue trembled in Ned's arms, realizing she could have been killed in someone else's domestic quarrel. She told Ned, "I know I should have waited for you men, but it was like Amy was calling me! That girl is someone's daughter. Don't you hope someone would do the same for Amy, wherever she is?"

"It's good karma," Ned agreed.

Years later, when Sue was attending a play at the Coconut Grove Playhouse, a woman approached her with tears in her eyes. "You probably don't remember me," she said, "but you saved me one night years ago. I just wanted to thank you and let you know everything has turned out right for me. I really think I might have been killed that night if it wasn't for you." Of course Sue remembered her.

When your child is missing, you never forget it, but to have it rammed into your conscience at virtually every moment can be especially debilitating. Almost weekly a young woman's body would be found somewhere in the state or across the country. Sergeant Gonzales would dutifully notify Sue that he was receiving dental records to match with Amy's, not realizing that he was causing more harm than good by keeping her so well-informed.

Sue's faded notebooks are full of scrawled notations, such as: *Sgt. Gonzales called to say a young woman's body was found near Orlando. Why doesn't he wait to tell me unless there's a match!*

She had nightmares every time she was told a body had been found, imagining what the girl's mother was going through.

Weeks turned into months, and suddenly a year had passed. The yearly Bike Week in Daytona was scheduled again, so Ned and Josh headed north to scout the gangs that would appear, hoping beyond hope that they would find Amy.

Fort Lauderdale was still the Mecca of spring break. Daytona, by contrast, was a small redneck town, known mostly for its racetrack and motorcycle races. Bike Week caused an invasion of thousands of rowdy bikers, all just one beer and one slanted glance away from killing each other. Anyone with any sense stayed away from Daytona during Bike Week. Locals locked their doors and stayed inside as much as possible, or left town completely.

When Josh and Ned arrived, they found that the bikers enjoyed a sort of self-imposed outdoor prison grounds, each club separated by fences of chicken wire, with armed biker guards at the entrances—a compromise with local authorities.

Ned asked the local police chief to escort them into the Outlaw compound to see if they could find his daughter.

The officer leaned back in his air-conditioned patrol car and laughed. "Are you kidding? I'm not sending any of my men in there!"

Frustrated beyond belief, Ned and Josh prowled the outside perimeter trying to get a glimpse of the women. But they were all stationed well away from the fence with many layers of defense between them and the outside. When they saw a lone woman stray, they would show her a picture, but always without any luck. No one would give out information.

Possibly so close, but farther away than ever.

A year had gone by. The world turned, and with it billions of lives continued their inexorable stories. But despite the whirlwind of bizarre experiences, Sue, Ned, and Josh were a family stuck in neutral—unable to mourn Amy's death, but also unable to go on with the normal day-to-day joys and heartbreaks of life, had they been able to confirm that she was alive somewhere, anywhere.

"We're torn apart," Sue told reporter Edna Buchanan at the time. "We still love each other, but we're a different family than we were. Sometimes we're afraid of talking to each other out of fear of causing pain."

Sergeant Mike Gonzales told Buchanan: "Sue Billig is still the same bright, talented individual she always was, but she's had experiences that no one like her has ever had. The uncertainty of what happened to her daughter is traumatic and ugly. It had to change part of her. I have never seen anyone go to such extremes to find someone. She's obsessed with it."

And she was. Anytime someone would suggest that she take a rest, a vacation, or imply that Amy was probably already dead, Sue would put it out of her mind. She felt as if she would somehow *know* Amy was no longer walking the earth. There was a connection that still felt very real and palpable. Certainly, if you believed the psychics—they all said that Amy was alive. If something had happened to her, wouldn't some evidence have been found? Judging from the Hell's Angels rock-pit debacle, these guys weren't always that good at disposing of bodies. Day in and day out, murder victims were found in fields, canals, and woods. No matter what people might say, it wasn't that easy to make somebody disappear forever.

And at every knock at the door, Sue would fantasize that Amy had returned. Every time the telephone rang, she thought it would be Amy at the other end . . . with a tale of woe and misery, but alive.

Sue spent virtually every waking and dreaming moment with her daughter on her mind. "I only feel alive when I'm searching for Amy," she told her friends and reporters. "The worst time is when nothing is happening. I get desperate because I think people will for-

get. . . . I look in the mirror and I don't recognize myself."

Frank Rubino shakes his head in disbelief now,
knowing all that would come later, and offers a smile
of respect. "Sue is just the toughest person I've ever
come in contact with," he says.

That was a year into the nightmare. How Sue would
keep going through a life that would become ever more
bizarre, like a twisted tale of *Alice Through the Looking Glass*, can only be attributed to pure willpower. It
really is better not to know the future.

5

The Billigs had just spent their second Thanksgiving without Amy. The holidays are always hard for families missing a loved one, and it was depressing for the Billigs, who could now look forward to an empty Hanukkah/Christmas season. As always, there would be many Grove parties and get-togethers, but this time they would stand among their friends, Amy's friends, trying to conceal the emptiness they felt inside. Everyone would remember how much Amy enjoyed special events and parties and being surrounded by her friends.

On November 30, 1975, when Sue was feeling especially low, she received a call before ten in the morning.

The voice was gruff, bearlike. "Mrs. Billig? You don't know me, and I can't tell you who I am."

Sue steeled herself. She had received many calls like this. She sat down on the bed, hit the record button on the tape recorder, and started writing automatically in her notebook.

"I'm a Pagan, and I've been in jail for a while. I just got out and I was going through old newspapers and I found an article about you. Are you taping this?"

"No," Sue lied. "We haven't received any calls worth taping for a while. I'm writing it down."

"Well, I see from some of the articles that you've taped conversations, so I'll make this short. Amy was my old lady for a while in Orlando."

"Is this Creature I'm speaking to?" Sue asked breathlessly. "Amy was supposed to have been with an Outlaw named Creature."

"I told you, I'm a Pagan. She lived with me in Orlando for a while. I got her from a guy named Bracket, not Creature. But I came back to Miami to get my bike and I got arrested. One of my friends was supposed to bring Amy back down, but the deal never went down. She was living underground with some hippie chicks—"

"And you're sure this was Amy? She said her name was Amy Billig?"

The voice grew harsher in defense. "Are you crazy? Of course she wasn't using that name. She had a fake ID, like everyone else. But I'm looking at her picture in the newspaper, and I'd know her anywhere. I don't know if she even knew who she was before. But I was good to her, I didn't beat her, Mrs. Billig." His voice quailed. "I loved her, Mrs. Billig."

Tears came unbidden into Sue's eyes.

"You have to meet me," she implored. "I have to hear more. Can you help me find her? We are not looking to put anyone in jail. We will keep everything confidential. All we want is to get her back. If we do, there's a reward of $2,000."

"How do I know you're telling the truth?" the biker asked.

"Check me out with your friends. Ask Satan. Whomever . . . We swear we won't bring any heat down on you. You have my word!"

"I'll check you out and call you back," the biker said.

"Give me your name—"

"I'll call you," he said, and hung up.

Sue and Ned paced nervously all morning until the next call two hours later. The biker had "checked them out," he said.

"So you'll meet us?"

"There's a Fina station on Krome Avenue, just north of Quail Roost Drive. You can't miss it. Be there at three P.M."

"How will I know you?" Sue asked.

"Oh, you won't be able to miss me," he told her.

Krome Avenue was really Route 27, way out in west Dade, pretty much a man-made border between development and the Everglades. The Fina was a fill-up station for farmers in the Redlands and Homestead, truckers headed north with loads of fresh produce, fisherman headed into the swamps trailing giant airboats behind pickup trucks, and vanloads of migrant farm workers who pulled up to buy beer. A thousand drug deals had probably gone down in the parking lot. If authorities weren't tapping the battered pay phones, they certainly should have been.

Ned and Susan pulled up in their station wagon and

turned the engine off. They opened the windows to a cool breeze washing in from over the swamp that smelled of mud and distant fertilizer. Sue was extremely nervous.

They didn't have to wait long. They could hear the popping echo of the Harley before they could see it. Soon, a hulking, black-leathered rider sped into view, then swerved into the gravel parking lot, spitting rocks from beneath his tires.

He stopped and looked around. His pale freckled arms stuck out like tattooed hams from his black vest with the Pagans' insignia emblazoned across the back. The tattoos were of an eagle, a naked woman, and others. A couple of lower ones had been burned off, showing rippled skin. Probably remnants of another bike club before the Pagans. Of course, he had the one percent tattoo branded on his knuckles. He had longish, red curly hair and sideburns, mustache, and a beard crawling over a meaty white face that looked fresh from prison. He scouted around and spied Sue and Ned, the one great anomaly sitting in the parking lot. They wouldn't miss him, and he sure couldn't miss them.

He cranked the handle and the giant black Harley with balding tires reared in their direction. He pulled up on Sue's passenger side and stuck his head down.

"Ever ride a Hog, Mrs. Billig?" he croaked.

Ned was incensed. "I'm not letting her go anywhere alone," he insisted, getting out of the car.

The biker looked at the slim middle-aged art dealer with thinning hair. The Pagan had killed men three times Ned's size and a thousand times meaner without thinking twice, and then done jail time with the worst sons of bitches in the country. Ned wasn't someone who would give orders to him. "You want any info about your daughter, you're gonna get it from me," he said without even raising his voice. "Now me and the little lady are going for a ride, and you'll wait here for her until we get back."

Sue got out of the car and slammed the door. "Ned, I'm going," she said. "It'll be all right."

Ned bristled. "We don't even know his name," he said.

Sue hopped on the back of the bike, no helmet, getting a painful burn from the muffler. "Ouch! I'll be all right," she said firmly.

Not many men of any size would have argued with the biker. Ned took a breath and prayed as Sue blew him a kiss. Suddenly, it was like lifting off in a jet. The giant motor blasted beneath her. She was caught in a universe of sound. Sue gripped the giant ribs in front of her as the bike exploded onto the road. Wind whipped her hair as she gripped the bike seat between her thighs and prayed.

She couldn't see the speedometer but guessed they must have accelerated from zero to 60 in a few seconds. The biker changed gears, the sound of the motor increased, and the diminutive five-foot-two-inch interior decorator cinched her eyes shut against the wind, knowing they were going at least 100 miles an hour.

Just as suddenly, the driver braked, leaned left and cut into a side road. She forced her eyes open, wanting to see where they were going in case she had to get there again—or if she had to get away. The road turned into a gravel drive lined with weedy sawgrass and half-smashed mailboxes nailed onto posts that jutted at various angles to the road. They passed a group of faded trailers with old rusted cars in front, tires piled here and there, and dusty dogs lazing in the sun. One looked up, started to bark, and thought better of it, scuttling away with its tail between its legs.

The Pagan pulled up to a medium-size trailer guarded by a giant, drooling mastiff hitched to a rusty chain.

Sue, a bit woozy, disembarked from the bike. The biker laughed at her. "Never been on a bike before, have you?"

She shook her head. "My leg hurts. But it was quite an experience." She took everything in. There was a rusted 1960s-era two-door Valiant parked nearby, trailing a taillight on wires. She memorized the license plate: 4-85026.

The large man pet the dog, which was growling at Sue, and pushed open the front door. It was littered with old pizza boxes, beer cans, and drug paraphernalia. The sink was piled with dirty dishes. Ashtrays had long ago been filled and had mountains of cigarettes piled in them.

The biker strode over to the chugging refrigerator and grabbed a can of beer from inside. "Want one?" he offered.

"Just tell me about Amy," Sue said, "I can't wait any longer. Describe her for me. I need to know that it was Amy you were with."

He sat down on a ragged old Barcalounger and took

a swig of beer. "Well, she's a skinny girl. Skinny all over. Especially her legs. She reads a lot. Always reading. She listens to music. Likes crap like that Joni Mitchell woman. She's definitely not like the other girls."

This all rang true to Sue, from the skinny legs to the music. But a smart man could have deduced some of that from the articles.

"But was she all right, healthy?" Sue demanded.

He swigged the second half of the beer down like water, then fetched another. "She'd been knocked around plenty by the time I got her," he said. "Had bruises on her face and knots on her head. I know she didn't know who she was anymore. Didn't remember her name or her family. So it's not like she's scorned you. She had a fake ID and I got her another one. She was afraid to do anything on her own. Say boo, and she cried. But she was so sweet. She hardly talked at all, but when she was alone she would sing a bit. Had a real nice voice."

"Tell me something else," Sue said. "There's information we haven't allowed anyone to know about, so we could identify her. What kind of rings did she wear?"

"I don't remember no fucking jewelry," the Pagan scoffed. "But she did have a thin, two-inch appendix scar, way down to her waist."

Susan gasped. "That's right! You're the first person to come up with that!" For the first time since the Majik Market, she felt she was really on Amy's trail.

"But I got to know," the man said. "All you want to

do is talk to her. You're not going to force her to leave?" He sounded upset. He was definitely in love with her and didn't want them to take her away.

Sue wanted to jump up and scratch his eyes out. Of course, the first thing they would do was bundle Amy up, get Frank Rubino and the police, and take her away from wherever she was. She'd been kidnapped and brainwashed as sure as any cult. Instead she spoke in a level voice: "It'll be her choice. We just want to know she's alive."

"You seem all right, lady. Got some spunk. I'll send a letter to one of my buddies whose doing time in Raiford. And we'll get you a picture of her so you know she's alive. Let me take you back to hubby now. He's probably about to die."

The bike ride back was just a little less nerve wracking. Before, she had no idea what type of situation she was headed into. But now she was okay. On the way back she kept her eyes open and actually smiled. This wasn't so bad after all. This biker seemed to have been genuinely nice to Amy—really seemed to want to help.

She told this all to Ned, who had been half out of his mind with worry. She wrote down the license plate number she'd memorized, and as soon as they were home, she called the policewoman, Ina Shepard, and filled her in on everything, including the plate number.

Ina called back quickly, her voice tense. "Was this guy about six-two and 225 pounds? Has an eagle and a woman tattoo?"

"Yes, that's him," Sue said.

"Well, the car is registered to a Paul Preston Branch, got a sheet longer than he is tall. Been arrested for auto theft, concealed weapons, assault, and—get this—he did eight years for murder. Got out, and got clipped for a second degree murder charge. Shot a guy in the head in a bar. Got off on a technicality. This is one mean and dangerous man you're playing with here, if it's the same guy. I want you to be extremely careful."

"If he was in jail, how did he have Amy?" Sue asked.

"Looks like he wasn't put in jail until July of 'seventy-four. That makes plenty of time for him to have had her. It's hard to tell from the records I have, but it looks like he probably got out last month."

When the biker called the morning of December 2, the possible murderer told Ned, "I'm sending a letter to Raiford today."

"Is this for the picture of Amy you mentioned?" Ned asked.

"We got a long way to go for that, pops," Branch said. "First we have to find where she's been put. Then we'll see what we can do after that. I might have to break some heads to get her back."

6

The holidays seemed brighter after they had received the new information about Amy. In fact, it seemed fitting they would hear something about her during Hannukah or Christmas. The family always celebrated both because they had so many friends of different faiths, and because they welcomed any cause for celebration. There was almost an air of expectation hovering in the house.

But after New Year's 1975, with no more contact from the mysterious biker, Sue began to think she was on another roller-coaster ride. It was time to apply some pressure to make things happen.

Ina Shepard was able to get Creature's arrest record. He was the Kissimmee Outlaw who supposedly had owned Amy when she was identified at the Majik Market. His real name was David Clark: six-five, reddish blond hair, 250 pounds, with arrests for assault, robbery, and assault with intent to kill. Another real nice guy. He sounded a lot like the mysterious biker who had taken Sue for the fast motorcycle ride.

Sue knew there was no way Ned would allow her to

go back to the trailer if she told him about her plans, so she arranged to go out with Father Hingston, who had accompanied them to the Denny's to meet the former narcotics detectives a few months earlier in October. Shepard and her partner would wait nearby in an undercover vehicle in case backup was needed.

It was a bright January day, with a brisk northern breeze that froze your ears and turned the sky a clear shimmering blue. Father Hingston drove a bright red Fiat convertible, a bit racy for a minister, but this was Coconut Grove, after all. He was in his fifties, with gray hair and a very respectable reputation. He kept reassuring Sue about Amy as he accelerated through yellow lights and wove through traffic as if he believed God truly was his copilot. There was no seat belt in this tiny car, either. "The congregation of St. Stephen's has been praying for Amy," he said. "How can God let something bad happen to her?"

Sue thanked him for his support, saying, "I hope you have a more direct line to God than I have, because I've been talking his ears off."

They met Shepard out at the Fina station and continued from there.

Sue had a sharp memory, and despite the trauma of her first ride, easily found what turned out to be the Sunarama trailer park, surrounded by a barbed-wire fence.

Shepard parked inconspicuously out by the main road as Father Hingston edged the Fiat alongside the battered trailer. The motorcycle was parked there, but the Valiant was not in evidence. Instead there was a blue pop-top van. Sue hastily memorized the license number, as she had with the Valiant. Hingston waited in the car as she walked up the aluminum stairs and knocked nervously on the trailer door.

The mastiff barked so loudly it seemed the walls would explode outward.

"Who's there?" came a suspicious snarl.

"This is Susan Billig, I was here the other day," Sue explained.

The sound of her nonthreatening female voice placated the man inside. "Shaddup, already!" he commanded the dog. The blinds inside the door window parted momentarily and a jaundiced eye peered out before the door cracked open. It wasn't the biker she had met before. This guy was wearing a similar black vest over a grimy T-shirt, greasy Levi's, and leather boots. He was much slimmer than the other biker, but still sported the requisite tattoos, including the one percent tattoo that marked him as a gang member. "You're that little chick's mother?" he said. "Who's the guy in the car?"

"Just a minister who drove me out here," Sue explained. "I don't drive. You know who I am?"

"Yeah, my buddy told me about you. He's not here."

"Can I leave him a message?"

"Come in," he said. "Sit!" he told the dog, which was pushing forward to make sure this was no invader.

"He likes chicks, so don't worry," the biker said.

"I met him the other day," Sue said, trying to lead the biker into conversation. Maybe he would spit out his friend's name. "He's the biggest dog I've ever seen."

"Maybe the ugliest, too," the biker said. He spoke to Sue in pleasant tones and promised to relay her message to his roommate. "Darnedest thing, him seeing your daughter's picture in the paper like that," the biker said. "He's been looking for her. He was just going through the old papers to see who had been arrested while he was in prison."

Sue wrote down her number again, in case the mysterious biker had lost it. "Please make sure he gets it," she pleaded.

"Don't worry, hon, he'll get it," the man said.

Hingston drove Sue back to the Fina station, where they joined up with Shepard. Sue gave the officer the license plate number of the van she had memorized before she headed home with the daredevil minister. While nothing had really been accomplished, Sue felt strangely expectant and enjoyed the wild ride.

She had just closed the door and put her purse down when the phone rang. It was the gruff voice of the mysterious Pagan.

"Mrs. Billig?"

"Yes, is this . . . I don't know what to call you. . . ."

"It's all right, you know who I am. I've located your daughter—"

Sue yelped with delight. "I had a feeling you would!"

"She's with another dude out on the West Coast," he said. "Problem is, he really likes her and won't give her back. He doesn't know what the fuck he's dealing with, though. Asshole thinks he can keep her. I didn't sell her to nobody. He thinks he can do whatever he wants, but he can't!"

"So what are we going to do?" Sue said, her elation slightly quenched.

"Me and my buddy are moving out there in February. It'll take a few weeks to close up the trailer, get a van to haul the bikes in—"

"So what happened? How did Amy get out to the West Coast?" she asked.

"She ran with this guy because she thought I was mad at her," the Pagan said. "But it won't be a problem getting her if I show up. He don't have much backup. He's not a popular guy because he's a bit of a snitch."

"Where is she on the West Coast?" Sue asked. "L.A., San Francisco?"

"No, not there. Let's just say a long way away, it's cold there."

"Do you need any help?" Sue said. "I'll do whatever I can do. I don't have much cash—"

"Keep yer money. I'll call you when I get out there."

"I feel like I can trust you," Sue told him. "You'll do what you say you're going to do. Let me know where you are, and we can come out there. It doesn't matter how far it is, we'll get there."

"Listen, if I get out there, and she wants to come home to you, I'll put her on the next plane out—simple as that. But how can she know what she wants to do, when she doesn't even know who she is?"

"Just let me talk to her," Sue pleaded. "I know her memory will come back if I can see her or talk to her. She can't forget her family."

The biker's gruff voice softened, becoming more human and less like a grizzly.

"You'll talk to her, I'll send you photos. I promise, if she decides she wants to come home, I'll let her."

* * *

It wasn't the ringing assurance Sue had hoped for, but it wasn't hopeless. She believed this guy because he wasn't asking for money and hadn't accepted her offer of help, whatever that might be. There was no request for expenses, such as the lawmen who had promised to help yet never left Miami. He had called her on his own initiative, because somewhere under that filthy black vest beat a heart that wasn't completely rotten. Somewhere, all these guys had mothers, she thought.

She called Sid Fast, telling him about the episode, minus, of course, the involvement of Shepard.

Sid's New York–tinged voice choked. "You're talking about a big guy with red hair, got tattoos burned off his arms and lives in a trailer off Quail Roost Drive?"

"Right," Sue said.

"Well let me tell you about this nice guy of yours. His name's Paul, from St. Petersburg." A retirement town near Tampa on Florida's west coast. "He's an ex–Hell's Angel, now a Pagan who sometimes rides with Outlaws. He's had to burn off the tattoos with battery acid so he won't get himself killed. His stomach is completely blasted with acid. Right now he's an executioner for the Pagans. Man has killed a bunch of people."

Sue had already been told some of this by the police, but hearing it again, she just about lost her breath. "But he really seemed like he wanted to help."

"The other guy you talked to out there is Pompano Red," Sid said. "He's an ex-Marine and Paul's best friend. Also been booked for aiding Paul on a murder.

Listen, the last time I talked to Paul, he mentioned Arizona. I'll check around and see what I can find out. I'll call you back tomorrow."

Sue knew the Valiant was registered to a Paul Preston Branch III. She'd written that down in her notebook.

Her next call was from Ina. "Looks like you found another guy who isn't exactly a choirboy, Sue. The blue van is registered to a Dennis Kenny, aka 'Pompano Red,' from Richmond, Virginia. Six feet, 155 pounds, blue eyes, red hair. He was arrested for murder in 1974, but got off."

Sue told her that Sid had identified the mysterious biker as Paul Branch, the Pagan executioner whose murder record Shepard had already brought to light.

"Some pair living out there," she said. "You be careful with these guys. No matter how nice they seem to you, remember these guys will kill someone for looking at them wrong, let alone if they figure they need the money you got in your pocketbook."

Sue was a mass of conflicting emotions. They'd been nice to her. Hadn't asked for money! She didn't know what to think anymore. Eventually, she told Ned what she had done, but didn't mention how bad Branch's record was. There was so much she had to keep from Ned these days, otherwise he would worry too much, which might keep Sue from doing everything she had to do.

Branch called a few days later at two A.M. and woke the couple out of a fitful sleep. Ned picked up the phone, but Branch insisted on speaking to Sue. He'd obviously been drinking. His voice was as harsh as a

Harley in need of a tune-up. His words were slurred. She hadn't heard him like this before.

"You little bitch," he cursed. "You're slicker than I thought."

"What do you mean?"

"You been checking up on me, I heard about it. Found out my name and who I associate with."

Sid Fast must have slipped up when he had tried to get more information.

"It's all right," she said, "you can't expect me not to be curious."

"Well, fuck you!" he shouted through the phone. "Now you figure out how to find your kid!"

Then an abrupt dial tone.

"Oh, Ned," Sue said, "we messed up. He's mad I asked Sid to check him out."

The phone rang; she snatched it up. Just the dial tone again.

Ned hugged her close. "Tell me what happened."

Again the phone. Again the dial tone.

"He's checking up on you," Ned said. "Seeing if you're dialing out to someone."

The phone didn't ring again, but Sue didn't sleep, either. All she could think of was that this fragile thread they had found had snapped so easily. If she closed her eyes she saw Amy with this brutal man, and knew she couldn't let him get hold of her again, no matter how nice he seemed.

Sue called Sid the next morning. The biker sounded pretty hung over.

"Why did you let Paul know I knew who he was! How could you!"

Sid groaned. "We were drinking together, and it just slipped out."

"He's furious, called me names and said he wasn't going to help us out. Now what are we going to do? He's our best hope."

"Don't worry. I'm gonna fix it with him," Sid said. "I promise. He was probably just really drunk and hopped up, paranoid, when he called you. He'll be all right."

"I expect you to fix this, Sid," Susan said. "He's the only one who sounds like he's got a legitimate line on Amy. You've got to convince him he can trust me."

"I will," Sid said. But there was a tone to his voice that left Sue feeling that he was trying to brush her off. She didn't trust him to fix it.

She sat down at the dining room table and wrote a letter to Paul in compact, legible script.

Dear Paul,

I feel I must write to you immediately, so that no bad feelings remain between us. I realized from your phone call last night that you are annoyed with me, but please understand my feelings. We are talking about someone we believe to be my daughter whom I love very much. When I went to the trailer I memorized the license plate on the white car and then asked an elderly man I know who used to work for "records" to check the ownership for me. I did the same on the blue van when I went back the second time. It was the natural thing for me to do. After all I don't know you & am trying with all my heart to find Amy. Re-

member this, I did go with you alone, & was not followed or wired. I swear to you, you can check out my behavior in the past. I have never gone to the police with anyone's name, and I have spoken with some pretty "heavy" people. I have done all the investigating myself, and through friends I could trust. One of these is Sid Fast, who came to me through a bail bondsman, who is a friend of mine, Joe Klein. He has bonded out bikers for a long time & been a very fair person. I never even mentioned your whole name to Sid, because I realized I didn't know it. Now be fair, tell me—if the situation were reversed and you were looking for your child, wouldn't you check out the license # if you could?

Again, if there is any way I can help you get to her, I will. If you need money, I will get it to you. But, I must know first that it is Amy. She can call me collect any time of day or night. I will go & get her alone, anywhere. Also, from what you have previously told me, she probably does not know who she is & is not too well, so it has to be handled carefully.

I can be trusted. Please check us out & contact me again.

Sincerely,
Susan Billig

The ink letters were spattered with a few tears. She walked directly to the Coconut Grove post office, kissed the envelope, and posted it with her prayers.

Her line to God's ear had apparently gotten a bit clearer. After a nervous and completely useless week, at three A.M. on January 18, a phone call woke her out of a fitful sleep. Sue had never felt so good as she did upon hearing the gruff voice, one that was much calmer than the last time she had heard it.

"I read your letter," Paul volunteered. "You should never have involved Sid or anybody else in this. Everyone's been to jail, everyone's got their own agenda."

"I'm sorry," Sue said. "I really am. But I already knew who you were. It wasn't him."

"This is what I get for trying to be a nice guy the first time in my life. Something like this always comes to bite you in the ass," Branch complained. "Man, I am such a dumb shit. Who the fuck you think you are, Sherlock Holmes?" he said.

"Nothing's happened," she said trying to placate him. "So I know your name? It's no big deal. Listen, I said I would help you. I can get you some expense money—"

"I absolutely don't want your money," he said. "Believe me, Sid wants your money. You'll hear from him, and he's gonna want something. From here on in, you let me do things my way and I'll reconsider our relationship and call you again."

Afterward, Sue hugged the pillow as Ned brought her some herbal tea. "What do you think?" he asked. "Is he back on our side?"

Sue sighed. "I got the feeling things were better between us. You know he feels macho helping us. He's got us in his power. I just kept telling him I was wrong and he was right. He liked that. I don't think he would even have called if he wasn't planning to help. He said he didn't want our money."

Ned gave her a hug. "That's good," he said. "Because we don't have any."

7

Laying all of their hopes for the well-being of their daughter and their family on the shoulders of a brawling, drunken biker-gang "executioner" who was a step away from jail at any moment, was a very impotent feeling. People often turn to God, alcohol, food, or chocolate—not necessarily in that order—in such stressful times. But Sue worried that in the time it was taking Branch to close shop in South Florida Amy could easily be spirited somewhere else. After all, it seemed she was always on the move. Just as the Billigs got close in Orlando, for instance, Amy had been snatched from their yearning fingers.

In February, after Ina Shepard's inquiries on Branch and Dennis "Pompano Red" Kenny, she called Sue to say Virginia authorities wanted to question Red about a case involving three counts of murder, robbery, and maiming.

"I can't believe it," Sue scoffed. "Branch is a big guy, but Red doesn't look like he could hurt a fly."

"Size doesn't matter," Shepard said. "Meanness matters. He knows how to handle himself—he's an ex-

Marine. The trailer is located in unincorporated Dade, so I'll have to get the Metro-Dade police to pick him up, but I'll try to get him transferred to Miami so I can question him before he gets sent to Virginia."

"But I told him I wouldn't bring the police down on them," Sue said. "They'll never tell me where Amy is! They're packing up to go out and get her."

"We can't leave a guy like this out on the street," Ina said. "It's not Branch, just Pompano Red."

"Promise me to be very circumspect when you talk to him. Don't mention my name or that I had anything to do with this."

Ina clucked her tongue and thought a second. "It's a difficult situation, but maybe Virginia will work with us—they owe you a big favor, since you led us right to him. Maybe if he can give us information on Amy, they'll let him plea down on some charge. This is the best way, Sue, we're bargaining from a position of power. I'll be very careful when I question him."

"Good luck," Sue said.

After the call, she went into the kitchen, mouthing a silent prayer as she poured herself a glass of wine. She knew this would be another night when she wouldn't be able to eat. She dialed her private detective, Frank Rubino, and filled him in on the situation. He would also try to question the Pagan when he was under arrest.

The phone rang again later in the evening. The Billigs had been pouring from a bottle of wine that became progressively emptier but did not take the edge off the nervous adrenaline pumping through their bodies. This waiting, always waiting, for phone calls—

somewhere in Dante's Hell, Sue thought, this must be one of the levels of Purgatory.

Ina called back later in the evening.

"Oh, thank God," Sue said. "I couldn't bear it much longer."

"We brought Kenny in," Ina said. "They were pretty stoned and didn't offer much fuss. We got lucky, too. Branch actually came in voluntarily to help his buddy out. I showed them pictures of Amy and said I was the detective on the case and that I was asking all bikers I came in contact with if they knew her."

"And?" Sue prompted.

"Red said, 'Oh, yeah, that's the Billig girl. Her mother came to see me at the trailer.' But he was just too strung out to get more information from. I then questioned Branch separately. I acted surprised to find out you had been to the trailer, and I think he bought it. He told me he had brought you out there, but changed his story a bit. Said he was only 'pretty sure' the girl he had known was Amy, and he didn't 'want to get your hopes up too much,' even though he could use the reward money."

Sue sputtered in disbelief. "That's exactly the opposite of what he told me," she fumed. "And exactly opposite to what I have on tape! He told us he could absolutely identify Amy from the pictures, and he even described her appendix scar. That information has never been published. He's just trying to distance himself from this, because he can't admit that he's part of a possible kidnapping. That's his out. Can we put more pressure on him somehow?"

"I can't charge him with any parole violations," she

said, "because he did all his time. He just can't ever own a gun again. He's still planning to help you out, though," Ina added. "He's on his way out to Oregon, but said he's stopping first in Omaha, Nebraska, to 'see the girl.' He said a biker named 'Dishrag Harry' has her, and that he thinks he knows where to find them, because they were staying with a guy named Pete. Dishrag Harry calls her 'Little Bits.' "

"Little Bits?" Sue sighed. Thinking about Amy as a biker babe was not comforting. "At least see if he'll give you the full name of this Pete, and any other information on Dishrag Harry. See if you can get his phone bills and see where he's been calling. Maybe Pete will be on it."

"I'll see what we can do," Ina said. "He's definitely not afraid of me, so maybe there's something I can charge him with that will loosen his tongue."

Paul was steadfast, however. He swore he wasn't going to snitch on anybody, and seemed to feel the information he had would be his "get out of jail free" card if anything happened in the future. It was a Mexican standoff. Sue became panicky as weeks passed and Branch's promised departure to Omaha seemed in danger of unraveling completely. If he didn't move now, she thought, Amy could be gone by the time he arrived.

But at least he was keeping in touch with her—that was something. By the first week in March, when time seemed to have come to a standstill and the weather had turned from winter to a tepid spring, Sue and Frank Rubino drove out to the Sunarama trailer park to confront Branch.

It was nine-thirty A.M., pretty early for a biker to be up, when they bumped into the dirt parking lot in Rubino's Mustang.

Branch threw the door open when they knocked. "Can't you ever come alone?" he yelled, and pointed at Rubino. "And you bring a cop with you?"

"He's not a cop," Sue said. "He's just a friend helping me out. He's a lawyer." Rubino had, in fact, recently passed the bar. "Can we come in?"

"In, out, what's the difference?" Branch groused. "I'm not going to tell you any more."

The interior of the trailer was dank, smelly, and looked like it had not been cleaned since the last time Sue visited. A pack of wild monkeys would have kept it in better shape. Newspapers, pizza boxes, cans . . . standard biker decor. The biker also seemed to be wearing the same clothes he'd been wearing when she saw him last; as if they achieved some level of petrifaction and stayed that way.

The big difference this time was in Branch's demeanor. Sue was glad Frank was there. Branch's face was red in apoplexy, with green veins pulsing in his neck and forehead. "You sure smell like a cop," he told Frank. "I can spot one a mile away. You a fed?" He breathed rancid air into Rubino's face.

The former Secret Service agent denied it. "I'm a P.I. who has been helping Sue," he stated plainly.

Branch pulled a beer from the refrigerator but didn't bother offering any to his guests. He swallowed the contents of the can and tossed it behind him, where it clanked against a pile of others. "This whole situation is fucked! I wish I'd never called you," he raged. "That snitch Fast must have ratted me out to the police. Now Red's in jail, and they just busted me a couple nights ago for a DUI, possession of a firearm, and, get this, having a broken speedometer on my bike! I had to bond out, and got it hanging over my head now. This whole thing is a pain in the ass."

"If you'd left earlier that might not have happened," Sue said. "Amy could be anywhere by now."

"I couldn't leave until I was ready. Now I have to deal with all this bullshit."

"I'm also a lawyer," Frank volunteered. "What if I straighten your life out? I'll do it for free if you'll go find Amy."

Branch's attitude changed. Even through the rage and the beer, he realized this was a good offer. "You any good?"

"Better than a public defender," Rubino observed.

"You got yourself a deal," the biker said. "You get me off, and I'll get you Amy."

Frank dropped by Sue's house the next day. He looked a little less sure of himself than the day before as he sat at the table and drank a cup of coffee. "He wasn't being honest with us, Sue," he said. "These are actually heavy charges. Two are felonies that carry up to fifteen-year sentences and might cost a lot of time and money to defend. His trial's set for next week. I'll see what I can do before that, but don't you think we should have more positive proof that this really is Amy we're dealing for?"

"Definitely," Sue agreed.

Because of the severity of the charges, Rubino contacted another lawyer, Rex Ryland, and brought him onto the case. Ryland lived around the corner from the Billigs, so he was easily accessible, and had worked extensively with elements such as Paul Branch.

Ryland was from deep-south Alabama, and he sounded like it. He had a wiry build, sported shoulder-length brown hair, smoked pipes and cigars, and wore cowboy boots to court. Before he had even graduated the University of Miami Law School, he'd had the good fortune to be hired by "Murf the Surf's" attorneys in Fort Lauderdale as a law clerk on the case. Jack "Murf the Surf" Murphy was the infamous jewel thief who in 1964 had robbed the 563-carat Star of India sapphire and other major jewels from the American Museum of Natural History in New York City. While Murphy was ultimately convicted and given two life sentences plus twenty years, the case had placed Ryland in front of the television cameras, where he enjoyed the limelight and the high-profile cases that continued to come his way after he graduated. Still, he also had a kind heart, and took Branch's case pro bono if it would help the Billigs find Amy.

Shepard made good on getting the phone records and mailed a copy to Sue, who forwarded them to Ryland. Days and weeks were going by, and she was getting ever more antsy. But the lawyer was snowed under and was barely able to return her calls.

Nothing was happening fast enough for Sue, but Branch's first trial finally came up on April 7. She went to court to watch the proceedings and hopefully exert her willpower on the legal system to come through for

Branch. A series of losers of all ethnic groups and ages were brought up one by one. DUIs, robberies, shoplifting, prostitution—some in the red overalls of prisoners who couldn't afford to be bonded out, others dressed in suits and ties, trying to look like they were not the menace to society that they were. Most cases were pleaded out or continued in seconds.

Branch still wore his black leather vest, but his T-shirt and Levi's were clean. Against his bulk sat a pudgy, worn-out woman in her thirties, with swollen eyes, wearing similar biker-babe clothing.

The imposing biker strode up to the bench when he was called. The judge stared at him in only mild disgust and asked how he pleaded.

"Not guilty, Your Honor," Branch said in a cordial manner.

Sue stifled a laugh.

Ryland asked for a continuance and was able to get Paul's DUI postponed for three weeks. Tomorrow, the harsher gun charges would be brought in a different courtroom.

They all had coffee at the downstairs cafeteria, and then Paul, still driving the Valiant despite his DUI charge, drove Sue back to the gallery in Coconut Grove. His girlfriend, Tina, said little and was relegated to the backseat.

Sue looked at her and tried to see Amy in her shoes. The woman probably looked ten years older than her natural age. She had the swollen face of a drinker and the glazed eyes of someone who just didn't care what happened to her anymore. Her skin had the pallor of someone who spent their days and nights in bars, and she squinted at the sun like a vampire. Pendulous breasts sweated against her T-shirt under the black leather vest.

Paul drove the several miles through Miami's grueling traffic as if there were no impending charges. "You have to do something really stupid to get stopped," he observed.

Sue neglected to remind him that he had in fact been stopped, otherwise he wouldn't be in the trouble he now found himself in.

The Pagan whipped the car through traffic on I-95. When three cars driving abreast blocked the lanes ahead, he swerved onto the shoulder, gunned the accelerator and passed on the far right side as he gave the drivers his finger.

"Please, Paul," Sue said. "If you get a continuance on the gun charge tomorrow, let me fly you out to wherever Amy is. You can get her and bring her back."

Paul spit out of the open window, letting the wind splash it against the windshield of one of the cars they had just passed. "Can't," he said. "One of the brothers got a funeral in Orlando on Saturday. Can't miss that!"

Sue wanted to scream. "I can get you back for that, it's three days!"

Paul stopped paying attention to the road and looked at her like she was crazy. "If I get her back for you, what's that going to do for my legal defense?"

"You can trust me," Sue said. Then: "Watch out!" as they almost plowed into a car they had overtaken way too fast.

Paul hawked a wad of something awful in his throat and spit it out the window again. "Tina, hand me a beer from back there!" he commanded. Then to Sue: "A friend of mine is leaving for the place in ten days." He grabbed the beer can that Tina held out, put it in his lap and popped the top. "He'll take pictures of Amy and send them back here. Will that put your mind at rest?"

"My mind won't be at rest until I have my child home in her bed."

"Take it or leave it," Paul answered.

The further continuance came through. Two weeks later Paul said his partner had already left on April 17, and would arrive at his mysterious destination shortly.

"But," he added, "he's pulling a heavy load—trailer with bikes and other crap in it and he's got some stops to make along the way. So don't be calling me every day. He'll get there when he gets there. Don't push too hard."

Sue took a deep breath but couldn't keep the anger out of her voice. "That's no way to talk to me," she scolded the big man on the other end of the phone. "I'm working hard for you, Rex is working hard to keep you out of jail, and you're not giving much back, mister. Now, God forbid something happens to you. What will I do? You're my only contact. At least write down where Amy is and put it in a safe place. Tell Rex where you have it."

Amazingly, Branch did not blow his top and hang up. He was smarter than that. "Okay," he said. "My trial comes up tomorrow. I'll talk to him then."

"Good luck in court," Sue said, meaning it.

"Let's just hope that lawyer you got me is as good as he says," Paul answered skeptically. "I been in front of plenty of judges, and had plenty of lawyers. None has ever been worth a damn. Red's back here now, though. He's got charges pending against him in Virginia, but right now they can't make them stand. But me, somehow I always end up with the cuffs slapped on my wrists. If Rex gets me off, it'll be a first."

But Ryland was every bit as good as he promised. He called Sue with a jubilant voice. "Got him acquitted on the DUI charges!" he said. "Paul was so surprised, I thought he was going to piss his pants. Said this was the first time a lawyer had ever won anything for him."

"That's great," Sue said. "Thank you so much. You've truly been wonderful through all this. Did you speak at all about Amy, now that the worst is over?"

"We still have the gun charge next Tuesday. I'll bring it up then," Rex promised.

Sue called Paul to congratulate him. "Can you believe it?" Branch whooped. "Man, that's a load off my mind!"

No thanks, no information offered about Amy. Sue was able to keep her cool and not blow up at him. Somehow she refrained from demanding the information about Amy. He still had the important gun charge hanging over his head, so she had leverage on him.

A few weeks later she called Branch at the trailer. Tina answered, sounding strung out, and handed the phone to Paul.

"I got a terrible hangover," he said. "So don't shout."

"Has your partner gotten to where Amy is yet?" Sue asked.

"Not yet. He's had car problems and now I've got to

go to St. Pete to scare up some money to send him. He's got a Polaroid camera, though. So as soon as he sees Amy, he'll send a picture of her."

Again, even though Sue had arranged for his legal defense, he wasn't asking for any money, so that reassured her that he was speaking the truth. She would have done anything to move things along at that point. The weapon trial had been postponed until June, so Paul wasn't about to disappear.

"Don't worry," Paul said, "everything's on track. It'll just take a few more days."

"I'm tired of always hearing a few more days, Paul," Sue complained. "String a few more days together and it turns into weeks. You know better than I do how she could disappear at any moment. It's taken you months to find her already."

"Look, lady," Paul said, "it'll happen when it happens."

Goading a biker with a hangover wasn't a good idea, but Sue couldn't help herself. Sometimes it seemed she was the only person in the world who was really looking for Amy. The idea that her daughter's sprightly, blithe spirit could be transformed into a soul as tragic as Tina made her ill. "I don't think you understand how much is being done for you between Frank, Rex, and me," Sue said.

"You think I care that much?" Branch said. "If I really wanted I could hightail it out of here and buy a completely new identity tomorrow. You'd never see me again. But I'm staying here, going through the court trials and everything. . . . Doesn't that mean something? I wouldn't be going through all this if I didn't

plan to keep my end of the bargain." He yelled off the
phone. "Tina, make me a Bloody Mary and roll a fucking joint. I can't stand this anymore." Back at Sue:
"Listen, when we find Amy, I think Rex should be the
one who comes out and gets her. You're too damned
emotional. When you see Amy you're going to break
down, and it might fuck everything up."

Sue choked back her first reply and took a deep
breath before replying. Tina must have finished making his liquid breakfast, because Branch slurped something noisily. "I can control myself," Sue said in a stern
voice. "I have complete control, and I think I've proved
that."

"You just keep it that way," Paul said. "I'll think it
over. My guy is almost there. I'll talk to you soon. Now
where is that fuckin' joint!"

Over the next few days, Sue went to pick up the phone
a dozen times to call Paul to find out if his friend had
arrived. She would start to dial. It even began to ring
once before she hung up. No, she couldn't make him
think she was falling apart. She tried to take her mind
off Paul, cleaned the house incessantly, made sure
Amy's room was gorgeous and ready for her return,
packed a suitcase full of her daughter's favorite
clothes, and made sure she had the latest photos and
news of Amy's friends. She would take Amy by force
if she had to, but wouldn't it be better if Amy came
home because she wanted to, because she couldn't
help but do anything else?

Sue had to prove she was as strong and in control as

she had promised. Her patience paid off. Paul called her two days later in the afternoon. He'd already started drinking, and his craggy voice was slurred.

"My buddy's out there. He's located Amy," Branch said. "Now it's just a matter of getting the picture."

"Oh, my," Sue said. Her heart beat a staccato in her chest. Her head felt like it was full of helium. Could it be? "When? When can he get the picture?"

"It's not so easy," Branch cautioned her. "The guy has her, he knows this guy is my buddy. He's trying to keep her hidden from anyone knows me, 'cluding my buddy."

"But you said your friend knows where Amy is?"

"In general," Branch said. "We're close. We're close. Very close."

Things were happening in rapid succession now. A few days later Rex Ryland called to say, "All charges against Branch have been dropped!"

"Just like that?" Sue asked. "I thought that weapon charge was serious."

"I found some procedural problems in the arrest. Once we got the DUI thrown out, the other charges stemmed from it. Everything's tainted now. It's a technicality, but that's how things work."

A tornado was spinning in Sue's mind. "That's great. Let's get Paul on a plane and fly him out to wherever his friend is to get Amy."

"Listen, kid," Ryland said. "I called out to the trailer the other day and got Pompano Red on the phone. He said Branch is really worried about you coming along."

"He told me the same thing. Get this straight: I am her mother, and I am going. Get that guy to send the pictures, and if it's her, like Paul says, let's go."

Ryland sighed. "You're a tough cookie, Sue. I'll call Paul now and give him the news, and we'll figure out what our next step is."

8

June in Miami meant rain. Days on end of thick, warm rain that flooded the streets and eventually turned your roof into a sponge. Combined with the summer heat, it made you feel like you were living in a natural steam bath. Tempers flared easily, and beleathered bikers like Paul Branch—especially those living in hot, rancid trailers—were definitely looking toward cooler climes. He wanted to get out of town and on Amy's trail as much as Sue wanted him to. So it was a desperate Pagan who called Sue on the first day of June.

"Mrs. Billig . . ." he began. Not the usual "babe" or "look lady," and the dozen other implied put-downs. His voice didn't even have its normal sound of a grinding transmission. "I really hate to ask you this, but I have nowhere else to turn."

Sue had never heard Branch speak so softly before. "Yes, what is it?"

"It's my bike. It needs repairs for the trip, but I just ain't got the bread. A friend of mine will do a complete overhaul for one hundred and twenty-five bucks."

"Paul," she said, "get your friend to send the Polaroid and we'll buy you a new bike. We haven't gotten anything from you."

"My guy is there. He's keeping tabs on the situation. The guy who has Amy isn't going anywhere without us knowing. But getting the picture is tougher than I thought. One hundred twenty-five bucks gets me there, Mrs. Billig. It's worth it."

"I'll meet you at the Fina station at three P.M.," Sue said. "We'll talk."

Though the amount of money he asked for was not considerable, the Billigs' finances were already operating on fumes. Sue called the bank president in charge of the Find Amy Billig Fund and asked him to release the amount of money in question.

The banker met her in the lobby with a check. He was the same generous man who had supplied the $30,000 to flush out the Glasser twins just weeks after Amy's disappearance. But it was also his responsibility to make sure the funds were properly allocated. "We can't give him any more than this, though," he told her as she slipped the check into her purse.

"I know," Sue said. "It's such a Catch-22 situation. If we give him money, we don't know if the information is legitimate or if he's just stringing us along. But if we don't give him the cash he needs, we may never find Amy. I've been struggling with it. But he knows we're not cash cows, and this is only $125. So it makes me think he's for real. If he gets us a photo of Amy, then really, he's holding all the cards. I'd sell the shirt on my back."

A friend drove Sue out to the Fina station and she got there a bit early. Branch was already there, bike parked in a line of shade under the roof overhang. For a biker, Branch was very good about making his appointments. So far he had usually called within agreed-upon parameters, and he always appeared where he said he would be, whether or not it was to his immediate benefit.

Sue held up the check, made out to cash. "Before I give this to you, you have to promise me something," she said.

He rolled his eyes and blew out an exasperated breath. He might have been a puppy dog during their earlier conversation, but a couple of drinks had hardened his personality in the interim. "What now?" he asked, his hazy blue eyes shifting into the distance.

"I know you won't tell me exactly where Amy is, but give me something. A territory. And I want you to tell Rex everything, under attorney-client privilege. Tell him exactly where she is, and with whom. Because if something happens to you before you get there, we're left with nothing. Someone's got to know. I've kept up my part of the bargain, and now I'm giving you money. It's not too much to ask."

His annoyed gaze lighted on her. A lot of heavy-duty guys would have pissed their pants had Branch, the Pagan executioner, looked at them this way, or dodged and run before going this far. But Sue felt nothing anymore. No fear. No bravery. No nervousness. Just purpose. She would attempt to manipulate the devil himself if it served to retrieve Amy.

"She's in Oklahoma," Branch sputtered. "A large town. The bike'll take a few days to fix. There's one small court thing we have to deal with on the seventh, and then I'm out of here."

Sue handed him the check. "It's a good investment, Mrs. Billig," he said. "I'm down to zero. Had to sell Tina for a credit card yesterday."

"What?" Sue said. "You sold the girl for a credit card?"

Paul shrugged and spit onto the pavement in the path of a man who was walking up to the front doors of the convenience store. The large redneck farmer snapped his head to look at the culprit, his eyes registering the monster in front of him. Then he put his head down and hurried forward. Paul let out an ugly chuckle. "Bought her for a credit card, sold her for one. That's how it works. I've sold 'em for a drink," he said. His eyes shifted appreciatively toward a mountain of Budweiser stacked in the store window.

Sue caught the glance. "Promise me you'll use the money for the bike!"

Paul scratched his crotch. "Yeah yeah. It's for the bike. I ain't using it for anything else."

Sue figured she was on a roll. "And you'll call me from the road?"

"I'll call you when I'm two days away from the destination. I'll check into a motel, and you can fly out and meet me there. Maybe you can bring Rex for company. I'll go get her, and I'll bring her back to you at the motel."

"Oh, Paul. Please, please . . ." She sighed, and tears

sprang into her eyes. She reached out and grabbed his hand, callused as his soul. "Tell me it's really going to happen!"

"Have I lied to you yet?" he countered.

Sue shook her head, feeling impotent as ever. "That's the problem. I really wouldn't know, would I?"

"I got no reason to lie," Paul said. "The legal stuff was important, but half the guys I know are living on fake IDs, so it's not the biggest deal in the world. If I was trying to con you, I'd be squeezing out a lot more than $125!"

Somehow, Sue believed this modern day pirate for whom lies were a living. She analyzed her feelings, knowing that even without proof, she would have given him much more money. As far as it went, she trusted him. She patted his hand. "You take care," she said, and admonished him like she was his mother: "And drive carefully!"

Sue and Rex met for lunch at a Grove restaurant the next day. He told her he would come with her to Oklahoma and prod Paul to leave directly from the courthouse if necessary. Per Sue's instructions, he would try to get Branch to confide in him as to Amy's whereabouts, as well.

On Monday, June 8, true to his word, Paul called to tell Sue he was leaving right after a breakfast of steak and eggs, and said, "I've filled Rex in on everything. I'll call you as soon as I check into a hotel."

Sue couldn't believe the words. "You've told Rex everything?" she insisted.

"Everything," he repeated. "See you in about a week."

Sue dialed Rex immediately. "Can't talk now," he said. "Meet me for lunch?"

They met at the Greenhouse restaurant in the Grove.

"Paul said he told you where Amy is?" Sue said the moment she sat down.

His voice was not as chipper as she had hoped. "He told me Tulsa, Sue. Says a guy named 'Dishrag Harry' has her. Full name is Harry Kramer. But said he didn't have an address. He knows who has her, though, and where to find him."

Sue's appetite disappeared. "That isn't much," she said. "Just some other scumbag biker name. We're no further than we were before."

"Kramer's a Pagan," Rex replied. "Has sandy hair and a tattoo of a Pagan god on one arm. Works in a downtown gas station in Tulsa. That's a lot of info to drag out of Paul in one day. Get Shepard to run Kramer's name and see if he's got a record here or in Oklahoma, and maybe we'll get some more information on him. Branch said it would take him a week to make the trip. We'll fly out Saturday, so we're already there when Paul arrives. When he calls back to Miami, Ned can tell him the hotel we're staying at. We'll save a day!"

Even though days, weeks, and months had passed without hearing Amy's voice, saving that extra day seemed like a brilliant idea. She couldn't even wait that long. "Oh God," Sue said. "I wish Paul had given you this guy's address. What if something happens to him along the way?"

"Branch has ridden a million miles," Rex observed. "He'll make it a thousand more."

Time is the strangest of human perceptions, always doing the opposite of what we wish. The next five days dragged mercilessly as Sue bought fresh sheets and a calico bedspread for Amy's room. She dusted and cleaned the entire house for the umpteenth time. Ned tried to get her to relax.

"No, sweetheart," Sue said. "I want everything to be perfect when Amy comes home. The exact opposite of wherever she's been. It'll be like starting life over again. We'll be a family again, instead of a group of relatives living together."

Ned smiled and hugged his wife. Someone had asked him recently how you stayed married for so long. "It's easy," he had replied. "You just don't leave." But it was much more than that, wasn't it? How couldn't you love this feisty bundle of energy? Always looking at the most optimistic side of everything. So sure she was on her way to find her daughter that she bought her new sheets and shampooed Amy's dog!

He wished he could be so positive. It would be wonderful to feel that way, for even a second. A moment of joy would mean so much. He wished he could go to Tulsa, too, but he had to stay and keep the gallery open. It was the only thing buttering the toast and paying the bills in some semblance of a timely manner. And someone had to be here to take the phone calls that still kept coming—and to wait for Branch's phone call as well.

* * *

Rex Ryland's friendship continued to know no bounds. He shelled out the money for both plane tickets, despite having to purchase high-priced business fares. Sue even had to fight for those, as all scheduled flights were booked on Saturday.

She called the authorities in Tulsa ahead of time and carefully wrote down the names of officers involved in biker investigations, the District Attorney's number, and even the name of a known biker hangout—the Anchor Bar.

By Saturday, plans included Rex, his wife Shannon, and their daughter Lee. Of course, luggage was lost, connecting flights were delayed, tickets didn't match up. It seemed like everything in the world was trying to keep them out of Tulsa. Good thing they were arriving early, Sue thought. If they were flying later in the week, when Branch was supposed to have Amy, and all this was keeping them away, she would have had a mental breakdown at the Dallas airport when Delta lost the Rylands' luggage. Sue arrived in Tulsa with Lee, expecting Rex and Shannon on the next flight.

The moment she hit the airport she ran to a bank of pay phones and called home. Ned informed her that there was still no word from Branch. They all checked into a downtown Holiday Inn, the last rooms in the place, because a convention of Jehovah's Witnesses were booked into the hotel. The "saved" walked around carrying stacks of the *Watchtower* in their arms and gazed at Sue and the Rylands with the condescending smiles reserved for the poor souls who wouldn't convert. Sue looked at the happy Witnesses. Of course, each person, no doubt, had weathered their own tragedies, but she couldn't help but wish that a week from now she could be as mindlessly blissful as they seemed to be.

The three ate a very late dinner of overdone hamburgers and wilted french fries while the Rylands' daughter slept fitfully on the settee. The conversation was focused on Sue's consuming fear that something terrible would happen to Paul, and they would never hear from him again. "If he doesn't call by tomorrow morning," Sue said, "let's find out where the bikers hang out and cruise the bars. Look for this Dishrag Harry. I can't stand it!"

"Calm down," Rex told her. It was a mantra that he repeated to her over and over again.

Sue looked at Lee, breathing deeply nearby, and could so easily picture Amy at that age. Could that innocent being in her memory have been transformed into an unwholesome biker chick and forced to live in some unfathomable horror? She knew there would be no sleep for her tonight. She'd only calm down the day Amy was home safe in bed.

By late morning of the next day, there was still no word from Paul. When Sue could stand it no longer, she said, "Come on, Rex, let's do something! Let's rent a car and drive around. Find the biker bars. You never know, we might see her. Stranger things have happened. I can't stand being cooped up in here!"

Sunday in Tulsa, bright arid light scorched the burned grass, and tree leaves barely rustled under a whisper of wind. It was an attractive city, though, built beside the wide Arkansas River, with forested parks along the riverbanks. Rex and Sue drove a nondescript

Chevy over flat, untrafficked, unfamiliar streets. It was a churchgoing town—a receptive environment for a Jehovah's Witness convention—with tidy congregations spilling out the doors of various churches. It was also a very western town, with men wearing cowboy hats and signs in diners advertising a breakfast of eggs, bacon, and grits for ninety-nine cents. The radio stations played mostly country-western songs. On others, fast-talking men preached about sin, salvation, and the terrors of Hell. Please send them money.

"We're a long way from Miami," Sue said.

A cacophony of mufflers erupted behind them, and a posse of black leather bikers, sporting chains, beards, wild hair, and wilder women clinging to their rear seats, blasted by on both the right and left like a herd of rumbling buffalo splitting past a large rock in the prairie.

"Follow them," Sue said. "Let's see where they're going."

The bikers quickly outpaced them, but they followed the general direction and found a large park along the river with signs advertising a rock concert . . .

And Bikers . . .

Flowing around the trees . . .

An inland sea . . .

Of bikers.

"This looks dangerous," Ryland admonished. "We can't go in there asking about Amy or Dishrag Harry!"

"Rex, if there's one thing I've learned, these people have mothers and sisters, too. Look at the way Paul has treated me. I'm not scared in the slightest. I'm going with or without you!"

Rex glared at her. "Well, I'm not letting you go alone. At least I'm used to these guys. They don't kill their lawyers."

They parked the car and joined the throngs of black-leathered bikers drinking beer, smoking joints, sporting guns sticking out of their boots and large knives in their pockets. Two Tulsa policemen sat in cruisers by the entrance, but they weren't getting out of their cars.

The music was loud, badly rehearsed covers of popular rock tunes. The bikers sang along with "Sympathy for the Devil" and "Satisfaction." All shapes and sizes of bikers. There were Outlaws, Pagans, and Rogues eyeing each other unsteadily, but knowing this place at this moment was neutral territory. Maybe they'd do business together. Make money, not war!

Susan walked brazenly up to a group of biker women sitting on the ground passing a joint and drinking beer. "Excuse me," she said in her sweetest voice. "My name is Susan and I'm looking for my daughter? Her name is Amy. . . ." She held out a worn picture.

A large biker with a huge beer belly rushed up. "Don't talk to my women!" he shouted.

"I'm just looking for my daughter," Sue said, holding out the picture.

The man swiped it away. "Any of these girls look like her? Now get out of here!"

Rex showed a photo around to the males. They looked at him like he was crazy for asking, said they'd never seen her, then turned back to their buddies and laughed.

For hours Sue strolled from group to group, studying the women's faces, knowing Amy would be older and might not look like herself anymore. But thousands of faces later—some bloated, scarred, scared, spaced out—there was certainly no match. She did find some women who would talk, but they looked at Amy's picture and shook their heads no.

"Well, can you at least tell me the names of some biker bars?" she asked. "I heard the Anchor was a good place."

"Yeah," said one, hair like a bird's nest, red eyes, and blue, broken veins across her nose. "There's a few. But the Keg is the best place. Everyone winds up at the Keg."

Tears flooded into Sue's eyes as the park cut across their rearview mirror. "Every biker in the state must be there," she said.

Bikers, bikers, everywhere . . .
But not a drop of Amy.

9

They waited at the hotel until Monday with no word from Branch. The Holiday Inn seemed like something out of a Fellini movie, with all the Jehovah's Witnesses walking around the lobby, spilling into the streets to attempt massive conversions.

Rex spent the day on the phone with his office, while Sue and Shannon drove around to gas stations all over downtown Tulsa looking for Dishrag Harry Kramer. Mechanics would look up from beneath a car they'd been banging on and fix her with a stare as vacant as a department store mannequin. "Harry Krymer? Dirshraig Hairy?" they'd repeat back, as if Sue was speaking a foreign language that they were attempting to translate. None had a Pagan god tattoo on their shoulder, either, that might identify them as the man she was looking for. "Yes, right," she'd say.

"I ain't never hairda anyone named Dirshraig. There's a Hairy over to the station 'cross the street. . . ."

Of course that wasn't Harry Kramer, either. Sue thought the town sign should read, "Tulsa, Oklahoma—Home of the Wild Goose Chase."

"It's just as I feared," Susan told Rex when they returned to the hotel to find out that Branch was still AWOL. "Something's happened to him. It's the way this search has gone from the very start. When someone writes a thesis on Murphy's Law, we're going to be their number one subject."

"It's a long ride, honey," Rex soothed her. "Keep your spirits up. Branch is too mean to have something happen to him."

"He might have gotten picked up by police, he might have been killed at a biker bar, or gotten into a drunken wreck," Sue said. "Why doesn't he call?"

"I have more bad news for you," Rex said. "I have to go back to Miami. Lots of emergencies to deal with. Another client got busted."

Sue knew what was coming next. "I'm not going back," she answered. "I'm here, and I'm staying put until we find out what happened to Paul. He could be here right now, and we wouldn't know it!"

"Come back with me. Ned is going to kill me if I come back without you!"

"Don't tell him you're back. I won't if you won't."

Rex shook his head. "God, you're a tough cookie," he said. "Promise me you'll at least stay in the hotel."

"Are you kidding? I'm going to find that Keg bar and see if Paul's hanging out there, and show Amy's picture if he isn't."

They conferred for a while and finally agreed that if Paul hadn't called by Wednesday, Sue would call the Keg bar and tell the bartender she was the secretary for a lawyer in Miami. They were looking for Harry Kramer because he was a witness who could get Pompano Red off an assault charge. "Remember, though, the big gang out here is the Rogues," Rex told her. "They deal with the Pagans, but you never know. And I want you to contact the police. See how they can help you. We don't want you to turn up missing, too."

Rex and his family hugged Sue after packing their luggage in the rental car that evening.

"I promise I'll stay put until Wednesday," Sue said. "And then I'll contact the police. But don't breathe a word of this to Ned, because he'll go crazy with worry. He'll insist on coming, and he's the easiest-going guy in the world, but when we find Amy, I'm afraid he'll just go crazy and try to beat the guy into pieces. You've been very dear friends, and are so good to me," she added.

Sue watched them leave, Lee waving sorrowfully in the rear seat. As hard as it was to see them depart, she knew it was just as hard for them go.

When Ned called her at ten that night, she made up the white lie to make him feel better. "The Rylands? They're doing fine," she said. In all the time they'd been married, before Amy disappeared, she'd never lied to him. But since then, she'd done it often so he wouldn't worry. Each white lie hung ever more heavily around her neck, like the dead albatross in "Rhyme of the Ancient Mariner," gradually growing heavier and more rotten. She knew it wasn't good for a relationship, no matter how noble the intentions.

By Wednesday morning the formerly reliable Paul Branch was proving that he was indeed a biker. Still no contact. Sue made all the calls that she had been saving up, to the police, the district attorney, even a lawyer who was a friend of Frank Rubino's. Everyone, including the police, seemed receptive and wanted to help.

Rex called at eleven P.M. "I heard from Paul," he said.

"Finally!" Sue shouted, her entire body shaking. She'd just fallen asleep a few minutes earlier. "Where is he?"

"Are you sitting down?"

"I'm in bed."

"He never made it past St. Pete," Rex told her. "Says his grandmother's in intensive care. She's the one who brought him up—she's like his mother. He doesn't know how long it will take him to get out there."

Sue was strong, and had become much stronger throughout this ordeal, lifting emotional weights, becoming a veritable body builder of inner strength. But everyone has their limit. The reservoir burst and she wept. "I am not leaving my baby in Tulsa," she cried. "Can't you pressure him to just fly in for the day? Let him know we were here, that I'm waiting here for him."

"I told him that. He's a strange character," Rex said. "Doesn't feel like he's put us out in the slightest."

"Well, it's time he started paying us back for everything we've done for him," she said. "Have him call me. I'll tell him a thing or two."

Rex was worried about Sue, but couldn't tell Ned that he had left her in Tulsa. So instead he visited one of Sue's best friends, Barbara, after the call, and got her to urge Sue to come home.

"You have to be crazy," Sue said to her friend. "This is the closest we've been to Amy in years. I can feel it, Barb."

"Rex really doesn't think Paul can be moved," Barbara replied. "He's worried about you staying out there alone."

"You tell Rex to get heavy with Paul. This is just too much. He has his grandmother, and I want my daughter."

Sue finally called Ned and revealed everything. That she was here alone, that Paul was in St. Petersburg, and that nothing was going right. Ned took it well, letting her cry into his ear as she apologized for not telling him the truth sooner. "It's all right, honey," he told her. "But don't try to protect me. It's not good. I trust you."

Sue decided if she was ever going to find Harry Kramer, she wasn't going to rely on Paul Branch, whose credibility had taken a dive. She didn't know how much to believe anymore. Ina Shepard called the Tulsa police and asked them to extend their help, so Sue met with two detectives. Of course, the first thing they wanted to know was, "Are you sure Amy isn't a runaway?" She gave them the details of the case and they promised to be ready if she needed some help.

Ned called on Friday the eighteenth with some good news: "Paul called Rex and told him he was leaving for Tulsa on Sunday." If that seemed a favorable sign, it got better the following day when Ned called again. "Sue, it really sounds promising. Paul has called Rex three times. He's dumped his bike, got a van, and he's already left! He'll be there Wednesday or Thursday. He says for you to stay put!"

Joy flooded through Sue's body, making her feel like she might levitate right of the bed. But alternating tidal forces of despair and happiness were almost too much. By Wednesday, when she hadn't heard any further news, she scrawled in her journal: *I hope I can hold out without falling apart. Maybe tomorrow!* Thursday was even worse. She wrote one word: *Zilch!*

She lay in bed not wanting to leave or use the telephone, in case she might miss the most important call of her life. Where was Paul? She didn't eat and didn't sleep.

Days stretched by with no further news. She felt stretched, too. Stretched and emotionally mauled. She decided to give Paul an extra week. On Tuesday she took a cab back to Tulsa police headquarters and met with Sergeant Larry Johnson and two detectives, Jack Powell and Charles Sasser. Right out of central casting, they were all hefty western cops with thick necks and military-style crew cuts. But their attitudes were very positive.

"If Amy's in Tulsa," Powell said, "we'll find her."

"But don't do anything to spook Paul," she told them. "I think he really is trying to help me."

The investigators agreed. Powell said, "Yep, Branch obviously has some feelings left, or he wouldn't have gone home to take care of his grandmother. So he must have some sympathy for you. We'll do everything very hush-hush and very low profile, and look for this Harry Kramer. Branch will never be aware that we're helping you."

The Billig family in New York, 1962 (*from left*): Amy, 5; Susan, 37; Ned, 39; Josh, 4.

Amy's seventeenth birthday in Coconut Grove, just before her disappearance in 1974.

(Photo courtesy of Susan Billig)

Sue Billig, after days of searching for Amy, just following the disappearance.

(Photo courtesy of Susan Billig)

The Dimensions art gallery in Coconut Grove in 1974, with the Billigs' 1954 Bentley parked in front. Amy was on her way here when she disappeared.

(Photo courtesy of Susan Billig)

Sue Billig tries to make the public aware of Amy's disappearance.

(Photo courtesy of Palm Beach Post)

Larry and Charles Glasser are escorted in handcuffs from the Fontainbleau Hotel after their aborted extortion attempt.

(Photo courtesy of Miami Herald)

Pagan biker Paul Branch circa 1972 after an arrest in St. Petersburg, Florida.

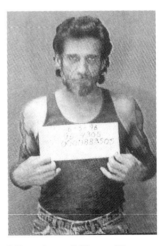

Mug shot of Harry Kramer in 1996. The biker had told authorities he knew nothing about Amy Billig.

Customs agent Henry Johnson Blair at his wedding in 1974, just twelve days before Amy's disappearance.

(Photo courtesy of Susan Billig)

Detective Jack Calvar riding his Harley-Davidson in Perrine, Florida, two months before being assigned to the Billig case in 1994.

(Photo courtesy of Detective Jack Calvar)

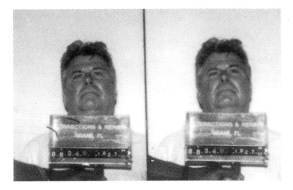

Mug shot of Henry Johnson Blair after his Miami arrest in 1995.

Henry Johnson Blair at his trial in March 1996 listens to an FBI recording of one of his sexually explicit telephone calls to Susan Billig. He is flanked by his attorneys William Norris (*left*) and Frederick R. Mann.

During trial, Sue Billig shows the stress of three and a half hours of grueling questions while recalling over twenty years of Henry Blair's telephone calls.

(Photo courtesy of Miami Herald*/Candace Barbot)*

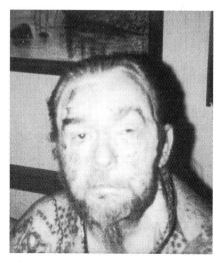

Paul Branch, still mean and ornery and dying of skin cancer, as found by Detective Jack Calvar in November 1997.

(Photo courtesy of Detective Jack Calvar)

Sue and Ned Billig in 1991, just before learning of their illnesses.
(Photo courtesy of Susan Billig)

Sue Billig poses for a *Herald* photo in Coconut Grove shortly before Henry Blair's trial in 1995.

(Photo courtesy of Miami Herald/Candace Barbot)

She felt as if some progress was being made now. She definitely had a good feeling about the authorities here. Unlike Orlando, they seemed to have a much better idea about what they were up against.

When she got back to the hotel, there was a message to call Ned.

"Paul called Rex," he said. "He got busted in Alabama and has been in jail! But now he's on his way."

The next night she had just hung up from the usual ten P.M. conversation with Ned when the phone rang again. "What did you forget, Ned?" she said, being cute.

"It's Paul," came the gravelly voice.

"Paul! Paul, you . . . why haven't you called me?"

He grunted. "I'm calling you now. Look, it's been a long trip, and I was in the slammer for five days. I'm on the outskirts of town, so get me a room at your hotel. I'll be there in an hour." The biker hung up before she could scold him.

Sue's funds were low. She looked at her credit cards, wondering which one would fit an extra room on it. She finally plucked one from her wallet and headed down to the front desk. A woman with thickly mascara'ed eyes and hair as fluffy as blond cotton candy chewed gum behind the desk.

"We ain't got no more rooms, ma'am," she said. "It's the Bicentennial Fortha July coming up, and the place is full."

Sue was so weary by now. Why couldn't anything be easy? she wondered. Not even this. "You must have something? A broom closet—anything," she pleaded. "This is very important to me."

The woman snapped her gum and looked at the reservation books. She made a face. "Weeeellll," she said, "the honeymoon suite is available, but only for tonight."

Sue laughed. "That's it? The only room you have is the honeymoon suite?"

The price was outrageous, of course.

Sue let out a sigh and weighed the credit card in her hand, as if to ascertain whether it could stand the extra expense. "Do it," she said. "I'll find something else tomorrow."

As late as it was, she would have expected the Jehovah's Witnesses to be in bed, but there were families checking in, the restaurant was full, and kids playing tag ran around the sofas and couches of the lobby.

When Branch strode into the lobby at eleven P.M., it was like a gunslinger had just entered a bar in a western town. He wore greasy jeans as stiff as cardboard. His vest covered a T-shirt that pictured a muscled hand labeled "Harley-Davidson," squeezing the brains out of three Japanese men labeled "Kawasaki," "Honda," and "Suzuki." His chains rattled menacingly as his boots left dusty prints on the carpet. A startled hush fell over the room. One little boy broke into tears. The front desk clerk, another big-haired lady, suddenly departed in the hopes this apparition wouldn't ask for a room.

Sue took a deep breath. "I can't believe you're finally here," she said.

He grinned. "Sometimes you gotta wait for the good stuff. You got my room?"

She waved the key. "You're staying in the honeymoon suite."

"Aw, shucks," he said. "I always thought you had your eye on me!"

Sue walked him up to the suite, noticing the nervous glances of the other guests and the disapproving glares from the front desk personnel hiding in the back office. The biker's body odor filled the elevator on the way up. Paul noticed the expression on her face. "That's five days of Alabama for you," he said.

"What happened?" she asked.

He shook his head. "Cops were just harassing me. I badmouthed one when he stopped my van."

"Have you gotten any more leads on Amy or Kramer?" she asked.

"I'll tell you the plan tomorrow."

"You don't have an address, do you?" Sue said.

"Bikers don't have addresses," Paul said. "Bikers are gypsies, we hang out until it's time to hit the road. But this is my specialty. I have found a lot of people who didn't want to be found."

Sue let Paul into his room. It was three times the size of hers, with a king-size bed and view of the city. A fruit basket sat on the dining table. "Don't get too comfortable," Sue said. "They're full after tonight."

Branch looked her up and down, and over at the bed. It was obvious what he was thinking. She slapped the key down on the dresser.

"Pleasant dreams," he called after her.

Back in the elevator, she started to shake uncontrollably. When Branch mentioned that he had tracked down people, she realized he meant he'd found and killed them. That night, in her journal, she wrote down everything that had happened. She hadn't seen Paul in so long that she had forgotten just how diabolical he looked, and she could easily imagine all the terrified Jehovah's Witnesses fervently praying in their hotel rooms to keep the evil at bay. But she also knew she couldn't write about the depths of terror Paul instilled in the people around him. These were notes that Ned would probably read, and that she would refer to over and over again. Anyone might see them eventually. She ended a paragraph with a simple, *He sure scares me!*

The next morning Paul called her at seven A.M. "I'm hungry," he said, his voice sounding like an engine grinding a piston ring.

Sue hadn't slept. Anytime she drifted into some semblance of sleep, visions of Amy swept into her mind and kept her heart racing. Now she felt like a beaten rug, and her body wanted to sleep all day. But the sound of Paul's voice seared her brain like a double jolt of espresso. She was already jumping out of bed as she said, "I'll meet you in the restaurant in ten minutes."

The biker's hair stuck out in various directions, and his eyes were red and watery as a basset hound's. Sue doubted he had done more than take his boots off to sleep. He swung his rancid gaze at the older waitress, who'd probably thought she'd seen everything in her life. She stepped backward in surprise.

"Coffee," he commanded. He scanned the plastic menu. There were pictures of pancakes and eggs with numbers next to them. He pointed at one that had a little of everything. It would have fed Sue for a week. "Gimme this," he said.

Sue ordered an English muffin. "So what's the plan?"

Paul said, "Coffee first."

He was going to eke this out by the second, she thought. He likes this. He's a sadist!

The waitress brought a small cup of steaming coffee. He opened his mouth and threw it down. "More," he said. "Bring one of those pots."

When he was situated with his coffee, he leaned toward Sue. He hadn't brushed his teeth in a week. "Okay, the first thing I do is check the bike shops. There ain't that many of them, and every biker ends up there for one reason or t'other. Don't worry, I want to find this guy as much as you do. He's got the girl, my bike, and . . . well, let's just say some other stuff. He knows I'm looking for him."

"If he knows you're looking, what's to keep him from gallivanting off? You said it yourself, you're gypsies."

Paul sucked up more coffee. The platter of food arrived. They ate big portions in Tulsa, and that was just right for Paul. Steak and eggs with grits was accompanied by a small mound of spongy pancakes. Sue received her muffin.

"I think he's been snitching," Paul said. "So he's lying low, not going anywhere."

Paul turned his attention to his pancakes, forking generous portions into his mouth while other patrons glanced at him furtively and whispered among themselves. Sue half expected some marshal to saunter over and say, "Hey, we don't like your kind in our town."

"Remember what I said about Amy. She's been living a complete different life than anything you can imagine, even though you think you've seen some of it. So don't expect *your* Amy."

Sue shook her head. She was glad she hadn't eaten anything heavy, because it wouldn't have sat in her stomach. "I know that, Paul. I'll take her in any form she's in."

"She may not even want to go with you," he said. "She may not even know you."

"You keep saying that, Paul. And it really upsets me. She's got to remember her mother. She's got a family. You can't erase seventeen years that easily!"

"That's what you think," Paul snorted. "Just remember what I've been saying, and be prepared. There's another thing. I gotta have some expense money. I'm tapped out."

Sue sighed. "Me too, Paul." She dug in her purse. "I've got $67 left." She handed him three twenties and a five. "That's all I've got, Paul. I'm living on credit cards."

"You can deduct it from the $2,000 reward money," he said.

An electric charge went through Sue's body. She didn't want him to know the $2,000 had been depleted during the search. Even his $125 in bike repairs had come out of it. "You always said you didn't want the reward," she reminded him.

He looked at her with savvy eyes. "Things change,"

he said. "Right now I need the money more'n I need the girl. That's lotsa money for a chick."

Paul finished his huge breakfast, while Sue was still nibbling on her muffin. He got up from the table. "Okay, gonna loosen the load a little in the bathroom and then I'm heading out!" he stated. "You stick around here, and I'll come back and fill you in later. Don't know how long it'll take."

"I could go with you?" Sue suggested hopefully.

Paul laughed. "You're a funny lady," he answered.

Sue waited by the phone all day. She watched morning news and Merv Griffin. She hated soap operas, but watched a couple of those, too, and wished her life was only as complicated as the poor souls plotting against each other on the tube. Paul finally called at seven thirty P.M.

"Shue, my girl," he slurred into the phone.

"You're drunk," Sue said.

"So what? I didn't have much luck at the bike shops, but one guy said the bike seemed familiar. I been asking around at the Keg now. I think I pinned him down."

"Where? Tell me, Paul. Just in case."

"I'll tell you when I'm good an' ready," he said. "Now you going to be there tonight?"

"Of course," Sue said. "I won't leave the phone."

"And we're cool on the two large, because I may have to promish shome of it around. Shpread the wealth."

"If you get proof positive about Amy, we'll get the money," Sue promised, her heart quaking.

As soon as she was off the phone she called Rex. "I

don't know what to do about the money. What if he finds her and then we don't have it?"

"Just follow the plan, Sue," Rex said. "We'll come up with the ransom . . . the reward, whatever it is. And if there's any problem, you tell him to call me. You hear? He knows you're low on cash now, so he's not sure. But if he hears it from me, he'll know you're good for it."

"I don't know what we'd do without you, Rex," Sue said, a grateful tear running down her cheek.

10

Paul found a cheap hotel for the night and was banging on Sue's door the next morning. The Pagan lumbered through the door and scoped the room. "It may not be the honeymoon suite, but it's better than the flea-bitten crap I crashed in the other night. Hardly a hotel room available in town!"

Sue wondered how he could live in a trashed-up trailer and then complain about any hotel room, no matter how modest, but she bit her tongue. "Please tell me you found Amy," she said.

Branch sprawled out on her just-made bed, his brutish body creating a dent in the mattress springs. "I'm going with a buncha Rogues to a concert at Wolf Mountain. Be thousands of bikers there, and Harry's not going to miss it. But . . ." He rubbed his fingers together. "I'm gonna need some gas money, babe. We're taking vans, so we can pool cash, but I gotta contribute my share."

"I'm at the end of my reserves," she said.

"So where's the two grand gonna come from?" Paul countered.

"That we'll get," Sue said without hesitation. "You can call Rex, and he'll vouch for that. But immediate cash is going fast. I gave you what I had."

"See if you can get some wired to you," he said. "Because I need something. I got some left from what you gave me, but I don't think it's enough. I spent twenty dollars on the hotel last night."

Sue sighed. "And you really think Harry's going to be there?"

"Bet your ass. This is a big gig. I'm going with some of his friends, and they say he's already on his way. He's riding with the Rogues now, I guess."

"I'll get you some cash," Sue told him. "But I have to get some real information soon."

"You'll get it," he told her.

She'd fantasized about being home by the July fourth weekend with Amy, but now realized that that idea was yet another dream that wasn't going to materialize. When Branch left, she called the maid to change the bedspread.

Sue arranged to get some additional cash but hadn't received it when Paul called at six-fifteen P.M.

The harsh voice grumbled through the receiver. "Been a change of plans. I started to get a bad feeling about being out in the middle of nowhere with a bunch of Harry's friends! I got someone looking for Harry at the concert, and the guys will call me when they get back on Monday. I got a German shepherd with me now, so I gotta stay in this fleabag place again tonight. You gotta come through with some more money. This place is depressing."

"Paul, just call Rex directly," Sue said. "He'll get you some money. I'm going to check out of here and go to the Sheraton by the airport." She gave him the number. "It's cheaper than here."

"Okay," Paul said. "Here's the real news. There's a big party planned for Tuesday night. I think Amy's going to be there, so you can get your act straight with her."

"Don't joke around, Paul," Sue said.

"I'm not joking. They say Harry's going to be there with his old lady. I can't wait to see her myself. It's been a long time."

"When did you see her first?" Sue asked. He'd always been hazy on this part. She couldn't bear the thought of Branch and Amy together, but needed to get the facts straight.

"Let's see," he said, his voice sounding like a bad connection full of static. He'd never be a singer, that's for sure. "I broke out of jail Christmas of seventy-three. I holed up in Orlando until summer of seventy-four, when I went back into the can in Texas. Bought her from a guy in Orlando."

"Who?" Sue asked. This was the first time Branch had volunteered this additional information. But the time line still fit. "Who was it you bought her from?"

"It's been a while," Paul said. "I think it was Bracket, but I'm not sure."

"But you're sure it was Amy?" Sue asked for the thousandth time, wanting to hear the reassurance that kept her going.

"Well, you know," Paul said, "how sure is anything in life?"

"What? After all this time you're not absolutely sure?"

"We'll know Tuesday," Paul said. "Won't we? Now be ready!"

Sue changed hotels. The Sheraton wasn't cheaper, as she'd told Paul, but it was near the airport. She wanted to get Amy on a plane home as soon as possible. If she got her, they'd be on the next plane out.

Sue waited, cursing the four claustrophobic walls of the hotel room, and prayed for the phone to ring. When it didn't, she called Paul's hotel room again and again. No answer. She'd psyched herself up for Tuesday, to meet Amy no matter what her condition, and convinced herself that this time it was going to happen.

Nothing.

She called Paul's hotel on Wednesday. The female clerk told her in a slow drawl, "That man checked out, honey! Last time we saw him 'round here was yesterday sometime."

Sue had a bad feeling about this. Panic rose in her gut.

Rex told her to "stay put" when she called him to report the news.

But the next day, even the lawyer had succumbed to doubt. Sue's friend Barbara called and told her, "Rex can't bring himself to tell you this, but he doesn't want to be responsible for Paul's whereabouts anymore. He wants you to call the police and come on home."

Sue felt betrayed. "He's been such a good friend,

how can he say that? I am not leaving here until I get some kind of answer."

She immediately called the police, and was visited that afternoon by Detectives Jack Powell and Ken Brown, who had already begun investigations after her interview at police headquarters.

They drank coffee in the restaurant, where the detectives accepted a few doughnuts. Sue couldn't help but smile.

Powell wiped his mouth with a napkin and said, "The good news is we showed Amy's picture around and a number of people said she looks very familiar. That's a good sign, Sue, because if these people could, they'd just blow it off. I swear there was one girl I could have sworn was Amy, but fat. It wasn't her, but she said that she definitely saw Amy at the Keg on Friday night."

Sue put a hand on her chest. Her heart was fluttering in her chest like a wounded bird. "I've had a migraine all day, and a dozen aspirin didn't help as much as that news."

Powell patted her hand. "There's some not so good news, too." He said. "We know who this Dishrag Harry is now, and he is a bad dude! Now that I've done some research, I see I've dealt with him before, when he had another ID. Anyway, two girls I spoke to swore Amy looks like the girl he has—but older and in very bad condition."

Sue nodded. "I've been told to expect that."

"They say she's very spaced out and—pardon the expression—has been passed around a lot."

"It's okay," Sue said, and sighed. "It breaks my heart to hear these things. But I'll take her in whatever condition she's in. The best news is that she's probably alive."

"I'll give you that much," said the cop. "With all the identification, if this isn't Amy, it's a dead ringer for her, and once we find her, you'll know for sure."

The detectives were unable to further the investigation over the weekend, but they picked up Sue at noon on Sunday to facilitate a tour of the biker bars. Unfortunately, even bikers in Tulsa were forced to recognize the sabbath, as all the bars were closed at the time. The detectives should have known this, as Tulsa had strict liquor laws and was a "dry" city.

Monday, July 12, marked Sue's one month vigil in Tulsa. But she was no closer than when she had arrived full of hope and optimism. Paul had never checked in again, even though she now had some cash for him to pick up. Detectives Powell and Brown were on other duty.

Here 1 month! she jotted in strong pencil in her journal. Those words reverberated in her brain.

"I'm just going to go to the bars myself," she said.

She dressed in jeans, sneakers, and a frumpy blouse, hid most of her cash under the mattress, and hailed a taxi. "The Anchor Bar," she said.

The cabbie scowled and pushed up the brim of his cowboy hat to see her better in the rearview mirror. "Lady, you don't look like nobody goes to the Anchor Bar," he said. "You know what that place is?"

Sue gritted her teeth. "I know," she said. "I'm looking for someone. It shouldn't be too rowdy this time of day."

"Suit youself," the driver said. "Don't say I din't warn you."

There were a half-dozen well-maintained motorcycles lined up in front of the squalid bar. Cars and vans parked at the curb looked like they were one fill up short of the junkyard. Sue walked from the brash Tulsa light into a dark, hot bar. There was a sort of wooden decor and some nets that made it look "anchory," perhaps, but that attempt had been made long before it had become a biker hangout. Now, Harley-Davidson emblems and other biker memorabilia were mixed into the fray, and even that looked grungy. There was a smell of beer and vomit that would never go away. A jukebox played Hank Williams.

When Sue's eyes adjusted, she noticed all eyes were on her. Several large men with hairy arms and green tattoos splattered against their muscles sat at the bar. Frizzy hair, ponytails, leather, beards, mustaches, boots—the same getups Sue had become so accustomed to seeing. Two were playing pool at an aged, scarred billiard table. Two others were frozen with darts in their hand. Several women slouched at cocktail tables. Smoke was a swirling fog in the air.

Sue took it all in, heart pounding her rib cage, blood rushing through her ears, and walked up to the bar. "Is the manager in?" she asked politely.

Obviously no threat, perhaps a liquor salesman or

even a lost Jehovah's Witness, the bar suddenly came back to life.

"You're looking at him," the bartender said.

Sue thought, Just like a movie! and explained her mission to find Amy. "I'm not the heat. I just want to ask people some questions."

"Free country," the bartender said. "Your funeral."

Sue took a deep breath and scouted the bar. The nearest guy looked familiar, and she realized she had met him at the rock concert in the park a month earlier. He was over six feet tall, broad-shouldered, with a sizable beer belly, and he sported a ponytail. He had about a week's worth of fuzz on his face.

"Yeah, I remember you," he said with amazement. "Lady, you have some guts. What do they say? Chutzpah? You been here ever since the concert?"

"The whole time," Sue said. "It's been a long month."

"My name's Paul Kline," he volunteered. "Yeah, I remember Klete was showing your daughter's picture around."

"Klete?" Sue asked.

"Yeah, a Pagan guy. About my height, reddish hair, from Florida."

"Paul Branch!" Sue exclaimed.

Kline nodded. "Yeah, that's his name. Here they call him Klete. Says he wants to buy a bike frame from me when he gets money from Florida."

"Have you seen Paul lately?" Sue asked.

"Not in a week or so," Kline said. "I'm getting awfully thirsty here."

Sue ordered him a beer. "What about Amy's picture. Have you seen her?"

Kline shrugged. "I don't pay attention to other guys' chicks. Ask the bartender, he sees a lot of them."

Sue showed the pictures to the bartender, Gary. He squinted at the photo under a fluorescent light. "Oh, yeah," he said. "I definitely think I've seen her here."

Gary passed the picture around to the other bikers, who glanced at Sue and shook their heads. The bartender said to leave the photo and call back later. If the girl came in, he'd compare it to her in person, and would tell Sue if there was a match.

Sue rode a taxi to some of the other bars on her list, but the bikers must have been on a run somewhere, because none of those types were around. She showed a photo of Amy to the bartenders and various patrons at the Keg. The detectives who had seemed so eager before were always out when she called, and never checked in with her. Deep into the evening she called the Anchor back. The girl finally came in at one A.M. Gary said, "She looks a lot like your photo, but this girl's from Scottsdale, Arizona, and has the accent to prove it. Definitely not her."

The price of hotel rooms and cheap restaurant food slowly maxed out each of Sue's credit cards. It was clear she would have to make an extraordinary effort in the next few days.

She complained to Detective Powell, asking him to arrange interviews with some of the people who had claimed to see Amy. "It's like you don't want me to talk to anybody," she said. He finally agreed to take her to interview a biker fringe member named "Shotgun," who might have some information.

They drove up to the house, a single-story wooden building with peeling paint, but a decent yard littered with kid's toys.

Of course, no one was home. Sue insisted on leaving a note with her telephone number on it, and even her Florida information. She no longer believed that Detective Powell would work seriously on her case.

She went through the same drill at a couple more houses and bars. Everyone had scattered and disappeared.

Back in her hotel room, at six P.M., the phone rang. A smoky female voice asked for "Sue Billings." It amazed her how many people, even with the name written right in front of them, added an unintentional *n* and an *s* to her name.

"This is she," Sue said.

"Yes, Mrs. Billings . . ." the woman said, sounding stoned. "This is Rosie. I'm Shotgun's old lady. I got your note."

"You've spoken to Detective Powell, then?" Sue asked. "You know why I'm here?"

"Yeah, he's filled us in," the woman answered, her voice dreamy. "Yeah, we know Dishrag. He was a Pagan, but now he's a Rogue. Now they call him Rags. . . ."

Sue wrote all this down in her notebook. "Rags? So you know him?"

There was rock music playing in the background. Rosie took a moment, and sucked a cigarette or a joint.

"Yeah, we hung with him in Peoria a while back. He has a monster Harley."

Sue described the bike that Paul said he had given to Harry Kramer for safekeeping.

"Yeah, that sounds like it could be it," Rosie said. "I didn't see your daughter myself, but people around say they know her. That's definitely his old lady. That's all I know right now. But I'll ask around." She sounded stoned. Stoned, but sweet. "You should know," Rosie continued. "Most the bikers 'round here really aren't going to talk to Powell much. Find yourself a detective named Grady McFadden. They trust him a lot more. I'll be in touch."

Sue immediately called police headquarters and left a message for McFadden. He met her in the hotel lobby that evening. The Tulsa detective was already versed in the situation. A good-looking guy, he was a bit hipper and younger than the previous detectives, with brown hair cut just over his ears. The Tulsa version of the Mod Squad.

"Yeah, I'm in good with the bikers," he said proudly. "I feel that Amy is here in Tulsa and that Rags has her. One of my contacts said she had personally seen a woman matching Amy's description riding with him. There's just too many people here who say they saw her. The problem is, we don't know where Rags is. He's lying real low. No one has seen him or his woman since Paul Branch came to town. My information is that everyone in town knows an enforcer is looking for Kramer, and he's in deep hiding. I don't know. I think there may be more than a bike and a girl in this. That guy owes Branch some drugs or money."

"It could be," Sue said. "He's awfully hot to find Dishrag, and at first he said he wasn't interested in the reward money. . . ."

"I'm going to have to find someone who'll turn on Rags," McFadden said. "And that means I'm going to owe them some favor or another. But he's definitely joined the Rogues, and I know some of his associates—guys named Sundowner and Cowboy. Now it's time you went back to Florida, 'cause this could still take some time. I will keep in touch with you there."

So many people had made so many promises. Sue could see that McFadden meant well, but once new cases and other pressures came up, just how long would Amy remain a priority? But she knew she had to trust him, because tonight's room rate was going to bust another credit card.

"I'll go," she conceded with effort. "But you have to promise me to stay on this."

"I will," he said.

She made arrangements to fly home the next afternoon. But she didn't trust McFadden entirely. First she went by Shotgun's house, where she met with Rosie. She was a simple hippie-looking woman in her late twenties, who wore necklaces and whose long brown hair was parted in the middle. Her old man, Shotgun, wasn't a full biker, but an "associate." Still, they were well-connected. And they could use the reward money.

Rosie said, "We're a lot more likely to find Amy than the police. We can go anywhere, and don't have to explain anything to anyone. Not the police, not the bikers. I've got some leads to follow. If it's Amy, she's calling herself Cheryl now. They call her 'Mellow Cheryl.' "

Total expenses for the Tulsa trip: $798.65. She would have spent a hundred times that amount, if she'd had it, and if she thought it would bring Amy back. As the plane banked above Tulsa, Sue looked down on the city. Somewhere, she felt, Amy was there, in one of the apartments or houses, and leaving seemed like abandoning her, giving up, and Sue had never given up on anything in her life. There was a wrenching feeling in her gut as the plane banked the other way and all she saw was sky.

It was great to sleep next to Ned again, cook Josh dinner, and to feel enveloped in the love of her loyal friends. Jasmine and honeysuckle perfumed the air, parrots flew over the yard, and the local peacocks strutted through the neighborhood, fanning out their colorful feathers. This was why Sue and Ned had moved there so long ago. But her mind and heart remained in Tulsa, a town she would never have visited in any other situation.

Two weeks later, on August 1, Rosie called. Sue's heart skipped the moment she heard that soft, stoned Oklahoma drawl.

"You're never gonna believe this," Rosie said. "Me and Shotgun got busted in Seminole, and they confiscated our van. I think the Rogues dropped a dime on us because we were following leads that Rags was there. Something real heavy's going down 'cause I never seen the Rogues like this before. They were real angry we were asking questions. But I spoke to a number of girls over there, said I was looking for my sister. They knew Mellow Cheryl and said she fit my description. She's from Miami! But how could she be my sister, because she had a different accent than me? I told them I had been living in Oklahoma for ten years now, that's why."

"Did you show them the pictures?" Sue asked, feeling her pulse race. She'd been depressed for weeks, and suddenly felt the veil lifting.

"They said it's her, and she's Rags's girl. He's somewhere else, and put her in Seminole for safekeeping. Don't worry, Rogues are different than some of the other bikers. They don't sell or beat their women, so Amy's probably all right. Our lawyer says we'll get our van back because it was an illegal search, but we're really gonna need that reward money. I think we can find her and lure her into the van. I'll call you in a couple weeks, after the trial and we get the van back, okay?"

Sue wasn't about to sit back now, however. She had meetings every day. The Dade County State Attorney, Richard Gerstein, set up a meeting with one of his top prosecutors, Janet Reno, who promised to help. Detective Gonzales was keeping in touch with the Tulsa police. Sue met with the FBI in Miami, who agreed that this girl had to be Amy or "a dead ringer" for her, and informed the FBI office in Tulsa of the situation, which put a full-time agent on the case. Wheels were turning, but were they moving the investigative cart, or just spinning in place?

Tulsa police weren't completely somnambulant. When they arrested a girl even close to Amy's description, they would wire the photograph. None were the right girl.

Paul Branch had dropped off the face of the earth. After all this, he was gone. No sightings by police, no calls to Rex looking for money. And Branch was still their best hope. Of everyone, only the enforcer could apply the pressure to find Dishrag Harry.

Rosie called again. "Rags is back in Florida," she said, "but Cheryl is still in Seminole, a town a couple hours south of here. The Rogues have taken possession of her. I've shown her picture around and everyone agrees it's her, but she's gained weight. But I've got a situation here. My ex-husband stole my kid, and I need $500 for a writ against him."

Of course, Sue thought. Everyone thought she was the golden goose. "The reward money is in a trust account," she said, "and I can't touch it. If I had any money left, I'd be in Tulsa right now!"

Rosie's voice deflated. "I understand. Don't worry, I'll keep on it. We'll find Amy for you."

Everyone was so sure. Everyone was so hopeful.

Sue called Rex, gave him the latest, and asked if he had heard from Paul.

"Still AWOL," he told her. "I just can't understand it."

"He's still our best hope, don't you think?" she asked.

"I certainly would have said so before he disappeared."

"I just can't believe he would walk out on me like that," Sue said, trying not to whine. "It just doesn't seem right!"

Soon after, Sue received a phone call from Tulsa's Grady McFadden. "We just arrested a bunch of Rogues, and I was pumping some for information regarding your case. There's a good reason Branch hasn't called you," he said. "Rogues say they killed him."

11

Paul Branch dead? It must have taken a large gang of Rogues to take on the canny biker. Sue fell into a depression and could barely eat dinner, just picking at her food at their round glass dining table.

She asked Ned, "Is it our fault for pushing him to go to Tulsa? He got killed looking for Amy. I feel responsible."

Ned, on his second pack of cigarettes that day, blew an angry burst of smoke from his lungs. "He got killed because he's a nasty guy, Sue. I'm sorry, and God, you know I prayed he'd find Amy, but I have to wonder if he just wasn't leading us on the whole time." Like many New York musicians, Ned had always smoked too much, but since Amy's disappearance, he'd increased his intake. Sue could bear breathing the fumes, but she'd never smoked a cigarette in her life.

"He couldn't have been leading us on. Pompano Red was up in Orlando and remembers him with a girl fitting Amy's description. He said he got her from a guy named Bracket. What we have to do now is go up to the Florida State prison and speak to Bracket and show him Amy's picture. Paul isn't the only one with contacts. All these bikers know one another."

Rex Ryland made preparations to go to the large prison outside Raiford and interview Bracket, whose legal name was Dale Preston Webb. Another biker told him to make sure to track down a guy named Juan "Geronimo" Jerry, who knew "something about Amy," who was now known as "Little Bits." Geronimo, a co-defendant of Pompano Red's, was presently serving a lengthy murder sentence in Virginia. The Little Bits name had come up before, in connection with Branch. Something tied all these guys together.

But Bracket was an Outlaw, and meeting with an Outlaw in prison wasn't so easy. No one wanted to be labeled a snitch because the Outlaw creed was, "Snitches are a dying breed." Anybody who was going to talk had to get an okay from Big Jim Nolan. Big Jim, not presently in jail, was hard to get a hold of, but he did agree to go to Raiford with Rex, since he also wanted to see some of the brothers.

He did admit to one thing that Sue thought interesting:

"Yeah, I knew Paul Branch," he said on the phone.

"I understand he was an enforcer," Sue said.

"I'm not going to get into that," Big Jim told her. "But you don't know everything about that guy, and I think a lot of people may be lying to you. But, as I told you, I'll go to Raiford with Rex, and we'll see what we can find out."

The Billigs were now looking at their third holiday season without Amy. Josh had quit high school and was working in the kitchen in a Grove restaurant.

While Sue's mind was wrapped up in the day-to-day search, helping Ned with the gallery, or taking on a quick decorating job to bring in a much needed cash infusion, in her heart she lived a Walter Mitty existence, imagining a life where none of this had happened; where Amy was doing great in college, was gushing about a new love in her life, had just been home, and the family had carved a turkey at the head of a feast-laden table lined with their best friends. In some parallel universe it was happening, and she was a silent voyeur to this other family's joy.

Sue was writing out some cards on the kitchen table when she received a call from Ina Shepard.

"Paul Branch is dead, right?" the officer queried.

"The Rogues killed him in Tulsa," Sue answered, the phone cradled against her neck as she continued to write.

"Well, then why did he just call Pompano Red's wife in Virginia to say he's on his way there to kill her? She's not into the biker scene at all, and I spoke with her before regarding Red, so she called me."

Sue dropped the pen. "Paul Branch is alive?"

"And mad about something," Ina said.

"I'll call Rex right away," Sue said.

Rex was harried, and was just leaving his office to go to court when Sue caught him. "Still alive?" he muttered. "Well, I'm not surprised. He's a tough bastard to kill. You know, I had a call the other night at three A.M., and there wasn't anyone on the other end. Somehow I had the feeling it was Paul. But why would he want to kill Red's wife?"

"If he calls you again, I want you to ask him why he

left me in Tulsa, and if he used to call Amy 'Little
Bits.' "

"Okay," Rex said. "I'll make sure to ask him. In the
meantime, see if Ina can track down Red. Time for
court, Sue, we'll talk later."

Ina Shepard called the Virginia authorities about Dennis Kenny, aka Pompano Red, only to find out that no
one knew where he was. She also checked Dade
records to see if he was registered there. No Dennis
Kenny anywhere.

On December 9, Rex called Sue. "Paul phoned me
late last night," he told her.

"So it's really him?" Sue said. Up until then, she
half expected to find out it was an imposter.

"Oh, it's him," Ryland said. "And mean as ever. And
he's got a good excuse for walking out on you in Tulsa.
Turns out the Rogues were just leading him on. A
bunch of Harry's friends dragged him out of a bar,
drove him across the state border, and worked him over
pretty bad. Busted both his kneecaps, shot him twice in
the abdomen, and left him for dead. Now he's almost
crippled and walks with a cane. Been hiding out for
months. He really must have been nearly killed. Takes
a lot to put the fear of God into a guy like him!"

The second week of December 1976, Sue drove up to
the Florida State prison with Rex and a biker named
Leroy Poss. The penitentiary is often simply called
Raiford by criminals, as it sits just outside the tiny
town of that name, which boasts a population of less
than two hundred. In contrast, the prison has a normal

population just over 1,100, with more than six hundred personnel to make sure they stay there. It's a maximum security prison, with an active Death Row where they execute prisoners on the famous electric chair nick-named "Old Sparky" because it has a tendency to fizz, and has actually set a victim's hair on fire. Poss had spent eighteen years in prison there for a crime he did not commit before Rex proved his innocence and got him released from jail. Make no mistake, though. Most of the inmates housed there are the most brutal of Florida's prisoners. As Florida authorities cracked down on the biker population, many of them were now calling it their "government sponsored vacation."

The prison is located about thirty-five miles north-east of Gainesville, through pine forests and cattle ranches. The landscape looks more like Texas than Florida.

Ryland steered a rented sedan under a sign reading FLORIDA STATE PRISON that arched across the two-lane road. They encountered two guard checks and tower-ing fences with huge rolls of razor wire on top. Leroy took a deep breath in the backseat. This wasn't bring-ing back pleasant memories.

The 1960s-era prison was blocky and nondescript, certainly not one of those Gothic brick prison build-ings so famous up north. It was as practical and un-adorned as a military base. They took a number, which corresponded with their previously requested reserva-tion. Sue was searched roughly by a matron, while the men were searched by a guard in a separate room, and they were then led through locked doors to a visitors' room with a bare wooden table.

Sue's main impression of Bracket was that "he was tall and mean." He didn't have long hair or a beard in prison, though, since they weren't allowed. All biker individuality had been stripped from him but his tattoos.

Bracket and Poss had known each other during Poss's prison days, so Bracket trusted his friend and was glad to see him. But he wasn't so sure about Sue.

"I don't know why I should be talking to you," he said. "Does me no good at all."

"You never did anything nice for someone else?" Sue asked.

"Not good policy," Bracket replied.

Poss chimed in here. "She's cool," he told Bracket. "She really isn't the heat, and they're not going to use any information against you. She's just looking for her daughter, man."

"I could really use some cigarettes," Bracket said.

"We'll put some cash in your commissary account," Rex told him.

"Why don't I begin by telling you what I think I know," Sue said. "Mainly that Paul Branch says that in 1974 he bought my daughter Amy from you after he escaped from jail and was living in Orlando. She may have been called Little Bits at the time, I don't know. He said she had other identification. She was kid—" She bit her tongue. "She disappeared from Coconut Grove on March fifth, 1974, and we have been told that she was later seen with Outlaws. Paul said he had written you here to ask what you knew about her, or if you knew what happened to her after he went back into jail.

He said he gave her to Dishrag Harry for safekeeping, but his friend ran off with her."

That got the biker to open up. "I never sold anyone to Branch," Bracket scoffed. "And Branch never escaped from anywhere! Sid Fast called me up here back in 1974 and I told him I knew the girl and she had been sold a few weeks earlier, but that's all I knew."

"Where? To who?" Sue asked.

"I'm not naming names," Bracket said. "I'm only talking to you because Leroy says you're cool and I can see you're sincere, so I'm going to tell you something. Branch did write to someone here named Scar, but that's all I can tell you."

It took some cajoling before he volunteered the name of Rolando Vilandre, a little guy, only five-three, with an appendix scar—a Pagan who had been busted with two girls in Orlando. One of the girls had stayed with Branch when she was released. "I think her name was Candy. Candy or Cindy," he said. "I think she's in Jacksonville with the Outlaws."

Sue showed him the picture of Amy. He nodded. "Looks like her, but she's very skinny, and has very skinny legs. What you do is get a picture of Scar and his fall buddies," the friends he was arrested with, "and get pictures of their old ladies. They're probably all in the same files."

Sue also showed Bracket photographs of several dark-haired biker women who, over the years had been checked out and dismissed as possible Amys, to make sure that the girl he was speaking about wasn't one of them.

"No," he said. He also gave them some other leads to check out, including another biker, incarcerated in another prison, named Cookie Monster Dave.

Breathing the stale prison air, feeling the dirty walls of indeterminate color closing in on her, absorbing the negative energy that seemed to imbue everything she touched, and being eyed by the soulless stares of men who had not seen a woman for too long, left Sue depressed.

There wasn't much upside to being a biker anymore, Sue thought, seeing how so many of them ended up dead or traded the open road and an endless horizon for inmate status and four walls. Indeed, this was the beginning of the end for the one percent biker gangs as they were then. By the 1980s, armed with new racketeering statutes originally passed by Congress to control the Mafia, prosecutors were going after bikers and drug smugglers with the same sort of fervor that had fueled earlier lawmen going after the likes of Al Capone.

When Sue returned to Coconut Grove, she attacked the phones again, calling the FBI and other authorities ostensibly to give them the latest leads, but really just to make sure they hadn't forgotten about her. Ina checked the prison records for Rolando "Scar" Vilandre, and found, interestingly enough, that his most frequent visitor had been Pompano Red. Vilandre had been arrested on charges of false imprisonment of a girl named Donna Witt.

"You see," Sue told Ned, "this is direct evidence these guys kidnap girls."

She hoped to get photographs of all of these women

to see if any, especially a girl named "Donna Witt," might know Amy.

They were able to track down Red, who was now living back in his Homestead trailer. Sue also found out the names of Scar's girlfriends.

Again, another New Year's. Sue's first entry in her notebooks under the heading of 1977 says it all. Amy's birthday. *1/9/77—Amy is 20 years old.*

Through the arrest records, Ina tracked down the mother of one of Scar's girls in St. Petersburg.

Sue called the mother, Martie, at her first opportunity. In a tired voice the woman said, "Yeah, she's one of Scar's girls, but Donna's hiding out because they're looking for her."

"I beg you," Sue said, "the next time you talk to her, have her call me. I just need for her to give me some information about one of the other girls who might be my daughter."

Sue did not get the feeling that her call was going to have a great deal of importance in Martie's life. So after hanging up she drafted a letter to Donna, detailing how she had been in contact with Jim Nolan and Paul Branch, and a number of other bikers who had tried to help her, and said any information Donna could add might be of great importance. She included pictures of Amy to jog Donna's memory.

Sue received the return call from Donna two days later.

"I can't talk to you," Donna said. "I'm really scared they'll grab me again, you don't now what they do to snitches, and I have two kids, a girl and a boy, nine and eight years old. . . ."

"If your information leads to Amy," Sue told her, "there's a very gracious reward. And even if it doesn't, I'll try to get you some money. I'm just looking for my daughter. Please—"

Donna interrupted. "I don't want any money. I looked at your pictures and think I worked with Amy in West Palm Beach about nine months ago. She called herself Susan Blakely, had short hair, and couldn't remember anything about her past except that she was from Miami. It wasn't the first time I met her, either. I worked with her in Orlando back in May or June of 1974. Then something happened and we all had to hide from the police. I went to jail and lost contact with her until West Palm Beach, like I said."

This fit in with the known facts about the Pagan killings in Orlando at that time.

"Would you please get in touch with Susan Blakely," Sue pleaded. "I'll even give you a calling card number so you don't have to pay for it."

Also, Sue knew, whatever number Donna called would appear on the Billigs' telephone bill. Donna also said she knew Paul Branch, and that he was also known as "Fat Rabbit." It was becoming obvious that Branch had many different aliases.

When Sue called Donna's mother again, a few days later, Martie told her, "Donna's very frightened, but is showing the pictures around and trying to get information for you. But she's very sure it was Amy, so maybe you should just be happy with that."

Bile rose in Sue's throat. Why did everyone think it was just enough to know your daughter was alive somewhere, living some miserable existence? "I have to see her," Sue said. "What would you do in my situation?"

Martie took a moment. "I'm just worried about my own daughter. But I do understand. Donna is trying to help you."

The next day a girl named Linda called collect from St. Petersburg. She had a sweet, mildly southern accent and sounded desperate, worried. "I have some information about Amy, Mrs. Billig," she said. "And I'd like to meet you. But there can't be any heat around and you absolutely can't tell anyone—especially Big Jim Nolan. I read your letter to Donna, and you dropped some heavy names, and it scares me."

Sue tried to soothe the upset girl. "Don't worry, I won't tell anyone. I had to drop the names to get Donna to answer me, let her know that if she talked to me she wouldn't be labeled a snitch."

"Okay," the girl said, whispering, as if there was someone in the next room who she didn't want to overhear her. "Donna doesn't want any part of this. You have to deal only with me. And it'll cost you $2,000."

Here we go again, Sue thought. "There's a $2,000 reward," Sue said, "but we must physically see Amy. It's not just for some information about a girl you say you saw in a bar!"

"I'm taking a bus down to Miami tomorrow," Linda said. "Meet me at the station in Miami. I'll call you and let you know what time I arrive."

Sue felt energized. The girl must have felt she had concrete information if she was taking such a long bus ride. It was a five-hour car trip!

* * *

When Sue and Ned picked Linda up at the Greyhound station the next night at eleven-forty, they found a nervous girl in her mid-twenties wearing sandals, hip-hugger Levi's, and a flowered peasant blouse and beads hanging between large breasts with no bra. She was attractive, with dark flowing hair, but skittish eyes, which didn't like to land on yours. Sue figured that with Linda's figure, and considering her friendship with Donna, she was probably a stripper, too.

For all her talk over the phone, however, Linda had a case of lockjaw when she arrived. She barely said more than her name, and seemed to be having second thoughts as they drove her immediately over to Rex Ryland's house.

The young informant sat on the couch and accepted a beer. Looking between them furtively, and down at the carpet, she took a deep breath.

"You came all this way," Sue said. "You must have something important to say!"

"I wouldn't have rode seven hours on a bus if I didn't," Linda retorted. "It's just that Donna's scared stiff that she'll get arrested on a kidnapping charge. She was already put away for a similar charge, unlawful bondage, with Scar."

"Yes, we know," Sue said, the point person for the small group. "Anything you tell us is in confidence," Sue assured her.

Linda gritted her teeth and came to some inner decision. "See, I'm in the group—the Outlaws," she said, "so I think I can find Amy for you, especially 'cause I'm not a biker's girl. There's a lot of talk about her, that she was taken off the road, and guys are worried that if she's ever found they'll get put away for kidnapping."

"Speaking as the Billigs' attorney," Rex said, "we're not going to press charges. All they want is to get Amy back."

"Yeah, I know," Linda said. "I'm going to need some expense money. Like . . . ah, $200 to get started."

Rex held off. "We'll be happy to give you money after we get positive proof of Amy. Two thousand reward money. More maybe."

"I'm broke," Linda said. "If I gotta go make money, I can't be looking for Amy. I'm not asking for much. Why would I sit on a seven-hour bus ride and another one back, just to get $200? I'm serious about this."

When Rex finally peeled off $200, he took an extra $100 bill and added it. "For good luck," he said.

Linda agreed to call them every forty-eight hours to check in. "I think she may still be dancing in West Palm Beach," she told them. "I'll go there tomorrow. She may have an old man by the name of Spooky or Spongy, something like that."

When Sue got home, she wrote in her notebook, *Now we wait!*

What the Billigs did not expect, however, was that Linda would be the catalyst for a whole new series of investigations that would weave yet another layer in the tapestry of lies and deceit. Was it because of the small amount of reward money involved, or was there something larger afoot? It seemed there was an entire underworld conspiracy intent on keeping the Billigs from finding their daughter.

* * *

Linda did prove more reliable in her calling patterns than some of the other biker types the Billigs had encountered. She missed a day, but called on February 10 at eight-fifteen in the evening. She'd no luck in West Palm Beach and had returned to St. Petersburg, where she'd flashed Amy's photo in the stripper bars.

"A girlfriend of mine says she saw a girl who looked like Amy, dancing in Satan's Den, here in St. Pete," she said. "I'm a bit worried, though, there are two escapees from Lowell and Raiford, and cops seem to think the first place they're gonna go is a titty bar!"

"Get a big guy to go with you," Sue suggested. Afterward, she called a friend in St. Pete, Jim Neiman, who was easily commandeered to check out the neighborhood strip joints for any sign of the Billigs' missing daughter.

Linda called breathlessly at nine-thirty the next morning. "I took pictures of a girl at a strip club," she announced. "Had to pay the bouncer fifty dollars to let me take pictures, so send me a postal money order, okay?"

Sue put her foot down. "If I sent money to everyone who sent me a photograph, I'd be out a million dollars already," she said. "We'll give you the $2,000 reward when we have physically seen Amy!"

"You look at the picture, and if it's Amy," Linda said, "then you wire me half, and I'll tell you where I found her. Okay?"

"Okay, okay!" Sue said in exasperation, and took Linda's address.

"I think it's her," Linda said.

Jim Neiman called hours later to say that he had shown Amy's picture around at the strip clubs, and workers at Satan's Den declared that Amy was working there. "They don't know where she lives, though," he said. "I'll go back tonight."

The two got into a conversation about Sue's recent investigations. When Sue mentioned the name Harry Kramer, Neiman, who was a motorcycle rider, exclaimed, "Harry Kramer! Straight, dark hair, about 160 to 170 pounds? Wears his hair in a ponytail?"

"Yes!" Sue said.

"He's here in St. Pete," Neiman told her. "Works on my motorcycle!"

12

Sue gasped. "Kramer is in St. Pete? Do you know how long we've been looking for him?"

"He's got a wife and kids. I've seen the wife, and she's not Amy."

"The story is he left her in Oklahoma," Sue said. "But if he's in St. Pete, she might be, too. Please take Amy's picture to him and see if the girl he had in Tulsa is her!"

"Absolutely, will do," Jim told her. "And I'll go by Satan's Den later, too."

Things were definitely heating up again, Sue thought. But she had to calm down. The trail had been hot before, only to cool down in quick and depressing ways. She couldn't allow herself to get too enthusiastic here. Good thing, too. The girl did not come into Satan's Den that night, and Harry Kramer could not be found. "He's suddenly gone underground," Neiman said. "He's not at the motorcycle shop, and I checked almost every bar in St. Pete, and I can't find him. I'll keep looking, though."

Ned had the gallery to keep his mind occupied during the day, but all this was pure torture for Sue.

Two days later Linda called to see if the pictures she sent of the girl had arrived. "I've also tried to contact Big Jim and some other Outlaws in South Florida," she said, "but the heat is on there. No one is around. Jim hasn't answered the phone in days."

"I'll call you the moment the picture gets here," Sue said. "I'm waiting by the mailbox."

The mailman delivered a sheaf of bills, circulars, and letters a couple of hours later. Sue hunted through the pile and found a thick letter with almost illegible handwriting scrawled across it, postmarked St. Petersburg. Her hands trembled so much she could barely rip open the envelope. Her heart raced and the entire world seemed to disappear around her as she slipped the photograph from the envelope.

The photograph was very dark and poorly exposed—the profile of a girl, long hair draped down, covering half her face. Sue could see instantly that this was not a secretly taken photograph in some dark nightclub, but a carefully choreographed fraud.

"Screw you, Linda!" Sue muttered to herself. "You little—" Sue hardly mouthed a curse in her life, and she stopped herself now.

Instead she tossed the photograph on the dining room table and called Donna's mother to see if Linda could be trusted at all, or if she was just another complete parasite.

Martie answered the phone, the television blaring in the background. "Linda? I don't know her. But Donna was passing those photos around to some girls she trusts, so I don't know what to tell you. I don't think she'd give it to some hustler. I'll see if I can get her to call you."

It wasn't until March 3, just a few days short of the third anniversary of Amy's disappearance, when Neiman called to say, "I found Kramer. He tells me he hasn't been out of the state in ten years, and that he did not steal Paul's bike, did not take his woman, and does not know Amy! I showed him the mug shot of Paul that you sent me, and he knew him instantly as 'Pagan Paul.' Said he had sold Paul some pot once, but that was the extent of their relationship. He also says he's never been called 'Dishrag' or 'Washrag,' or anything of the sort. I believe him, Sue. I think Branch may have made everything up."

Sue had to fight for a breath. This was not the news she had hoped for, or expected. "So how does his name come up all the way in Oklahoma?" Sue asked. "It wasn't just Paul. Everyone, including the police, said they knew Harry Kramer."

"Must be another Kramer around," Jim said. "And I found that girl at Satan's Den," he said, and lowered his voice. "Sue, there's really quite a resemblance—could be her sister—but she isn't Amy."

It was amazing. Another Kramer? One who fit the description that Paul had first given her? At least more than one girl fitting Amy's description floating around? Either there was an amazingly coincidental world of doppelgangers out there or something really fishy was going on—or maybe both.

By now Sue had had enough of this nonsense. She commandeered a friend, Loraine, to chauffeur her up to Glades Correctional Institution in Belle Glade, a four-hour trip, to interview Rolando "Scar" Villandre.

They started early in the morning, driving up Route 27, through the sod and sugarcane fields of Central Florida. The narrow, two lane road was one of the most dangerous in Florida, with convoy after barreling convoy of Mack trucks hauling tons of perishable produce at top speed. Even driving 65 mph, the trucks came towering behind you, blasting their horns and speeding by in the opposite lane, whether there was a passing zone or not. There was a terrible accident along this road at least once a week, especially when it rained or when the sugar fields were being burned and smoke cut the visibility.

The women's stomachs were in knots by the time they arrived in Belle Glade, a farm community on the banks of Lake Okeechobee, one of the poorest areas in Florida. They passed shanty communities with zinc roofs, every bit as poor as slums in Jamaica, where many of the laborers were shipped in from.

Built in 1932 as a prison farm to grow vegetables for other institutions, this prison was even shoddier than the one in Raiford. But the security procedures were not as stringent, being a medium security prison, and their body search was hardly more than perfunctory. Scar was brought in to see them without much delay. He was a wiry Latino with close-cropped hair, a face that had been bitten forever by adolescent acne scars, and, of course, the requisite biker tattoos. To be really different, Sue thought, a biker should refuse to get tattoos. That would show their independence!

His speech was barely clipped by a Spanish accent. Just enough to know it was there. He looked at Amy's picture and shrugged his shoulders. "Me? I never saw her. I don't know what date you're seeing on the records, but I been in jail for that false imprisonment charge since February 1974, and I don't know her."

"But you do know Paul Branch and Pompano Red?" Sue asked.

Scar looked at her with a pained expression. Plainly, he did not like to talk about his associations.

"Red is a frequent entry on your visitor list," Sue said.

He snorted in disgust. "So what?"

"Listen, I'm just looking for my daughter," Sue said, giving the familiar litany. "Check me out with people like Jim Nolan or Red. We're not the heat. Jim was actually very kind to me, and put out some feelers. Unfortunately, there's a lot of heat in South Florida because of war with the Hell's Angels."

The familiar names slowly seeped into his consciousness and quelled his paranoia. Sue wasn't an outsider anymore. She told him about Paul and the trip to Tulsa to get his feelings.

"I don't think Paul would string you along for that kinda money," he told her. "I think he was probably telling you the truth. Pro'ly not all of it," he added. "But I don't think he lie to you. Maybe there's another Harry Kramer. I don't know."

After a generous hour and ten minute conversation, he finally realized he wasn't going to get rid of Sue too easily, and that she'd insist on seeing him again if he didn't help her. "Okay, already," he pronounced. "I'll write some letters and see what I can find out for you."

As always, the next day Sue sat down and wrote Scar a letter outlining their conversation and what she hoped he might accomplish for her, and sent it off directly. Somehow, people who forgot about you the moment you exited their presence, or hung up the phone, could be prompted to make heroic efforts on your behalf with a letter in their hand. When a person held that letter, it was as if they could feel the energy that had gone into the act of writing it, which somehow transferred into their own minds to a greater extent than any mere conversation.

Also, she realized, letters were very important to prisoners.

At the end of the week, Sue received a call from Sid Fast. She hadn't heard from him in a while, and told him she was very glad to hear his voice. His calls always turned out to be important.

"I know you've been looking for Paul, and I wanted you to know he's back living with Red in the trailer."

"Back with Red?" she said. "Have you seen him? I hear he's near crippled."

"I haven't seen him myself, but someone else has. He's walking with a cane. He sounds like he's really strapped for cash, so I don't think you should trust him."

"He nearly got killed for me," Sue said. "And there's so much I have to ask him. I found Harry Kramer in St. Pete, but I don't know if it's the same Kramer that Paul was chasing. I've got all sorts of conflicting information now. Branch says he escaped from prison in seventy-four, and someone else claims he didn't. It's very important to get this all straight!"

"I'm just giving you my feeling," Sid said. "Take it from the voice of experience. I'm not saying you shouldn't have trusted him before. But he's gotta be pretty desperate now!"

Sue hung up the phone, clenched her fists and called Rex. "I don't know who to believe anymore!" she cried. "You call Paul and tell him to meet with me. He owes us, big-time!"

She was expecting to hear back from Rex the next morning when the phone rang. Instead, the voice was female.

"It's Donna," she said.

Her mother had pressured her to help Sue out some more. "I found Harry Kramer," she said, duplicating the information Sue already had. She also mentioned the look-alike at Satan's Den who Jim had already dismissed.

"Oh," Donna said in a relieved tone. "So you don't need me?"

"Of course I do," Sue responded. "Tell me more about where you knew Amy from."

Donna realized she wasn't getting off the hook so easily. "Last place I remember seeing her was a place called Sneaky Pete's in Hallandale. She wasn't dancing. Was a cocktail waitress . . ." The information was instantly suspect, as Donna had told Sue she had last seen the purported Amy in West Palm Beach. She had the feeling that Donna was trying to give them disinformation. Anything that would keep her from getting further involved.

Thus, another week was spent tracing dead-end leads, finding the former owner of Pete's, and showing Amy's picture to the girls there. Of course, no one had seen her. Another week of not finding Amy. Another week when Amy might have been found somewhere else if Sue had not been purposefully sent in the wrong direction. It was actually starting to look like a conspiracy to keep her away.

Further evidence of such a conspiracy seemed to come just days later. A Coconut Grove attorney, Martin Blitzstein—who often represented bikers and was also one of Branch's lawyers— met with Sue at the Billigs' home.

Blitzstein was a New York type, with a feisty can-do attitude. He came by the house, took a tour, scoped Amy's room, perused all the photographs on the wall, a virtual shrine to Amy, and gave Sue a hug.

"If the boys have her," he said, "I will get her back. Pompano Red owes me his life!"

Whether this contact drew the death threat or the culmination of all the other phone calls, no one will ever know. But suddenly someone was getting very worried. Rex received a three A.M. phone call from an unknown voice that he relayed to Sue the next morning.

"Definitely a biker," Rex told her. "He said he heard I could be trusted, so I should inform 'that lady with the daughter' that she was 'throwing names like Jim Nolan and Paul Branch around,' and she better quit— or else she's going to end up being used for target practice in the Everglades. Sue, you are really starting to piss people off. These guys don't make light threats. I'm begging you to slow down."

The words went through Sue's brain and amounted to nothing. If she stopped looking for Amy, she was as good as dead inside anyway. But coming from such a good friend, it was hard to take. "I am not quitting," she said. "I am going to continue doing whatever I have to in order to find my daughter. What if this was your daughter who disappeared? You'd do whatever you could, and you'd never stop! I know you, Rex."

This was becoming a mantra among her friends and in questions asked by reporters. Why do you keep going? Why don't you just accept that Amy is gone? Sue rarely responded, but in her mind she would ask, How could you be so heartless? How could you live knowing a person you loved so much had disappeared and probably didn't even know who they were?

Rex didn't fight her, though. He knew the depth of her commitment to the search. She filled him in about Blitzstein—and Rex said that if Blitzstein was as "in" with the bikers as he said, having him involved couldn't hurt.

Blitzstein reported a few days later. He had explosive information, but his voice had taken on a completely different tone. It seemed he was no longer Sue's advocate, but had jumped sides.

"Sue," he said, "first thing is, Amy's alive."

Great words, but Sue was instantly suspicious about the tone. "Alive?" she asked, excited, yet more apprehensive than ever.

"She's in New Jersey," Blitzstein said. "But she's there because she wants to be there."

"Impossible!" Sue interrupted. "If you knew her—"

"She doesn't want to come home," he interrupted. "She's a biker girl now."

"I still want her to come home. If she comes home and decides to leave again, that's her business, but she's been brainwashed. She needs help, and we'll get it for her."

"You don't understand," Blitzstein explained. "She's a different person now. She is not the angelic, innocent Amy that you remember."

"Marty," Sue said, "we will do anything to get her back. I don't care what it is. If everything goes smoothly, there doesn't have to be any heat involved. We don't want to send anyone to prison. But at this point we are prepared to get the authorities involved and throw some heavy weight around!"

Blitzstein seemed to make a decision. "Okay," he said. "I'll help you get her back, but be prepared for the worst. You may need money to buy her back."

"Absolutely," Sue said with conviction, not knowing where she would obtain the cash. "Whatever is necessary. We'll go up there as soon as you locate her."

Blitzstein paused, obviously mulling the scenario in his head. He decided it would be better to keep the Billigs in Florida. "You stay put for right now. I'll get her for you, and bring her back by force. If necessary," he continued, "in chains."

* * *

Sue was a whirlwind. She contacted a doctor who specialized in deprogramming cult members. Her neighbor across the street, a lawyer named John Lazarus, drew up "Baker Act" court documents, in which a judge declared Amy incompetent, giving Sue and Ned the power to place her under emergency psychiatric care.

Blitzstein was suddenly out of the office all the time, distancing himself from the situation. He directed calls to his associate Granville Tracy, a former biker who worked for him. Granville knew virtually everyone involved in the case, so he hit the ground running, but ran straight into a stone wall of silence. Red wouldn't give him any information, Paul had disappeared and was again rumored to have been killed—or in Nashville, if still alive.

Blitzstein himself shut up and did not appear to be assisting Granville with whatever information he originally had.

Sue was outraged. "I feel it is morally wrong for Martin to withhold any information he has at this point!" she declared. "Other lawyers I've talked to say he could be charged with assisting in a continuing criminal enterprise if he refuses to talk!"

Granville traveled considerably trying to gather information. He arrived in Coconut Grove from Richmond, Virginia, and met the Billigs at the art gallery. He didn't look like a biker at all. Instead, he was a light-haired, all-American type. Picture him playing rugby at Yale, rather than wearing chains and biker leather.

"I showed photos of Amy to a dancer in Richmond," he told them. "She recognized them as being 'Loco's' girl, a strict vegetarian, who was also a dancer in Miami. They were all living at the Sunny Isles Hotel on Miami Beach!" he said. "I also showed the pictures to Red's wife, 'Banshee,' and she said the same thing!"

Blitzstein dodged Sue's calls until her friend Barbara pretended she was a potential client and was put through to him at his Coconut Grove offices. When she confronted him about dropping the Billig case, he denied that he ever told Sue he would get Amy back.

Sue finally strode unannounced into Blitzstein's modestly furnished Coconut Grove offices, located in an elderly concrete office building that has since been demolished. She was surprised at his cordiality.

"I'm sorry, Sue," he told her, "I really am. What's happened is Pompano Red has disappeared, and that's what's holding everything up. But I'm going to take care of it anyway. The big thing we have to offer the person in New Jersey State prison who knows Amy is in my services as a lawyer."

While he didn't name names, Sue got the feeling that the New Jersey prisoner was "Loco" who she thought had been transferred from Virginia.

A couple of days later Red appeared, and Blitzstein called Sue to tell her the two of them were traveling to New Jersey to talk to Loco. He wouldn't let her accompany them.

She didn't hear from Blitzstein for weeks. Ina Shepard was sick, and the FBI was having trouble locating what prison Loco was in. Sue sat down at the phone and called the Department of Corrections in every state down the East Coast from New Jersey until she found out that Loco was actually locked up in Richmond,

Virginia. At that point she scrawled in bold, angry script in her journal:

It has now been 1 and $^1/_2$ months since Blitzstein said it would be two days before I had Amy back!

On August 22, Sue wrote a letter to Loco promising to find him legal help if he could provide information about Amy.

Three days later Paul called Rex at midnight. It was such a surprising call, with new information, that Rex woke Sue up as soon as he hung up with Paul.

"Sue," he said. "Branch says he's calling back in a few days, and to get your questions ready for him. He also said to tell you to get yourself ready to travel."

13

Paul should have said "Hurry up and wait." Maybe he was trying to get the Billigs to appreciate him, or he simply went off on some long bender. But he did not call again for an agonizing six weeks. Sue phoned Rex daily, asking, "Have you heard from Paul? What could have happened? Have there been any biker shootouts where he might have gotten himself killed?" Paul had become increasingly unreliable, but this was extraordinary even for him.

During this time, Sue, who had never stepped foot in a topless club before Amy's disappearance, became an expert in Dade County strip joints, tracking down yet more topless dancers who swore Amy had worked in a club called the Apartment in North Dade three and a half years earlier.

It was late afternoon, and dancers undulated on circular stages, while slavering men gaped at their breasts and shoved dollar bills into their G-strings. Some patrons wore work shirts or business attire and would soon go home to their wives and make excuses for being home late for dinner. The female manager brought

Sue into the back room, where half-naked women with large, perfect breasts sat on break, cigarette smoke swirling around young, pretty faces with old, tired eyes.

Sue shook her head in amazement, thinking how surrealistic and unbelievable her life now seemed, and wondered if it would ever be normal again.

One girl scanned the picture of Amy and blew out a long stream of smoke. "Sure, I knew her," she said. "A biker used to bring her in with a half a dozen other chicks, belonged to Big Jim Nolan. The biker would come in after their shift and take all their money. One of the girls, I remember, was Denise. She's fat, with hanging tits and is hooked on smack. Wears thick glasses. The last time I saw her, even the bikers didn't want her no more. She was like living in cars or something."

Sue sighed. These poor girls, she thought. "But the girl who might be Amy—she wasn't that bad, was she?"

The girl brushed a stray hair from Sue's face and frowned. "Bikers don't treat their girls very well, sweetheart," she said. "They really break their girls so they don't know anything but working for them. Give us your number and we'll call you if anyone knows where Amy is. What will you do if you find her?"

Sue smiled wanly. "Love her."

The girl nodded. "That's what she'll need. Listen, try a couple places in Fort Lauderdale—the Playmate and Take One."

The manager also agreed that Amy's picture looked like one of Nolan's girls.

It was maddening, all the loose ends, close calls. Could Amy have been living so close to home, when half the city was looking for her?

When Sue checked the Lauderdale clubs, no one remembered Amy. The turnover was high, and there had been several generations of management and dancers since the time in question.

Sue came home exhausted, late in the evening. She, Ned, and Josh ate dinner together, and Sue told them about her frustrating day. "I'll go to the dancer bars with you," Josh said, too eagerly. Sue and Ned laughed. Sue gripped Ned's and Josh's hands and took a deep breath. "Promise me we'll never lose our sense of humor," she said.

"Who was joking?" Josh asked.

The phone rang at four A.M.

Sue groped for the receiver and groaned a sleepy "Hello." Four A.M. calls, while annoying, were pretty common.

"It's Paul," came the familiar, gritty voice.

"Paul?" Sue said.

"That's what I said," he grumbled, obviously drunk. The word "said" sounded more like "shed." But after six weeks Sue wasn't about to put him off now.

"You want your daughter," he said. "She's a long way away. Harry Kramer split from Tulsa last summer and brought her to Seattle."

Sue turned on the light, reached for her notepad and sat up in bed, instantly alert. Ned glanced at her and closed his eyes again. He'd seen this a hundred times already. It wasn't that he had given up looking for

Amy, but he'd long ago stopped listening to any of these late night crank calls, and he was completely over Paul by now.

"A guy who knows Harry Kramer in St. Pete said Harry claims he hasn't left Florida in ten years," Sue said.

In the condition Paul was in, it took him a while to process information. "He's lying or it ain't the same guy," he said. "Kramer's about six feet with dark brown hair. Got a panther tattooed on his arm? That the guy?"

Sue admitted it didn't sound like him.

Despite the early morning hour and his inebriation, or maybe because of it, Paul was more garrulous than usual. He volunteered information that conflicted with his previous testimony. Earlier, he had claimed he bought Amy from Bracket, which Bracket had denied. Now he volunteered that he had actually bought Amy from Kramer in Orlando, and left her with someone else—a Puerto Rican guy. He didn't say who, but from that description it sounded like Loco.

When Sue questioned him directly, he said she was right.

None of it mattered anymore, though, because he said, "She's in Seattle now, dancing at some dive two blocks above where the ferry lands, fucking a bunch of Injuns and niggers for money."

Sue cringed. "I don't want to hear that kind of derogatory talk about people from anyone, even you!" she admonished the biker.

He laughed in his scary, guttural, voice. "Fuck 'em!" he said. "I talk to them like that right to their face. If they don't like it, I'll kill 'em. Anyway, she's real burned out and looks old. Don't look for anyone under thirty. Now you hear this, this clears any debt I have to you. This is it. You're never going to hear from me again!"

Sue didn't know what to believe anymore. Now she had conflicting information that placed Amy simultaneously on opposite sides of the continent. So, while she and Ned figured out how to pay for a trip to Seattle, Sue waged the war on two fronts, formulating a brilliant plan to check out the dancers in every club in Miami.

She called Ina Shepard to inspect the "health cards" for every woman dancing in Miami clubs. Shepard thought that was a great idea, and said she would notify the records department. A clerk called back and said such a review would have to be cleared with the FBI first.

Sue called the local agent, Peter Fleitman, who had been handling her case. As so often before, individuals in authority who had once been helpful suddenly decided there was no upside to continuing the case. Fleitman surprised Sue by saying, "The Bureau has done all it can to help you. Amy's probably dead."

Tears sprang into Sue's eyes. From day one, officials had downplayed the case and shuffled their feet, rather than sprinted. Police had labeled her a runaway and said she'd come home in a few days. There were no fingerprints on file because no technician was sent to dust Amy's room. Police were afraid to go into the biker area in Daytona to search for her. Again and again leads had been dropped.

"Please don't abandon me," Sue pleaded.

"Well, we consider this a missing persons case," Fleitman told her. "From here on you should find help in the private sector. Face it, Sue, it's time to quit."

Sue's heart started beating in a strange pattern, and she was suddenly out of breath. "I can't quit," Sue said. "I love my daughter, and love never quits."

The next morning a Lieutenant Storms called from the North Miami Police Department to tell her there were thousands of pictures, but he had put a girl on detail to pull information on the ones who had worked in the Apartment.

"This is really wonderful," Sue said. "When can I see them?"

"You can come up and look at some of the cards this afternoon," he told her.

"You don't know how grateful I am," she said.

But from the time she had spoken to Fleitman, her heart wouldn't stop beating strangely. She had barely hung up the phone when a pain shot through her arm and made her drop to the ground.

Ned heard her scream, and came running into the living room from the kitchen. "Oh God, honey, what's wrong?"

The room came back into focus and the pain subsided. "I think it might be an attack of some kind," Sue said. "I'm all right now. I have to go look at photographs."

Ned wouldn't hear of it. "I'm taking you to Jackson Memorial right this second! Let's get you right into the car." He kissed her cheek forcibly and helped her to the door. "I don't know what I'd do without you," he said. "We can't let anything happen to you."

Jackson was only ten minutes away. An emergency room doctor listened to her heart and said, "We've got to put you in intensive care immediately."

"No," Sue protested. "I have to go look at photos at the police department. Please wait until tomorrow. I'm feeling fine now, I really am."

"I'm not letting you out the doors, ma'am," the doctor said. "It's for your own good."

She stayed the night, but sneaked out the next morning and took a cab up to the police station. She went through a pile of pictures, none of them Amy. She left a copy of Amy's picture, as they promised to "pull more." She went back to the hospital, where a Dr. Gardener told her she had heart disease and needed a bypass operation.

"Are you kidding?" Sue said. "I won't have anything of the sort! I don't have time for this."

"You're going to have to make time," the doctor said. "Or you won't have any time left."

Sue spent a week in cardiac intensive care after the operation. While other patients might have watched television or caught up on their reading, she spent the time on the telephone making plans to travel to Seattle.

The Billigs sold some of their last treasured paintings by David Levine, Aaron Shikler, and other major artists whom they had known from New York, to pay for tickets to Seattle. Sue arrived in the early evening on November 16, 1977, with Artie Saewitz, the husband of one of Amy's friends. He was a nice Jewish boy, with thinning hair, but an athletic build, who worked in his family's fabric store business and had never consorted with bikers.

What a change from Florida! Almost as far away from Coconut Grove as you could get in the continental United States. While Artie went to check out the rental car, Sue was already in gear. A man with a ponytail and tattoos on his hand was picking up a girl on the same flight.

"Pardon me," she asked. "Are you a biker?"

The man looked down at her over a crushed nose and split lip from a recent fight. "What about it?"

"I just want to know some of the biker bar hangouts around here," she asked. "I'm looking for my daughter."

He picked up the woman's bag and said, "Check out the Blue Moon and Century Tavern." They walked away, but he slung another couple words over his shoulder. "Good luck."

A wet, icy Pacific breeze froze their cheeks the moment they walked to their rental car. She had requested a simple, unobtrusive car. What they found was a sporty red and white Mustang. "Well, this will be inconspicuous!" Sue said.

They checked into the Olympic Hotel and brought their bags to their room, but Sue wasn't the type to waste precious minutes settling in. She called the Seattle police to make an appointment for seven A.M. the next morning, then said, "Okay, Artie, ready to check the bars that Paul mentioned?"

The ferry was easy to find, and so was the area that Branch had told her about—a neighborhood along

First Avenue with strip joints advertising "beautiful girls" and adult bookstores with XXX signs plastered over covered windows. The West Coast version of Times Square. Drug dealers dressed in black leather leaned against dirty walls, eyeing the traffic meanly—wary for cops or clients. Girls in tight clothes congregated on street corners and motioned to men who drove by.

"Park the car," Sue said.

"Here?" Artie said.

Sue pointed out a particularly nasty looking place, the Red Lion. "We're going in."

Artie gulped. "We could get killed in a place like that!"

"Don't worry, I'll protect you," Sue said.

The bar was crowded with bikers, hookers, pimps, and Alaskan Indians. An entire herd of cows had gone into making the black leather and boots worn by this crowd. Rock music blared and a basketball game showed on a television above the bar. A pinball machine clanged in the corner, and the sound of a billiard break shattered the air, followed by a yell of disappointment.

No one paid attention to the Miami couple as they wended their way to the bar. A giant bald bartender with an earring took a while to make his way in their direction. "What you want?" he shouted over the music.

They ordered locally brewed beer and sat on cracked wooden stools that had been polished by leather for many years. "What now?" Artie asked. "Are you gonna show people Amy's picture?"

"Not yet," Sue said. "I've learned a few things about doing this. We can't just come in and push too fast. We'll come back tomorrow and get a bit friendlier, buy some rounds. Tonight we just get them used to looking at us."

Sue could barely sleep, and woke up before dawn. She finished breakfast and decided to take a taxi to the station to let Artie sleep in, since their bodies were still running on Miami time. She arrived early to see Sergeant Skagen, with whom the night sergeant had arranged the appointment.

The shift was just arriving and the offices were still pretty empty when Sue arrived. Skagen was a bright woman in her late thirties with short-cropped hair. She wore civilian clothes and had a very cold demeanor. Sue was an invader from the East.

Billig sat beside Skagen's desk and was offered a cup of coffee.

"So I understand you're looking for your daughter?" Skagen said. "She was supposedly kidnapped by bikers?"

"That's right," Sue said, sipping her coffee. "She may be with the Pagans or the Outlaws or being passed between both. We've had conflicting information about that."

Skagen clucked her tongue. "Well, I'm afraid you're way off base here. We don't have any Outlaws or Pagans in Seattle."

Sue just about spit out her coffee. "I saw bikers all over the place," she said.

Skagen leaned forward and rapped her knuckles on

the desk. "Nothing organized. We don't abide that here."

Sue handed the sergeant photographs of Amy and Paul Branch. "That's my daughter, you can see she's no biker type. She was kidnapped. The man is Paul Branch, a Pagan, and he says he used to 'own' her. He says she's been brought here by a guy named Harry 'Dishrag' or 'Washrag' Kramer.' "

Skagen looked at the photos carefully. "I'll be happy to post the information, but as I said, we don't have any Outlaws, Pagans, Hell's Angels, or anything here. Can't keep people from riding motorcycles, though. I'll go show this to some of my officers and be right back."

She left the desk and headed into another room where some sort of roll call was taking place. Sue scanned the area, reading the duty roster on the blackboard, with crimes and names and codes she did not understand listed on it. Typical police room. Then on Skagen's desk she noticed a note, apparently written by the night duty sergeant who had taken Sue's phone call. Sue could read it upside down:

She seems nice, but drops names and will do any-thing to get her way. But she seems like a nice lady.

Skagen returned without the photos. "You have copies, right? I've posted them, and we'll make copies and have our officers keep a look out, but I can't promise much."

Sue motioned to the note. "I couldn't help but see

that," she said. "I don't appreciate the telephone analysis."

Skagan glanced at the note and grimaced. "Sorry about that, but you do seem like a nice lady. We will try to assist you if we can."

Sue could feel the brush-off as viscerally as if Skagen had pushed her out the door.

When she arrived back at the hotel, a flustered Artie was at the front desk trying to see if she had left a message for him. "I was looking all over for you! You had me worried."

"I thought I'd be back before you woke up," Sue said. "We had a long day yesterday." She told him about her reception by the police. "Looks like we're going to have to rely on ourselves."

No matter what had happened to Amy, Sue felt as if her daughter's basic personality could never be transformed. Amy would still be a vegetarian, drink herbal tea, and listen to Joni Mitchell. She would enjoy shops and art and music. Driving around, they happened on Pike Place Market, a large indoor and outdoor farmer's market and bazaar, with stalls, shops, and restaurants right on Puget Sound. It was aged, but brightly painted, and actually the oldest continuing farmers market in the United States. The weather had grown nicer and hundreds of people shopped, while musicians strolled the sidewalks.

"Here! Here, Artie," Sue said. "It's just like Coconut Grove. If she's in Seattle, she'll come here."

They parked the car and were walking across the

street when Sue spotted a Native American woman. "Was that girl at the Red Lion last night?"

Artie said she looked familiar.

"Great," Sue said, "finding a girl alone is the best way."

Billig intersected the young woman—short, with long dark hair, wearing jeans, a red checkered blouse, a wide leather belt, and boots. "Excuse me?" Sue said, and introduced herself. "I think I saw you at the Red Lion last night."

The woman cast a suspicious eye on her, looking Sue up and down. "Maybe."

Sue dug out a picture of Amy from her purse and explained for the thousandth time in her short career as a self-taught detective that she was not "the heat," and only looking for her daughter.

"Sure, I've seen her, right here," the woman said.

Sue could hardly constrain her glee. "You're positive?"

"Absolutely," the woman responded. "Not too long ago, either."

"Where? Have you seen her anywhere else?"

The woman shook her head. "I'm really not into saying any more," she said, ducked her head down and bullied forward as if forging into a gale.

Inside the market, they found a shop that sold herbal teas. When Sue showed the owner Amy's picture, he said, "She comes in every Saturday. Yeah, I'm positive."

Sue was more excited than she had felt in a long

time. Saturday! Today was already Wednesday. "If I hadn't been in the damned hospital, we'd have been here to see her!" Sue complained.

"Calm down," Artie said, "you just had a bypass operation, and we're running around like maniacs, drinking in biker bars at night. Don't give yourself another heart attack. If we're this close, we'll find her."

"Let's go back to the Red Lion now," Sue said. "It'll be calmer and we can talk to the bartender."

Apparently, people did a lot of drinking in Seattle, because there were plenty of people inside. The bartender was different, a smaller, friendlier looking guy with long hair and a beard. His name was Ralph.

He scanned the picture with interest. "Yeah, I know her," he said. "Why do you want her?"

Sue explained that she was Amy's mother, and that bikers had been helping her locate her daughter.

Ralph wasn't convinced. He made a motion with his fingers and said, "Gimme some names."

Artie was looking nervous, but Sue had been through this before. "Big Jim Nolan, for one," she name-dropped. "And Bracket in jail in Florida. There's lots more."

"Just a second," Ralph said. He took the photo and showed it to a large guy, also with a beard and ponytail. The guy glanced at Sue, nodded, and said something back to Ralph.

Ralph returned. "I gotta be sure there are no police involved," he said.

"All I want is my daughter. We're prepared to buy her back," Sue said.

"Buy her back, eh? Well, that's interesting. Give me

your number and I'll let you know when I can put it together."

Sue left the bar feeling as if she were walking on a cushion of air. She held Artie's arm and just about skipped. "We're going to get her, Artie. I can feel it!"

Artie was beginning to enjoy himself, and seemed glad to be a part of this terrible situation's denouement. He could imagine coming home to Coconut Grove with Amy. It would be so wonderful!

When Sue called Skagen and told her everything that had happened, even the sergeant said, "You've done really well!"

Sue called Ned and told him everything, so excited she was stumbling over her words. Her mind was way ahead of her lips. "That's fantastic, honey," Ned said. "You keep on like this, and you'll have a whole new career as a private eye. Or we'll make you a character on a television show—a veritable Miami Ms. Marple!"

14

The trail was the freshest yet most elusive that Sue had come across yet. This was the day she had been waiting for—Saturday. The day Amy was supposed to frequent the herbal tea store.

When Sue and Artie returned to the Pike Place Market area and showed Amy's picture to more of the shopkeepers, a bookstore manager nearby said he was sure she was a customer, clerks in a drugstore said she came in occasionally, usually wearing overalls and a backpack, and waiters in a restaurant recognized her as well.

When Sue asked them to describe the girl in more detail, the bookstore manager said, "Well, she had a funny sort of uplifting walk."

"She's here, Artie!" Sue cried. The information about Amy's unique stride was almost as good an identification as Paul's recalling her appendix scar. Sue gave everyone her name and contact numbers. She was so close she could almost smell her daughter's perfume, and every dark-haired girl on every corner drew her attention.

They kept a good lookout on the herb store, but the manager had to shrug his shoulders. "I guess she's not coming today," he said.

Back at the hotel, Billig called the police and spoke to another sergeant, and relayed the newest information. "Please be on the lookout for her," Sue asked. "I really think she's here." She also asked about bikers again, saying some bikers from the Red Lion were also on the case.

This officer was more forthcoming than Skagen and admitted there were some bikers around. "But just Hell's Angels and Banditos. There are no Outlaws here."

In the early evening, Sue and Artie returned to the Red Lion. It was already crowded and noisy, with a lot of the same faces from their previous visit. But it seemed as if, while Sue and Artie had been gone, these people had just been here drinking. An angry Native American man wearing a flannel shirt with rolled up arms, exposing his tattoos of skulls and knives, slammed a baggie of marijuana down on the bar in front of a muscled black man wearing Army-style fatigues.

"Tarragon, motherfucker!" the Indian said.

Ralph, not paying attention to the escalating fight, brought Sue and Artie their beers. "I got feelers out, and told people about buying Amy back. I ain't heard nothing yet."

The black man turned slowly. "Who you calling motherfucker?"

"Who am I looking at?" the Indian said. "I paid good money for weed, and all I get is herb!"

Ralph turned to the nearby drug dealers. "Hey, guys. Take it outside!"

The Indian smashed a bottle on the bar, sending glass flying into Sue's lap. He held the jagged edge up to the black man's throat.

"Let's get out of here!" Sue said, and they made for the door.

The relentless Sue made Artie drive back to a restaurant district where they had obtained some information about Amy earlier. A young woman at the drugstore said a girl named Willow Treeland fit Amy's description, and gave Sue an address of a nearby apartment building.

The entire three floors were dark, as if the building had been cut off from electricity. No one seemed home in any apartment. A mailman, still making deliveries, said Treeland had just moved. Back at the hotel, Sue called directory assistance and found a new listing for Treeland. She dialed it immediately, and a woman answered.

"Yeah, I'm Willow," the woman said. Not enough words to know if it sounded like Amy.

"This is Susan Billig," she said.

"So?"

"Does the name ring a bell?"

"Not really," the woman said.

Susan explained who she was and why she was calling.

"Well, it's not me," the woman said. "My parents live right here in Seattle."

Sue asked her to describe herself, to see if the multiple sightings of Amy might be Willow instead. "That's kinda hard to do, isn't it?" Willow said. "I have long brown hair, and, well, I'm pretty fat, okay?"

That didn't sound like the girl people had been describing. They spoke a bit longer. Willow's boyfriend, Mike, said he knew some Florida Outlaws in town, and his buddy John suggested that Sue check the tattoo parlors and a few strip clubs, but they were all closed that night.

"It's like Tulsa," Sue said. "Does every town in the West roll up the sidewalks on Sunday?"

On Monday, Sue and Artie went off to check out more bars. At the Rainbow Café a female bartender looked at Amy's photo and snapped her gum meaningfully. "Yeah, I know her. Goes by the name of Vicky. Runs with a biker from the Zudmans club." Her gum cracked an exclamation point.

"You're sure?"

"Well, as sure as I can be. But I can't tell you where to find them."

A gray-bearded biker wearing leathers at least twenty years old had been listening. "Check out some places on Pike," he said. "Unique Café and Chi Chi's. You'll find 'em."

On the way back to Pike they found one of the tattoo parlors people had mentioned. An old man there shoved a voice box against his throat and intoned mechanically, "Try Custom Tattooing. The Outlaws run the place."

"You mean they go there a lot?" Sue asked.

The old man was annoyed. "No, they own it! Florida

Outlaws come here and take away our damned business!"

"And you're sure they're Florida Outlaws?" Sue asked. "Everyone says there aren't any here."

The leathery tattoo artist raised a cigarette to a hole in his throat, sucked in smoke and blew it out his nose. He obviously liked to disgust people. "They're from Florida, all right," came the buzzing words. "Got rings and T-shirts that say so."

The Outlaw tattoo parlor had a lock and chain securing the door shut. The windows were so dusty it looked like someone had sprayed liquid snow on them one year and never wiped it off. They couldn't see inside.

From a pay phone, Sue called John, the friend of Willow's who had seemed fairly knowledgeable about local bike activity, and asked about the Zudmans, whom she had been told Amy was with.

"Yeah, I know the president of Zudmans—a guy named Roach. They're not a violent group. Mostly they just party and get high. I'll set up a meeting for you."

"Listen, if they're decent people, tell them I want to see the girl I've been told about."

"No problem," he said.

The next day, Sue met with Skagen again.

"You said there weren't Florida Outlaws here," Sue said, "but there are. They own a tattoo parlor, for Christ's sake."

Skagen seemed apologetic about the misinformation about the bikers, and even a bit more helpful now. The sergeant searched police files and found a Harry

Kramer listed as an area biker, but there was no "street name" such as "Dishrag" listed, or even a present address.

Two days later the Outlaw tattoo parlor had still never opened its doors. Obviously, it was not a place that was meant to do any business. Sue met with Skagen again, asking her to pull the occupational license of whomever owned the place. They also spoke about the Zudmans. Skagen said, "Yeah, they've got a club called the Mink Farm. But do not go there! I don't want to send you home in a bag. We'll contact the sheriff's department."

Sue laughed. "If you knew just a portion of what I've done, you wouldn't be telling me that," she said.

The occupational license was listed to a Loretta Clayton and leased to a man named Jack Hunt. Sue and Artie drove to the address—a run-down house with peeling paint and rotting window frames, with junk strewn around and a pickup truck in the front yard. When Sue got out of the car, a rat nearly ran across her foot and dodged under some rusting debris. She yelped. Artie, sitting in the red Mustang rental, looked apprehensive. "I'll tell you right now," she said. "This is the place."

Artie said, "I'll stay here."

Sue trod up to the weathered door and knocked. The door swung open to reveal a tall, bearded biker wearing a veteran leather jacket with Outlaw colors. He held a large revolver pointed at the floor in his left hand.

"You must have the wrong address," he said.

Sue quickly explained her presence, and the man admitted he was Jack Hunt. "Please, may I speak with you?"

The man gestured to Artie in the car. "That the FBI with you?"

"Him an FBI agent?" She laughed. "No, that's my friend Artie. I don't drive, and he's very kindly come all the way from Florida to help me."

Jack gestured for Artie to come in. He looked reluctant, so Sue shouted, "It's okay!"

Inside there were about a dozen tattooed men and women dressed in biker garb, T-shirts, leather vests, Levi's, and chains. The whole Outlaw posse at Jim Nolan's could have been teleported here, and hardly anyone would have known the difference. A five-year-old girl wearing pajamas welcomed them inside. "My name is Patsy!" she said.

"My daughter," Jack said. "And that's my wife Patricia." He motioned to a woman with frizzy dark blond hair and sharp features. Two large black Labradors nosed forward and tried to stick their noses in Sue's crotch. She pushed them away, but they persisted, wagging their tails, until Jack shooed them into the living room.

Jack had let them inside, but he suddenly had a lot of questions. Sue worried she might not get back out so easily unless she answered them correctly. "So you said some bikers in Florida were helping you find your daughter? What're their names?" Jack asked.

"Well, there's Big Jim Nolan, for one," Sue said. "Bracket, up in Raiford, and Scar in Belle Glade."

Jack nodded. "Well, those are the right names, but why in the hell are you in Seattle?"

She told him about Paul Branch. "He said this lead was his final payment to me," Sue said.

Again Jack nodded, and relaxed. "Get these guys a beer," he told his wife.

Sue told him about their adventures in Seattle so far as Jack studied Amy's photograph.

"I have to say, Willow does look exactly like Amy, and she's not that fat. She's real spaced, like she dropped too much acid. Talks in real sixties slang and listens to music all the time. Sings to herself a lot, too. Got nice teeth—you notice that about her."

Another biker named Chris knew her, too. "I'd say she looks ninety-eight percent like this picture. Her old man is a guy named Mike Martin, and he's real good to her."

Jack passed the photo back to Sue and plucked Patsy up and put her on his lap. "Yeah, but if Willow is Amy, she belongs with her family. I know a doctor can help, if it's her. We'll go over to Willow's house and see if we can take some pictures and show them to you."

They met again at four P.M. outside the tattoo parlor. Jack was there, driving the pickup truck. "You checked out with Nolan," he said. "So we're going to help you out. If Willow is Amy, I'll grab her, even if it means I gotta blow someone's head off. If it's not her, and she's anywhere in the Outlaw nation, we'll get her back."

Sue felt an overwhelming surge of gratitude. "You have a daughter, so you know what this means to us. We will be so grateful to you, Jack."

He smiled, showing strong, but yellowed teeth, gray in the corners. "Tomorrow's Thanksgiving," he said.

"Why don't you spend it with us? We're going to have a great dinner."

She patted his hand. "Thanks so much, but I really get depressed on holidays. Let me see how I feel and we'll call you tomorrow." Later she wrote in her diary, *If bikers can be good guys, these people certainly are!*

Artie was all for hanging out with the Outlaws on Thanksgiving, but Sue wasn't so sure. "I feel awful you're not home with your family, but I don't think we should get too chummy with the bikers. And you never know what will happen if they start getting drunk."

She felt blue after speaking to Ned and Josh, but also energized because she might be close to Amy.

"Next Thanksgiving, we'll have the whole family eating dinner here," Ned told her. "I'm sure of it."

But on this Thanksgiving, Sue and Artie spent an hour in a bar with the cast of a musical that was doing a road show.

The next day they drove out to Jack's house to see if the bikers had seen Willow the previous night, as they had promised. Sue was already out of the car running before Artie had even turned off the ignition. She jogged up to the door and knocked heartily to be heard over the sound of music inside. The dogs barked and Jack opened the door, looking a bit stoned, hung over, but not unhappy.

"Come on in," he said. "Take a seat. You wanna beer or a toke? Man, you should have come over last night. What a bash!"

As before, the house was full of other bodies in various states of dress and wakefulness. The sounds of a couple in the throes of passion emanated loudly from the other room.

"It was really nice of you to offer," Sue said, "but I get depressed. Did you see Willow? Were you able to take pictures?"

Jack shook his head. "They were partying with the Zudmans. We passed by, but couldn't figure out any way of taking photos without the Zudmans getting suspicious. But she really looked like Amy to me." He turned to Patricia and Chris. "What'd you guys think?"

"I'd say it's her," Pat said, stroking her daughter's head. "Hair, skin, teeth, her body shape. She's not that fat. And she's got that walk you talked about. If it's not her, I think she's the girl you've been following from Miami. If it's not her, you should just give it up."

Sue shook her head. "I can never give up. Not unless I see her, or bury her."

Jack sucked on a beer. "Okay, we'll see if we can lure her and her old man and the Zudmans over to the Cedar Bar tomorrow night. You be there already, and if you walk out, we'll know it's Amy, and we'll decide how to grab her. But figure out what you're going to do if she freaks and won't leave town with you."

"I hope to God it comes to that!" Sue said.

"We have some great leftover Thanksgiving food," Pat said. "Why don't you stay for dinner?"

The turkey proved succulent, with excellent gravy and homemade cranberry sauce. All the bikers were extremely friendly.

Pat and a few of the other biker women made a living as topless dancers. A girl named Debby was showing everyone a butterfly she had just had tattooed on her chest. Finally, two guys named Chow Hound and Tank said Amy's profile picture looked just like Willow.

Besides the biker clothes and the bare-chested Debby showing off her tattoo to all the men, Sue thought this was not that far off from normal. Then a car pulled into the driveway, lights skimming across the curtains.

The men jumped from their chairs. Guns appeared from pockets and from behind pillows, and everyone rushed to the windows with weapons in hand. Sue's heart jumped into her throat and she almost choked, but Artie looked strangely excited, his eyes focused on the big revolver that Jack held in his hand.

Jack let the curtain fall back. "Go back to dinner. It's just a turnaround," he said.

By Saturday night plans had changed a bit. The Zudmans weren't interested in going to the Cedar Bar and had their own party planned. Sue and Artie met the Outlaw group at Jack's to finalize their actions.

"You're never going to mix in with the bikers," Jack said.

"But I'm the only one who can recognize Amy," Artie said. "I have to go with you."

Jack smiled. "Then you gotta blend in. If you go in without colors, someone's gonna stomp you. Pat, what can you do for the man?"

Pat rustled up an Outlaw T-shirt and leather jacket. "They'll fit," Jack said.

Artie was nervous but excited, changing into the biker clothes. "How do I look?" he asked.

Sue laughed. "I wish I had a picture!"

Jack shook his head. "Not enough. We gotta get you some chains and stuff. And you gotta walk with some umph! But don't look anyone in the eye for too long. We don't want to get your ass out of a knife fight."

"Knife fight!" Artie blurted. "I don't have a knife."

Jack reached into his pocket and came out with a stiletto-type knife. "You can't go in with no protection."

Sue looked around and saw all the guns sticking in the men's belts. "Will the other guys have guns, too?"

"Of course," Jack said. "No one's going to a party without one. Good way to end up dead."

Sue grabbed Artie's arm. "I think you should stay here. We'll figure out another way."

"I'll be all right," Artie said. "We gotta get this over with. My dad and my wife are going crazy back home. And I know Amy, so this is our best bet."

"Please, Artie."

"I'm going," he told her.

Jack stayed behind to keep Sue company while the crowd jumped into trucks and vans. Billig guessed bikers didn't always need motorcycles to be a bike gang, but it seemed strange that only a few men were actually riding machines.

Sue watched the taillights disappear into a mist and threw a kiss after them.

"Make yourself comfortable," Jack told her. "They'll be a while."

The minutes stretched to hours. Jack was very sympathetic and said he knew the entire story. How a girl had been taken from Coconut Grove. He said he knew Harry Kramer, who was now living in Portland, Oregon, and "that son of a bitch Paul Branch." He made a pistol motion with his fingers. "I'll fucking kill him if I ever get the chance. He's not the kind of guy you ever turn your back on." During the conversation, as he learned more about what Sue had been through, he promised, "If Willow isn't Amy, I'll follow this up for you. I'll use whatever powers I have to get the truth."

A dimestore clock on top of the television ticked the seconds, and Sue watched the minute hand slowly revolve. Three hours, and she was getting nervous. "It's all right," Jack said, toking a joint, watching an old biker B-movie on television. The bikers on the tube were stupid and mean, and Jack laughed at them. "This is what Hollywood thinks is a biker?"

Late in the evening a couple of motorcycles rattled into the driveway, followed by the truck and a couple vans. Jack rushed to the window with his gun, and put it away when he saw the visitors were friendlies. The horde barged into the house, drunk and raucous, but with no bloody noses or bruises.

Artie came in behind them and shook his head. "I'm sorry," he said.

"You're sure you saw Willow?"

Artie nodded. "Looks a lot like her, but she's not. It's been a while, but I'd know Amy anywhere."

Sue wiped a tear from her eye. She hadn't realized how much hope she had invested in Willow. "I wish I had gone," she said. "Can we go back? I have to be sure."

Artie gripped her shoulders. "It's not her!" he told

her. She fell into his arms, and he hugged her. "We've done our best. It's time to go home now."

Just as they were leaving for the airport the next day, the phone in their room rang. It was a biker calling from the Blue Edge Lounge.

"This is Darryl, I met you at Jack's," he said.

"I remember you," Sue said.

"Well, I got a girl here looks like your daughter. I'll hold her here until you come by. But come quickly, because I don't know what I'll do if she makes a fuss."

Susan and Artie threw their bags in the trunk of the Mustang and rushed over to the bar. By this time they knew where every place was.

Sue ran in, fingers crossed, her heart pounding. She recognized Darryl, who sat beside a girl in a back booth. The young woman matched Amy's description and was quite the knockout, but Sue could tell from the door that this was not her daughter. She walked the rest of the way to the booth.

Darryl left them together. Sue spoke to her for what seemed hours, with the girl crying now and again and admitting she was a runaway. She wouldn't tell Sue her name or age.

"If I had a mother like you, a mother who loved me, I'd go back in a minute," the girl wept.

"Believe me, she loves you," Sue said. "A sweet, gorgeous girl like you? How couldn't she? You may not know it, but she does. Please, tell me where you live. Come to the airport with us, and I'll buy you a ticket home. You don't want to be all alone out here. Things can happen." She told the girl all about Amy. "I would want someone to do the same for her."

The girl shook her head. "My mother doesn't want me. I can't go home."

Sue hugged her and wrote down her name and number on a napkin. "You keep this. If you ever need a mother, you call me from anywhere collect."

As the plane blasted from the earth, Sue watched another city slip beneath her wings and thought about the sweet runaway and about all the lost people in these cities she had visited.

And, right now, she felt as lost in her own life as any of them.

15

The trip to Seattle was a watershed event in many ways. While it did not end the search for Amy among the biker subculture—as clues and sources would continue to explode into existence, sending the Billigs into a frenzy of activity, only to have all clues fizzle into a vacuum just as suddenly—it did mark the culmination of a four year investigation and a need for some soul searching. Just how long could they continue their efforts? Could they devote their lives to their daughter's rescue, or did their human and financial resources have an end?

They closed the gallery. This was a heartrending decision on their part, which meant they were giving up hope that their family life would soon return to normal, and conceding that the search for Amy was not a sprint to the finish, but a marathon. Ned got a job managing another store for a salary.

Next, the financial costs caused them to lose their home on Poinciana, Amy's only home in the Grove. They moved into a much smaller cottage around the corner. In between all of this, Sue would find interior design jobs to keep up a cash flow.

Sue had kept Amy's room just as she'd left it all this time, dusted and neat. One time when she thought Amy had been found, she bought new Bill Blass sheets and a nightgown to welcome her home. Now she packed Amy's artwork, books, clothes and all the stuff of a teenager's life into a few boxes from the dry cleaners and carried them to the new house. She couldn't believe how compact it all was. "My daughter's entire life fit into a few boxes," she recalls. She couldn't summon the emotional strength to tape the boxes closed. Josh had to tape them and bring them up to the attic.

"If I take them out," Sue told him, "it will be like creating another shrine. It will be like saying she's dead."

Sue walked back to their former house to show the new occupants a photograph of Amy in case her daughter should ever return home looking for them. "It was the most devastating thing," she told Ned. "I never wanted to leave there. It was Amy's home!"

About this time a nationally syndicated television crime show aired a segment about Amy's disappearance. Hundreds of people, from bikers to housewives, telephoned or wrote in to say they had seen Amy here or there. One man claimed to be Amy's husband and was tracked down by an investigative reporter, only to find the man had no connection to Amy. A man in Ocala swore he had seen Amy with a biker three years earlier. Weeks and vast amounts of energy were wasted in dealing with inefficient police from the area following up the useless information.

On Amy's twenty-first birthday Sue cooked a small

dinner and cried. "She's no nearer to us than she was four years ago!" She told Ned, "But I feel like there is some connection that if she was no longer on this Earth, I would know it."

Ned continued to be her anchor in this confusing maelstrom. "Then she must be alive," he said. "We have to keep looking for her."

Rosie, from Oklahoma, called on June 8, saying she had just met Amy at a Texas gathering of a motorcycle club called the Banditos. "It was like looking in a mirror," she said. The girl called herself Sharon, but "had an accent just like Sue's" and "couldn't remember where she was from." The girl even had the secret appendix scar like Amy's. But Rosie suddenly stopped calling and could not be found.

Prosecutors finally turned Bracket against Big Jim Nolan in the Hell's Angels murder case and allowed Sue to meet with him in a secret locale in Fort Lauderdale. Bracket told her Paul Branch was the common denominator between all biker/Amy links and suggested Sue "hire some heavies to beat it out of him!"

But the worst moment was when Bracket shook his head and told Sue, "Don't you think it's time to give it up?"

Sue had heard that from so many people now, from authorities to bikers, from friends to inimical callers who told her "Amy was a sex slave now."

But those words just drummed against her consciousness like so much static. "I won't give up until I find her grave or I find her."

* * *

In many ways, the Billigs were only able to live their lives between telephone calls, like some couples who only talk during commercials. Each lead subsumed the entire focus of their lives for however long it took. Each blamed themselves for Amy's disappearance, starting with the ironic move from New York to Miami to get away from crime.

"How could something like this happen among all this beauty?" Sue would ask as they took one of their rare walks to Coconut Grove's famous Dinner Key Marina and sat on a bench watching the boats, the rigging slapping against the masts.

"Amy loved that sound," Sue reminisced. "It sounds like hundreds of bells tingling."

The couple still tried to get out and see their large circle of friends. Rex Ryland, who became good friends with the Billigs, says, "Ned always had a smile on his face, no matter how badly he was feeling inside. Everyone in the Grove knew him, even many people who he didn't know back. And whenever people would ask about news, or how he was feeling, no matter who they were, he always said something positive."

But home life was difficult, Sue says. "Talking just hurt too much, so we hid in silences."

Josh rarely spoke about Amy anymore, even though it plainly hurt him deeply. "People would say 'poor Sue and Ned,' but never 'poor Josh,'" Sue says. "And that must have been difficult for him. Now, I realize the despair he must have endured. Why didn't I spend more time with him? He must have needed me, but couldn't tell me about his pain. He seemed to become a different person, as though he didn't deserve the things he had."

By now Josh was becoming a self-taught stonemason. He and a friend began building coral rock walls, and he liked the feeling that he was helping to protect people. He was pained by his father's drinking, which became a friction between them, so he didn't like to spend a lot of time at home. His observation now: "I think my father had a lot of sorrow." Their best times came when they would accidentally meet at the grocery store and "just go up and down the aisles shopping, talking to the friends we'd meet."

Theirs was also a difficult kind of celebrity. "We didn't want to be martyrs," Sue says, "but we were famous because of a tragedy. People would ask, 'Haven't I seen you on television?' And usually I would just say it must be someone else. Or people would say, 'It's so good to see you going on with your life,' and I'd say yes, because that's what they wanted to hear."

Ned became increasingly depressed. His doctor gave him Halcyon and doubled the dose when Ned said it wasn't working. The drug made it difficult for him to concentrate, and he lost his job. So, in March 1979 the couple went to Longboat Key for five days of rest and recuperation, their first vacation in years. They returned feeling refreshed, having made some decisions about how to continue their lives. They would never forget Amy, but they couldn't forget their son, either. They would never stop searching for Amy, but they couldn't lose themselves in the search. It was a fine line that would be difficult to ascertain, but they would try.

But a man who called himself "Hal Johnson" was waiting in the wings, and he had other plans.

When they returned home, *Miami Herald* reporter Edna Buchanan updated the story. As usual, this prompted a new deluge of phone calls and letters, many of which were sympathetic prayers, others suggesting they contact certain psychics.

One call was very disturbing. An angry man who Sue immediately imagined as a biker threatened, "Listen, lady, you better keep your mouth shut unless you want more problems with the rest of your family."

Sue had by now heard several of these. They were very scary, but she'd learned to deal with them. "Thank you for the warning," she said, and hung up the phone.

Sue and Ned were developing a true love-hate relationship with the telephone. It was the lifeline that might solve all their problems, and it was the one thing that made their lives miserable.

Hal Johnson, with an earnest-sounding, mildly southern voice, was going for the latter. He introduced himself politely on the phone, saying he was from Fort Pierce and was staying at a local Ramada hotel on business when he read the newest article about Amy. "I saw a girl who looks very much like Amy hanging out with bikers on Fisherman's Pier," he told Sue.

There was something very practical and firm in his voice that made Sue believe he was not the type to spread false hope. "Would you come down to the gallery my husband manages in Coconut Grove and look at some photos there?" she asked.

"I'd be glad to, Mrs. Billig," he said. He got the address and made the appointment for the following day during lunch hour.

Sue and Ned brought the photographs into the store and waited patiently for the visitor who never came. When they called the Ramada Inn, they were told that no one by that name was registered.

But Johnson did call again a few days later, apologizing for standing them up. "Listen," he told them, "she will be posing for me and another artist in Fort Pierce on Thursday. If you want to see her, come by." He gave her a phone number and an address—913 Ohio Avenue—along with instructions on how to get there. "You take U.S. 1 to Searstown, and the first light past that is Ohio. You can't miss it."

Sue thanked him profusely before he hung up. But as soon as she hung up she turned to Ned. "Something doesn't sit right with me about this."

"Call the number back," he said.

Sue dialed the number Johnson had just given her and received a recording. "We are sorry, but the telephone number you have dialed is not in service. Please try again."

Sue's next call was to the Fort Pierce Police Department. The officer she spoke to, Fred Brosilow, was familiar with her case and left immediately to drive past the address. He called back shortly later, saying, "There is no 913 Ohio, Mrs. Billig. It stops at 911 and starts up again at 1002. I also checked and can't find any listing for a Hal Johnson. There's a Harold listed at a different address."

Brosilow suggested they contact FBI agent James Franklin, who was in charge of that area. Again, there was another frenzy of phone calls getting everything set up. Eventually Ina Shepard convinced the FBI to provide backup while she and Fort Pierce police provided surveillance of Sue. FBI agent Harold Phipps, newly stationed in Miami, set up watch as well.

Sue spent another sleepless night and rose at dawn to make the two hour ride to Fort Pierce before rush hour with Ina, with whom she was becoming good friends.

The sun broke through high cumulus clouds in the east, spreading a golden spray of light slanting across the highway. Someday, Sue hoped, she would be able to enjoy such a dawn again, breathing deeply on a beach while nursing a cup of coffee. Simple pleasures were some of the things she missed most in her life. But that would have to wait for another time. Now they were racing up the highway her expectations peaked, throat dry, blood pressure high.

The directions were easy to follow. They first went to the FBI office to meet Franklin, and from there to the police station to allow the authorities time to coordinate their surveillance. One agent sat in a car; another dressed as a meter reader walked from house to house.

The neighborhood was one of modest middle-class CBS houses, with green lawns and hedges of hibiscus and Surinam cherries. Sue and Ina, dressed in simple jeans and blouses, walked up and down Ohio Avenue knocking on every door and ringing every bell. Sleepy looking octogenarians, with coffee cups in hand, answered the doors.

No Hal Johnson here, honey.

No Amy.

No girl. No artists.

While most were retired folks, some younger people were mixed in. At number 608 an obvious biker answered the door.

"No Hal Johnson," the guy groused. "Would you throw me that newspaper?"

After they had exhausted all the addresses, Ina turned to Sue. "I'm really sorry, but it's another goose chase," she said.

Back at the police station, a Captain Parker said, "Really, Mrs. Billig, it would be much better if you would go back home. We'll see if we can get some information on Johnson and look at Fisherman's Pier for you."

"My God," Sue cried. "What is this Hal Johnson doing to me?"

Parker shook his head. "Go home, he'll probably call again."

Little did he know just how prophetic those words would be.

The next day she received the call from Johnson. "Why didn't you come?" he berated her. "She was there!"

Sue protested, "I came, the address didn't exist."

"We were there," Johnson said.

"If you saw her, tell me how she looked," Sue asked, trying but not succeeding in keeping a pleading note from entering her voice.

"Oh, she's beautiful," Johnson said. "Very nice body. And she's got great tits!"

"Don't talk like that, I'm her mother," Sue snapped.

"And she's got a beautiful mouth," Johnson said. "She knows how to use it!" He hung up.

Sue held the phone in her hand, looking at it with revulsion, feeling as if something unbearably slimy had touched her.

Feeling violated.

Feeling scared.

By May of 1979, the country had a lot more on its collective consciousness than the small story of a missing daughter. The country had just recently recovered from the shock over the mass suicide of 909 people in Jim Jones's cult in Guyana. Iran's Ayatollah Khomeini had overthrown the Shah of Iran and was brewing fundamentalist hatred against the United States. The Sandinista revolution in Nicaragua was about to topple the Somoza government. Three Mile Island was nearing a nuclear meltdown. And Golda Meir, British punk rocker Sid Vicious, and disco were dead.

And then there was the story of a missing girl, which Edna Buchanan began work on for a cover story in the *Miami Herald's* Sunday magazine, *Tropic*.

Rosie Harrington finally called back from Tulsa in the middle of July.

"I'm so sorry, honey," she said in her Oklahoma accent. "But the reason you couldn't call me back in Texas was that some shit went down and the Banditos ran us out of town. A heavy-duty guy was killed in Fort Worth and the police were trying to get the Banditos for it. The Bandito who had Amy is named Tramp. She called herself Cheryl and said she was like from all over. When I specifically asked if she was from Florida, she said, 'I don't know. I think so, maybe.' "

But that was the extent of the information.

I don't know if she's lying or not! Sue wrote in her diary. It was so frustrating not to know.

So far, Amy and the Billig family's story had been compelling to bikers, criminals, and the best of the community. Now, at a wedding in New York, an acquaintance sidled up to them and said that Mafia don Santo Traficante and Meyer Lansky had heard about the case and would try to help them with Amy. Nothing ever came of it, but it is interesting to see how the story touched the hearts of such a wide range of people.

And Sue's hopes continued to be fueled in so many ways. In August a friend sat her down in front of an acclaimed tarot reader and psychic. During the reading, Sue matter-of-factly asked, "Will I see my daughter?"

The woman, who Sue had been assured had "no idea who you are," looked up and said, "Your daughter is alive and you will see her again. She was taken from you by strange people—a counter or subculture group. Strange people . . . She's with a large man who has long hair and a beard, and they are living in a sandy area. Your daughter has a memory block from the trauma of being taken and doesn't know who she is. But you will see her again."

The tarot reader told Sue that Josh "was a creative person who works outdoors with his hands, but will eventually go into law. He has hopes of seeing Amy, but finds it very hard to speak of her."

By this time, Josh was a working stonemason who

did work outdoors most of the time. But he would never study law.

The woman also told Sue, "You will be traveling very soon on a lead. You should place more ads in magazines." At this point an advertisement was running in *Easy Rider* magazine.

Just a week later Sue and attorney Frank Rubino flew to Orlando to meet with a biker, Redneck Jim, who claimed he had seen Amy in Nashville three years earlier with a biker named "Roadblock" at a National Run. Redneck Jim had taken lots of photos, which they scanned, but they could not find anybody who looked like Amy. Of course, the photos were not of the best quality, and many faces were simply blurred in the background.

Sue kept thinking about the tarot reader's predictions, and insisted on driving past the Outlaw clubhouse. An Orlando lieutenant who had set up the meeting with Redneck Jim told her not to go. "There's a guy there named Calo who's a maniac and'll cut your throat as soon as look at you."

Rubino promised he wouldn't let Sue get out of the car, and they drove by. The house was located in a "pretty area of very clean homes," Sue remembers. "But when we got to the Outlaw address, the house was painted completely black. They were outside lounging on the grass, wearing their black leather and working on their bikes. Of all the bikers I'd seen so far, these were the scariest, meanest-looking bunch I'd ever seen."

They drove past a couple times and didn't see anyone who resembled Amy. Sue took a deep breath and told Frank, "If the psychic's right about finding Amy, it's going to happen sometime in the future. Not today . . ." She scanned the bikers one last time, looking at each girl closely. "Not today . . ." she whispered into the glass.

Buchanan's Tropic article was published on September 9, 1979. The article was by far the most detailed and moving to date, interspersing Amy's poems and describing the impact on the family. Sue told Buchanan, "I only feel alive when I'm searching for Amy. The worst time is when nothing is happening. I get desperate because I feel like people will forget. The last five years have been like thirty. I look in the mirror and don't recognize myself."

Response to the article was phenomenal. "The phone rang off the hook for two weeks," Sue says. She mailed copies to most of the bikers she'd spoken to over the years, including Hector Garcia, Sergio "Cono" Cuevas, and Loco. Cuevas called collect from prison and said he wanted to help, that he had two daughters himself. He promised to write other Pagans in jail and gave her the names of some women who might have known Amy.

The article was reprinted in other newspapers and more leads poured in. An Outlaw biker gal named Christy from Charlotte said she had partied with Amy, who called herself "Sunshine," for two weeks recently, and said they were on their way to Fort Lauderdale. Sunshine didn't know how old she was but loved poetry and had a scar on the side of her face from a time "when she had it out with her old man." She wore boots, a Bob Seger T-shirt, and had long shiny hair.

Shortly afterward, a Dania, Florida, convenience store clerk called to say a girl answering Amy's description had bought food because she had "two hungry Outlaws outside." First Fort Pierce, now Dania, a small town south of Fort Lauderdale on the way to Miami. Again the psychic's prediction seemed to be coming true, and Sue, despite her skepticism from years of hearing psychic predictions, felt her excitement growing with every day.

Amy, "Sunshine," it didn't matter. Amy by any other name was still Amy.

Could she be coming home?

16

In case Amy came looking for them at the old Coconut Grove address, Sue walked the few blocks over to their former residence to inform the current owners. As she approached, she heard a rumbling noise. Walking faster, she arrived to find bulldozers heaving the kindling of their old wooden house into large Dumpsters. A wave of sadness surged from her solar plexus into her chest, becoming a flood of tears. She knocked on her former neighbor's door.

The woman answered, and Sue fell into her arms. Her friend didn't understand. "Did they find Amy?" she asked.

"The house . . ." Sue sputtered.

"Oh, they're building a new one," the neighbor said. "Isn't that nice?"

"That's Amy's home. She won't know how to find us!" Sue said.

Before she returned to their present cottage, Sue made sure all the neighbors would be keeping watch in case anyone who might possibly be Amy came wandering through. "She may not look like we remember her," Sue told them. "So call me if any woman seems to be searching here for something." It was a quiet street where neighbors knew each other, and a stranger would stand out.

Sue walked the neighborhood day after day, visited Amy's favorite shops in the Grove that were still around, always in anticipation. But if Amy were headed south, she did not make it to Poinciana Avenue. Within the next several months more psychics introduced themselves. One man came through their house and declared that Amy was very much alive but didn't know who she was, and said the Billigs would have to go get her themselves. He saw her in an area with cactus plants, close to a desert, possibly Arizona.

But Hal Johnson said he knew exactly where Amy was. Sometimes he would call several times a night, sometimes he didn't call for weeks.

Sue went back through her telephone logs and found several calls from the early weeks after Amy's disappearance. When she thought about it, his measured southern tones, she recognized the voice from that earlier time.

Now Hal Johnson was calling again, with variations on the same theme. "I've trained Amy, she's my sex slave."

Sue demanded that he give her concrete information that would identify Amy conclusively. He wouldn't answer.

Instead he would just continue: "I've smoothed her out. She knows how to please."

"I won't listen to that," Sue would tell him. "I want to know if she's okay."

"She knows all the sex games," came the measured voice.

It was a voice that would eat into Sue's mind and keep her worried at night.

If there was ever a time for the Billigs to change their telephone number, it was now. But they couldn't bear to do it because it was the only number Amy knew. If she ever did try to get in touch, it would be the number she called. Indeed, police and other institutions around the country had that number on file.

There were other cruel calls as well. A young girl phoned and wailed, "Mama, it's Amy, Mama."

"This is terrible," Sue said. "You're not Amy, and how would you like it if someone caused your mother such anguish?"

The girl still tried to convince Sue that she was Amy, but just repeated information from the newspaper. She didn't know any intimate details that Amy would know.

But it was Hal Johnson who haunted Sue's nightmares and whispered to her in her sleep. Ned would try to console her or grab the telephone away to shout at the man, but Johnson would simply hang up, leaving the dread words in his wake.

In a matter-of-fact voice, as if reciting a grocery list, he said, "She was kidnapped from Coconut Grove, brought to Fort Myers, sold to a motorcycle gang, and taken to Canada. From Canada she was unloaded in London." He said he had trained her as a sex slave.

And then he would hang up and not call again for days or weeks.

Other leads inevitably popped up. The couple hunted St. Petersburg for a girl who said her last name was Billington and gave a birthdate near Amy's. Pictures of a murdered woman answering Amy's description were mailed from police in Orlando. Sue opened the envelope praying that it was not her daughter. It wasn't. While Sue was gratified, she still cried. "She's still someone's daughter, and she's probably buried somewhere under an assumed name and her parents will probably keep on looking for her. It's so sad."

Because Amy's disappearance, unfortunately, was not unique, Sue received letters from all over the country from parents asking her to keep watch for their daughters as well.

One poignant letter came from Helen Sinagub in Palm Springs, California, who felt a striking kinship to Sue, since her daughter Naomi had disappeared.

I have been praying and wondering what happened to my daughter Naomi? At times I feel that she's no longer alive. I have no proof. My feelings are mixed. . . . I feel caged in and helpless. I have been told so many things by the Hollywood police . . . they don't care. There are so many, many thousands of girls missing, to them it is all the same, only a different name.

After reading and rereading your story, I can pretty much tell that you are a very brave and courageous lady; your search has taken you into many strange and dangerous places. May God watch over you and may your search for your beloved Amy bear the fruit of your labor.

Since your search has taken you into so many places, perhaps you have seen a young girl, now 25, small, 5'2", dark hair—large brown eyes? Maybe?

It is exactly five years since I have heard from her. God only knows if she is alive, or needs help or if she is ill . . .

Sinagub enclosed pictures that Sue memorized. If she could even bring home someone else's daughter, well, that would be a gift almost as good as bringing home Amy.

A reporter from the now defunct *Miami News*, Phil Stanford, brought renewed energy to the case when he tried to trace the Banditos in Fort Worth, Texas. Eventually, he traveled all the way to Cement, Oklahoma, to find a man who had called the Billigs saying that Amy was his wife and mother of his son, but that they couldn't talk to her because the biker gang wouldn't let her.

After all his effort, Stanford found this was all just another cruel hoax.

And there were many more, keeping the family running from town to town, police station to police station, only to find somebody trying to extort $10,000 or to satiate some whim.

These phony calls were always draining.

Sitting outside on the terrace, exhausted, Sue told Ned, "I always feel so empty when these things go down. I promise myself I won't get too anxious, and then I find I'm thinking of nothing else but her, my baby."

On August 12, 1981, Sue wrote about another South Florida kidnapping that would shake tears out of the nation. *A small six-year-old boy was abducted from a Sears store, and a few days later his head was found in a canal. I was devastated. . . .*

That little boy was Adam Walsh. John Walsh, the victim's father, would go on to become the host of *America's Most Wanted* and start the Adam Walsh Foundation. Sue craved to do something similar, but her life was kept in constant turmoil by the never-ending search.

About this time, prosecutors were making major strides in putting the Outlaw Motorcycle Club members behind bars. In Tampa, several biker women testified against their old men and succeeded in getting five of them found guilty of white slavery.

This gave the public a glimpse into the true brutality of the clan.

The Outlaws originated in Chicago and had followed Big Jim Nolan to Florida sometime in the mid-1960s. There, in their prime, hundreds of bikers would sometimes swarm the highways across Florida. No law enforcement official ever successfully infiltrated the organization, because initiation rites included felonies and rape. Additionally, members greeted each other with mustached, open-mouthed kisses, something that police officers would shun. Gang justice was swift and cruel, honoring the slogan, "Snitches are a dying breed." Body parts of bikers who broke the code were found across Florida, many of them around Daytona.

Sergeant Robert Faulkner, a Broward County sheriff, told the *Miami Herald* at the time, "Big Jim Nolan was shrewd. If he could have put his brainpower to work on the other side of the fence, there's no telling what he could have become."

One Outlaw murder charge that struck Sue particularly hard: Naomi Sinagub, the former "old lady" of Donald Joseph "Gangrene" Sears, was murdered, her body eviscerated and thrown to the sharks. She was never found. Sue found the letter that Helen Sinagub had written to her years earlier and cried. Cried for the poor girl, her family, and what it might mean about Amy.

The trials broke the back of the Outlaw organization. It still survives, but is a shadow of its former dangerous self.

The convictions affected the search for Amy as well. Bikers who were notoriously closed-mouthed anyway now became stone-silent. Too many girls had testified against their old men, too many trusted brothers had turned on their brethren—who cared about some lady looking for her daughter?

Every time a skull was found, Sue had to deal with the possibility it might be Amy, praying it wasn't, but knowing that if it was, the search was finally over. Once, a Florida State University anthropologist even reconstructed the facial features of a skull from which the teeth were missing, so a dental match could not be made. Months later, the answer: "Definitely not Amy."

Information came through biker channels that "Loco" was the last person to see Amy alive in Orlando. Granville Tracey, who worked for New Jersey lawyer Martin Blitzstein, had interviewed Pompano Red's wife in Richmond, Virginia, who also claimed that Loco was the last person to see Amy.

Josh went to Bike Week at Daytona Beach and searched again in 1983. Again no luck.

Importantly, Sue found that authorities did not have Amy listed in national databanks, and that she could only be found in the Florida missing persons computers. When she went to a meeting of a missing persons task force, attended by then State Attorney Janet Reno, Metro Police, the FBI, and the Florida Department of Law Enforcement, she felt they had a patronizing attitude and "gave me the same platitudes I always heard."

Sue set her shoulders straight and shook a finger at the panel. "When Amy disappeared, no one took it seriously," she said. "The police work was awful, no one lifted her fingerprints from her room until it was too late. Her picture should have been sent to every police agency in the country. Over and over again the FBI referred me to local law enforcement, who would have to start from scratch again. It might be too late for Amy, but not for all the other children that might fall into the crack the FBI has created."

Sue's tirade might have had some effect, as procedures became more streamlined afterward. When a trucker called in a tip that he had seen Amy in Sparks, Nevada, Harold Phipps at the local FBI office teletyped Amy's picture to Sparks and Reno authorities within fifteen minutes.

Meanwhile, Hal Johnson was still calling, usually late at night, sometimes waking the couple up.

The tenth anniversary of Amy's disappearance had been an emotional day for the Billigs. Sue went to bed with a pounding migraine headache, which she said was caused by tears petrified in her head. But there would be no rest. The phone rang well after midnight. Ned answered, but the caller insisted on speaking with Sue.

"It's been ten years," came the voice. "Where do you think Amy is?"

"Oh, God," Sue pleaded. "If you have her, tell us where she is. If you don't, please stop calling and give us some peace!"

"Amy's doing well," the voice said. "She's getting very good training, and will be sold to some new rag-heads in Saudi Arabia."

Sue screamed, "Give me some information! I'll meet you anywhere. We'll pay anything to get her back!"

"Not more than the ragheads," Hal Johnson replied calmly, and hung up.

Police traced the calls and discovered they had been initiated from four pay phones in the Miami suburb of Kendall. But when they staked out a particular pay phone, the culprit did not return.

The police told Sue they didn't have the manpower to stake out all four pay phones all night until he called again.

Johnson also seemed especially canny, as if he could spot the police surveillance. If they were staking out one phone, he would call from another, then hang up and run long before police could arrive.

When a man in Texas said his former girlfriend, now dead from a brain abscess, looked like Amy, it took months battling red tape and an intercession by Florida governor Bob Graham to have the body exhumed. Finally, the news came in. The poor girl was, of course, not Amy, any more than the previous bodies had been.

Still, the news hit Sue hard, as she scribbled down in her diary, *But where is she? Is she in some other grave, somewhere? I feel empty.* Now she says, "Many of my efforts may have been for naught, but if it makes other people realize what they can achieve, then it was worth it."

It had been over ten years of constant activity from March 1974 to September 1985. During that time, people had raised families, built businesses, traveled the world, written works of genius, played music, enjoyed meals, felt sorrow, fallen in love, and survived all the things of human life.

Sue just felt empty.

By 1985 the world had become a very different place since the years of Amy's disappearance. The country's shift toward conservatism, with Ronald Reagan at the helm, had turned the Age of Aquarius on its head.

Teenagers rejected the old ideals of "peace and love," traded in their blue jeans and flowers in their hair for the dominatrix look and identified themselves with the "Material Girl"; the Cold War against what the President had termed the "evil empire" was in full stride; AIDS had changed everyone's ideas about the innocence of sexual relationships; and the incipient War on Drugs had forced small bands of Robin Hood–style entrepreneurial drug smugglers to organize into large, rich, and dangerous organizations.

Here, Rex Ryland made some unfortunate headlines. It turned out that the lawyer who had become such a great friend and helped so much in Amy's search had been leading a double life. In September 1985 the forty-three-year-old criminal defense attorney, who had become a Miami celebrity for taking high-profile cases, was arrested and charged, along with thirty-eight other defendants, with operating an international drug smuggling ring that grossed some $64 million from 1979 to 1982. Under this new world order, Ryland's transgression was treated much more severely than it might have been a few years earlier. He was disbarred and sentenced to sixty-five years in jail for his participation.

Before he was sentenced, Ryland accepted his guilt, saying, "I put a lot of good years to get where I was, and in a matter of months it was all over."

Serving most of his time in Talladega, Alabama, he was finally paroled in the year 2000, after fifteen years in prison, and is currently a freelance paralegal in Miami.

By contrast, when Big Jim Nolan, forty-five, was

convicted as a "dangerous special offender" on charges of racketeering and conspiracy stemming from his years as head of the South Florida chapter of the Outlaw Motorcycle Club, he received fifty years. The club had been accused of murder, drug dealing, and extortion.

The ongoing search and the increasing public awareness of child abductions had made Sue a frequent guest on news programs and television talk shows. Each time she appeared, she did it in the hopes that other parents and children would be more vigilant and that other families would be spared the Billigs' experience.

On December 9, 1987, Sue was a guest on *Oprah*, for a show on "Forgotten Americans." She was one of six mothers who appeared.

Oprah asked sympathetically: ". . . the things that your heart and mind can imagine are far more damaging to your own spirit than what actually happened or is happening to [Amy]—am I right? Because I guess you imagine the worst?"

Sue's answer was directed toward some unknown person who might be watching the show: "What I keep hoping is that somebody out there knows something, and since Amy has been gone thirteen years, the statute of limitations is over and they'll come forward and give us some information about her, whether she's dead or alive, and that's what we hope and pray for. And that's why we keep on looking and going on anything public in the hopes that even if she doesn't know who she is, that she sees a picture of herself and says that could be me, I have no background, I don't know where I was when I was little, I don't know what I used to look like, and say I want my family, they want me, and I have to find them again. If there is anyone out there, please contact us."

When Oprah seemed to think of Amy's case as being parallel to parental abduction, Sue tried to disabuse the talk-show host of the thought: "It's terrible when a child is gone, but when you know that your ex-husband or wife has them, it's terrible but you know the child is alive and is being fed. I don't know that my child is warm or being fed or even alive, and I think it has to be separated. I think the government should step in and do something for all these hundreds and thousands . . . of children. . . . We're not getting help from anybody. Everything we had to do we had to do ourselves. . . . Children taken by strangers should be helped by the FBI, and we cannot get help from them."

Sue also appeared on *Geraldo*, the *Today Show* and many others, in the hopes of delivering her message to authorities and whomever else might be listening.

By now the Billigs had to wonder if all their investigations during the years had been worthwhile, because Hal Johnson continued to call, and he seemed to know so much about Amy. He talked about her looks, her appendix scar, the music she liked. . . .

Ring . . . Ring . . .

"You know who this is," came the voice. "I'll meet

you at the Taurus restaurant tomorrow night at eight and give you pictures of Amy," he told them. "You and your husband alone. No police. Be there."

The Taurus was an old Grove hangout just blocks from the Billigs' house in the South Grove.

They spent the day in agitation, of course notifying the cops, who promised to be there undercover.

"What will he want, Ned?" Sue asked.

"It doesn't matter," Ned told her. "We'll get whatever he wants."

And then Sue thought about it. "He kidnapped Amy or knows who did. Ned, he picked the Taurus for a reason. He knows where we live. He could be watching us right now. He could be anybody. A person in the store, the guy behind you in the car. He could bump you in the street, say 'Excuse me,' and you would never know."

"We have to hope they catch him," Ned said.

The Taurus was so close, they walked there in less than ten minutes and arrived fifteen minutes early. It was a wooden pub and restaurant on the southern tip of the Grove business district, shaded by thick banyan trees. They knew the bartender and half the other people there. Ned ordered a beer and told the bartender, "Don't pay any special attention to us." They took chairs at a table where they could see the door.

Friends and acquaintances waved from varnished wood tables. They waved back and searched the faces they didn't know. Could it be the man with gray hair hunched over the bar? Was it the guy with the beard and the leather vest? Not quite a biker, but someone who wanted to look like one. He looked familiar, but maybe that was because he'd been watching them. Was he looking at them too hard?

The nervous couple kept vigil on the door, a shiver slipping down Sue's spine every time someone entered. The bearded guy slapped a bill on the counter and departed.

Ned tapped his watch. "It's eight now."

The minute hand crept inexorably around its arc.

"This is nerve-wracking," Sue said. "It could be anybody!"

A man entered, tall and gangly, with bad skin, deep-set eyes, and wild hair. He looked around, went to the bar and ordered a beer.

"It's him," Sue said. "I'm going up there." She jumped from the seat before Ned could stop her and strode up to the man. "I'm Susan Billig."

The man looked surprised. "Oh, hello . . . I'm Dr.—" The name didn't concern her. She knew instantly that she was wrong. Not a shred of recognition had passed across his eyes. She went back and sat with Ned.

And sat.

Hal Johnson could be any of the single men at the bar, silently laughing at them, but if so, he was too wary to approach. They even stood on the outside deck for a while, in case he wanted more privacy.

"What kind of man would kidnap a girl in the first place?" Sue cried in disgust. "He's a coward!" She raised her fists in the air. "Coward!"

They took a cab home. Just in case. On the few

minutes' trip home, Ned hugged his wife and said, "It's all right, honey. Just stay calm. Stay calm."

But Hal Johnson would make sure they would never feel calm again.

17

False leads continued to come in regarding biker women who looked strikingly similar to Amy but were not. A couple of women's names kept on coming up: "Mute" and "Sunshine," for instance. Almost everyone who identified Amy's photograph usually said she did not speak very much. A habit such as that could easily lead to a nickname of "Mute." An equally strong coincidence was the name "Sunshine." Amy had written many poems that included references to sunshine, so it seemed a possibility. Girls often had more than one nickname, as did their old men, however, so it was entirely possible that Mute and Sunshine were several different women, or even the same one.

The Billigs were kept constantly on edge trying to keep track of it all. Many families might have been torn apart by the circumstances. There were always a hundred decisions to be made about how to allot their meager resources for the continuing search, and it was a source of tension. But the Billigs were soul mates, destined to be together, and were resolved that no matter how hard life might be, they would face it together.

Josh married in 1988, and he and his wife Michelle, a schoolteacher, had a daughter, Elizabeth, who Ned and Sue doted on. There were also the normal family crises that all families have to deal with: fevers, accidents, school. But always, even dealing with the minutiae of life, the dilemma of Amy's absence was felt. Did it help that from the time of her infancy Elizabeth bore a striking resemblance to her missing aunt? While all their friends could see the similarity, the family seemed to be in denial about it.

And from day to day, week to week, there was always Hal Johnson.

"Do you know what Amy's doing to me now?" he would say. "She has a great stomach, great muscles, she's keeping herself very nice."

When Sue's mother died, she received the expected calls from friends and family. But Johnson made sure to add his voice to the choir to taunt her about it.

Time marched on. George Bush was elected President, the Berlin Wall was torn down, the USSR was dissolved, Boris Yeltsin was elected president of Russia, the Gulf War made the Middle East erupt in flames in 1991, straining the world's nerves and starting an international recession—and, throughout it all, Johnson continued to add his brand of torture to the Billigs' lives.

But there were moments Sue was still determined to enjoy, like her and Ned's forty-fifth anniversary on March 26, 1992. Sue made reservations at a fancy restaurant in the Grove, one of their favorites where they only went on special occasions. Unfortunately, she had been feeling a bit lethargic at the time and her breathing was shallow, and so she made a routine visit to the doctor. He said he wanted to see her again to discuss some test results. Ned drove her to the office on their way to lunch.

Sue couldn't believe it as the doctor fixed her chest X rays to the light. There were large, dark blobs in her lungs.

The doctor held her hand and squeezed. "I'm sorry," he said. "The tumors are inoperable."

Sue was outraged. "Cancer? I haven't smoked a day in my life!"

"Secondhand smoke," the doctor intoned softly.

A freight train howled through Sue's head, drowning out the sound of her own thoughts. Her voice seemed a very long way away. "How . . . how long?"

The doctor shook his head. "I'm very sorry, Sue. I give you maybe four months to live."

The words echoed in Sue's ears. She fell into Ned's arms, but didn't cry. She wasn't worried about herself, but in agony that she would never see Amy again. "I'm not satisfied with that diagnosis. I'm taking this to a higher authority!" she managed to quip.

The doctor's stern expression didn't change. He wasn't the joking type.

"Secondhand smoke?" Ned asked. He had smoked three packs a day for years, especially since Amy disappeared.

"It's a recent finding," the doctor intoned. "It carries more carcinogens than primary smoke that is inhaled through the filter."

Ned put his head in his hands. "Oh, God. Honey, let's go home and get you some rest and figure out what to do."

Sue would have none of it. "We are keeping our reservation, and we're not going to have the slightest mention about my immediate demise all day," she commanded. "I'm not listening to some doctor that doesn't even have a sense of humor!"

The next time Johnson called, she told him.

"Please, I've got cancer," Sue told him. "They don't give me long to live. If you've really got Amy, let me see her."

The plea received no sympathy. Sue didn't write this conversation down, but the answer, she remembers, was something like "Maybe you can meet us for a mother-daughter team before you die."

Ned, however, refused to believe the doctor. "I am not just going to let you die," he said. "We're getting another opinion."

The second doctor agreed with the first.

Then Sue's dentist referred her to a more youthful, more courageous doctor who was prepared to remove the tumors. "You're trying so hard, I really want to give you a chance," Dr. Young told her. "There's absolutely nothing to lose."

Sue endured a few weeks of debilitating chemotherapy first, which made her deathly ill and did not reduce the tumors. The prognosis was not positive, but she kept telling herself, "I'm not ready to die. I'm too busy to die! I will not die until I find Amy!"

There was nothing else to do but go under the knife. Feeling weak and miserable, barely able to stand, she insisted on leaving a clean house and buying burial plots that were only a few miles from the house. If she died, she didn't want people having to trek too far to visit her grave.

They operated on one lung first. She woke up feeling the worst pain in her life. It lanced right though the morphine and could be felt even in her sleep. When the doctor told her he thought the operation had been successful and that they could operate on the other lung in six weeks, she laughed painfully, saying, "If I'd known it would hurt so much, I wouldn't have let you do the first one! I'm not letting you touch me again!"

But despite the pain, she felt grateful to be alive, and had a very positive attitude. When she was released from the hospital after the second operation, the couple was able to celebrate Sue's "imminent survival."

But in January 1993, just when Sue was beginning to strengthen and the couple began to make plans for the future, Ned was also diagnosed with lung cancer. Like Sue, he was given only a few months to live. Unfortunately, he was genuinely inoperable.

"The instant I heard he was sick," Josh says, "all of the problems between us dissolved. All I wanted was for him to get better. And we really were able to heal things. It makes you wonder what all your problems were ever about in the first place. When he was dying I was holding his hand and said, 'We love you.' I really wanted to say 'I love you,' but he smiled, because I think he understood what I meant."

Ned would never lose his sense of humor, even in the most painful moments. "He could still muster a joke until the moment I kissed him good-bye," Sue says.

Near the end, Ned took her hand and said, "Don't think of it as losing a husband. Think of it as gaining a closet."

Josh remembers that Sue bought Ned a new pillow. "I've been asking for one for years," he joked. "I have to die to get a new pillow?"

And while Ned lay dying beside her, "Hal Johnson called over and over again to torment me about it," Sue remembers.

Even as he expired, Amy was never far from Ned's mind, either. Just minutes before his time on earth was up, he gripped Sue's hand, searched her face with milky eyes and said, "Never give up looking for Amy."

Sue remembers, "Losing Ned was such a blow, a tremendous test of inner strength to me. Not only did I have to continue the search alone, but now there was nobody I could open my heart to. We had always been there for each other, trying to lessen the pain that we both felt."

The publication of Ned's obituary was a surprise to many in the community who had not known that he was sick. Sue was on the phone for hours at a time, welcoming the company in any form it came. Except for one.

After tossing the first handful of dirt on Ned's coffin, after weeping and saying prayers to send her loved one to God, the phone rang two weeks later.

"Ned's dead, isn't he," Hal Johnson said. "You're alone now, aren't you?"

"What do you mean by that?" Sue asked. "Why do you keep taunting me? Please leave me alone. . . ."

Johnson's voice breathed evilly. Then, "You better watch out," he said.

18

Hal Johnson kept any sense of normality from entering Sue's life. Even as she recuperated from Ned's death and dealt with her own painful recurrences of cancer and the necessary chemotherapy treatments, his calls came ever more frequently.

He had Amy, he told her. He was training her as a sex slave. . . . She would alternately hang up or plead for more information. After so many trails had turned to dust over the years, Johnson seemed to her the only road left that might lead to Amy. No matter how disgusting the calls became, there was one consistent theme—Amy was alive.

Sue notified local police and FBI agent Harold Phipps of the continuing telephone calls. He couldn't take over the case completely, but he could assist the locals. Cold case detective Jack Calvar took over Amy's case file and, along with Phipps, set up a more sophisticated trace and recorder system on Sue's telephone. The calls were still being initiated from several telephone booths in the Miami suburb of Kendall, southwest of Coconut Grove. But as before, every time police arrived, the caller was long gone. Surveillance proved fruitless, as Johnson kept one step ahead of police and always seemed to use a different phone than the one being watched.

Calvar took a great interest in the case. A Miami police officer for twenty years, he'd been hearing about the Billigs throughout his career. "I felt an instant sympathy for Sue and her family," he says, "and for Amy, a lovely girl who had vanished so long ago. I just wanted to do everything within my power to find her."

The detective was six feet of burly tenaciousness, sporting a thick mustache and a shaved head. He liked to ride Harleys himself, sketch architectural buildings in Europe, and had studied everything from Sherlock Holmes to metaphysics.

Sue felt that if anyone could think outside the box and come up with new leads, Calvar could. He was a friendly and gregarious man who could easily have been a character actor in different circumstances.

Calvar did have other cases, but working with Sue, he tracked down bikers who had been associated with the case over the years. They were harder and harder to track down, as some had been absorbed into the Witness Protection Program, others had died of alcoholism, been murdered, or were long-term prisoners who didn't want to be labeled snitches.

One of the most important leads he finally tracked down, however, was Paul Branch, now living in Gordonsville, Virginia. He made the trip up to the small town, and found a large unadorned trailer with several dogs in the yard.

"He was in terrible shape," Calvar says. "He was fat and bloated, had a terrible case of skin cancer, and was hooked to an IV. He had large pizzalike lesions everywhere on his body, pustulating through old tattoos. It was really sad-looking. Oh, God, it stunk in there. Branch maintained that everything he had told Sue was true, but that he'd lost track of Amy and never seen her again. I really thought I was going to find something and was very disappointed."

He returned to Miami feeling as if there were no other leads to follow but Hal Johnson. "Why else would this man be so obsessed with Mrs. Billig for so long?" he asks. "I really wanted to get him."

Phipps, the tall, paternal FBI agent who had been of so much help in previous years, assisted Calvar and Miami police. After Ned's death, he became very close to Sue, giving her his home number and visiting often when Sue became too terrified to be alone. Josh and his family moved next door, but her son worked long hours, did not always return until after dark, and was sometimes out of town.

"Sue was a dear, sweet woman," Phipps says, "and I wanted to do everything I could to make her feel safe and provide some protection."

But for all the law enforcement muscle that was allocated to the case, Johnson was a wily coyote who slinked from shadow to shadow, phone to phone, always slipping out of any trap that was laid for him.

"It was incredibly frustrating," Calvar says. "He was definitely someone who had knowledge of surveillance techniques. I had a feeling that he was enjoying this, that he was out there watching us watch him."

In 1993 a puzzling call came from Johnson. Sue was able to keep him on the phone for some time, but in the end the telephone company had no trap-and-trace record for the call.

"Damn," Calvar said. "He must be using a cell phone."

Cellular telephones were especially difficult to trace. At the time, there were several dozen cell phone companies operating in Florida, and there was no technology available that could pinpoint where the calls originated. While a cell phone meant that some private user with a name, account, and ultimately a home address might be tracked, no judge would issue any sort of shotgun subpoena for so many communications companies to search their records.

And Hal Johnson knew how well camouflaged he was. Now that he could apparently call from anywhere at his convenience, he called more frequently, at all times of the day and night.

Sue kept up a brave front and didn't tell her closest friends about the constant harassment, or the fear that the telephone stalker instilled in her: that he could be any stranger in the street, the man walking his dog, the driver of the car that seemed to pass her house too slowly, or the friend she ate breakfast with.

"I might be willing to trade you for Amy," he said to her one night.

"Anything," Sue said. "Meet me during the day someplace."

There was a pause as Johnson pondered the suggestion. Sue had stopped listening to his threats and taken
the offensive. "Let's get some basic things straight," he
countered, trying to regain control of the conversation.

"Go ahead," Sue said in a pragmatic voice.

"Are you willing to go?"

"If I can have proof that Amy is alive. Yes."

"Are you willing to leave everything?" His voice
was questioning, cajoling, conjuring up images of being transported to the far corners of the earth.

"Yes, I am—if Amy is alive." Sue was irritated.
Johnson had made so many promises before, from the
time in Fort Pierce in 1979 until now, always trolling
the bait, never trying to set the hook.

"Do you understand what that means?" His voice
was businesslike. "You don't get your period anymore?"

"No. I'm not getting into this with you."

The voice was relentless. "You still have both your
tits?"

Sue couldn't believe what she was hearing. He knew
she had cancer, and wanted to know if she was healthy
enough to be worth trading for. "I have everything,"
Billig shouted. "And I'm not getting into a personal
discussion with you."

"Well, my clients want two generations of tits to
play with," Johnson said, taking another tack. "They
want mother-daughter teams."

Sue was shocked into silence for a moment before
she could answer. "What do you mean?" she asked.

"They want you," he said. "I'll be your trainer.
When you're ready, take out an ad in the *Miami Herald*

that says, 'Elderly woman seeks younger, masterful man.' "

"I will do no such thing," Sue replied.

"Watch out, Amy doesn't have long," Johnson warned. "We've cut her tongue out. And we're going to do more!"

Sue's heart stopped for a moment, then crashed against her chest. Sue cried out that she would meet him anywhere, anytime. "Tonight, at midnight," he said. At Dadeland, a shopping mall several miles away. "Alone."

Sue called Harold Phipps at home. They only had thirty minutes. Phipps, who lived in Kendall, set the blue light on his dashboard and sped over to Shorty's Barbeque, a restaurant on U.S. 1 near Dadeland. "I got there in about three minutes," he says. A nervous but angry Sue took a taxi and met the agent in the parking lot.

Mike Hernes, a Coral Gables police detective who Phipps knew, also hightailed it to the scene after a call from the agent. A marked patrol car would wait nearby. "I'll pose as her son," Hernes said, "since I'm a bit younger." Phipps would hide, fold his large frame into the backseat and provide backup. They drove to the Dadeland Mall in Hernes's black four-door Ford Explorer.

"It's really going to happen," Sue said. "He's finally going to tell me about Amy! I have a good feeling about it this time."

Phipps gritted his teeth and held back any comment, but if Johnson showed, he was prepared to run him to the ground. By this time he was almost as angry as Sue. The two men wore bulletproof vests, and made Sue put one on under her blouse. Both men had guns, and there were more weapons on the seat. It scared the hell out of her, and she realized this situation could become serious.

It was almost midnight when they arrived, and the giant lot was dark and empty besides a couple of cars, lit by spots of amber crime lights. Hernes parked well away from the other vehicles, in front of the Burdines department store, as Johnson had specified, and they waited as the seconds ticked by.

No one.

Sue's hopefulness quickly crumbled into frustration. "I can't believe it. He's lied to me again!

"I'll get out and walk around the car, so he can see it's me," she suggested. "But I'll get back into the car immediately."

She jumped out of the Explorer and walked around the car. Besides the cars rushing past on Kendall Drive, an always busy thoroughfare, there was no movement. She raised her fists in the air and shouted, "Come out you coward! You . . . you bastard! I'm here, like I said I would be!"

Her only answer was her own voice echoing against the building.

"*Psstt*. Get back in here!" Hernes said.

Sue marched over to the other cars. "Are you there? Where are you?"

Hernes jumped from the car in alarm, flashed a light into the parked cars, and hustled her back into safety.

They waited another fifteen minutes, but no Johnson

came to gloat. "He's out there," Sue said. "He's watching us!"

Sue got out again, ran to a large Dumpster, and climbed up to peer inside. But there was just construction debris, no human garbage inside. Being good police officers, Phipps and Hernes checked out several places where Johnson might be observing the scene, but found nothing.

"It could be a way to get you out of your house," Phipps said. "We'll go back with you and make sure it's safe."

Phipps's suspicions were unfounded. Johnson was not waiting for Sue at home in a closet or behind the shower curtain.

But while the police were still in her home, the phone rang.

"Why didn't you come to Dadeland?" Hal Johnson asked.

Sue motioned to Phipps and mouthed, It's him!

Phipps motioned her to keep him on the phone and pushed the record button.

"I was there!" Sue said. "You never showed up."

"You blew it, just like you did in Fort Pierce," Johnson said.

"I was there!" Sue cried. "You're a coward and didn't meet me!"

But Johnson had gotten his kicks for the night. "I'll call you tomorrow," he promised, and hung up.

Johnson had done it again—left Sue with a mind-numbing migraine that kept her in exhausted pain all the next day.

Phipps had had enough of this, and showed up with

Miami detectives later in the afternoon. Sue struggled to the door to let him in. The agent was carrying a small case. "What did you bring?" she asked.

Phipps held up the case and smiled. "Newest technology," he said gleefully. "State-of-the-art cell phone tracer. Let's set her up, boys."

Now anybody can purchase a caller ID that shows cell phone numbers. But it was cutting-edge stuff at the time. They disconnected the old recorder and plugged in the new machine. Phipps called Sue's number and checked that his cell phone number was properly displayed. It was not the instantaneous process it is nowadays; it took a few minutes.

"It works!" Sue said.

"Now we just wait," Phipps replied. "This is going to be good."

Sue invited the officers to sit down for coffee. While everyone sipped from their cups, the telephone rang. A sound of cymbals that only she could hear reverberated in her head. Oh God, can they finally get him? she wondered.

Phipps motioned for her to draw out the conversation.

"Tell me what Amy looks like," she mumbled softly after Johnson greeted her.

"She has no lines on her abdomen," Johnson purred. This was exactly what he loved to talk about. "She has a great mouth. She really knows how to use it. . . ."

"I'm her mother," Sue said. "I don't want to hear that."

"My client's put in a special order, he wants you and her together. Are you ready to give up everything?"

Johnson asked, obviously reverting to his previous conversation, in which he had told Sue he would take her away.

"Yes," Sue replied. Johnson, of course, couldn't see her beatific smile. She was smiling because Phipps was giving her the high sign.

Johnson's number had popped up on the display.

Even though they had the number in hand, there would be no midnight bust, as the number itself meant little before they could find out who it belonged to. And finding the owner would prove more difficult than they thought. Calvar brought the information to Assistant State Attorney, Andy Hague, who filed a subpoena against Bell South Mobility to issue the identity of the phone.

Hague was a compact, athletically built former diver, with square shoulders and the tenacious personality of a pit bull. He had successfully prosecuted everything from Colombian hit men to a gang of murderers who made international news for preying on tourists who they followed from rental car lots. He had attended high school in Coconut Grove and had mutual friends with Sue Billig, but hadn't known the extent of everything she'd been through.

"When I heard about the agony that she had endured," Hague says, "I knew I had to find this guy if I could. My biggest motivation was that I thought this guy knew what happened to Amy."

Even with a subpoena in hand, Hague was frustrated. Records were decentralized, and he had to machete through a forest of bureaucratic inefficiency, fighting with the company's "office of compliance," only to find out the number was issued by AT&T Wireless. Hague worked after hours and on days off until he finally got the records he wanted. The number was one of about a dozen leased to an import/export company with an address on Miami's posh Brickell Avenue, a wide boulevard lined with office buildings along Biscayne Bay. In its heyday, South American drug lords had stashed more than $20 billion in surplus narcobucks in Brickell banks.

As soon as he had the information, Hague drove by the address. When he finally found the proper building, he wanted to scream.

It was a Mailboxes-R-Us.

It took weeks to subpoena the records of the mailbox drop, which was rented by a company called Yaro. With that information, Hague contacted the Florida Secretary of State's office to ascertain who the company officers were. With their names and Social Security numbers in hand, Hague had an Auto-Trac background check performed, only to find out that these were all false identities.

"By this time," Hague says, "I was really getting uncomfortable. No one could be so buried unless it was someone in law enforcement." This time he subpoenaed the actual records of phone calls made by the phone. Sure enough, Susan Billig's phone number was on the list.

"I had to be very cautious and not go in like a bull in a china shop," Hague says. "If it was part of some kind of undercover operation, I might blow somebody's cover and get someone killed."

He began calling numbers on the sheet. A few were beepers. He looked at one that had been called repeatedly after hours, and tried that one. It rang once and was picked up.

"U.S. Customs," a woman answered cordially.

19

On October 27, 1995, Hague persuaded Bonnie Tischler, the Customs Special Agent in Charge, to confide that the mailbox was a "drop" for an undercover operation, and that the cell phone in question was assigned to one of their agents. "But our phones have been cloned a number of times," Tischler informed the prosecutor, "so anybody could have initiated the calls."

Yeah, right, Hague thought. "My mind was racing in all directions. I really couldn't believe this could be a law enforcement officer." He told her they wanted to interview the agent immediately, then beeped Harold Phipps and told him the news. "I'll meet you at Customs!" He also informed Jack Calvar and Lieutenant Hernes, who said they would be there.

The Customs building was located against the Miami River just opposite downtown Miami. From their windows, they could watch every freighter that chugged up the waterway, many constructed with secret compartments filled with cocaine. It was only a ten-minute drive for Hague, so he arrived well before the other investigators, and was greeted by Tischler and two Customs Internal Affairs agents. "It was not a warm reception," Hague recalls.

The cell phone in question, he was told, was assigned to Henry Johnson Blair, a top supervisor in charge of undercover operations, and a highly decorated agent.

"The hair stood up on my neck, and I got tunnel vision," Hague says. "I was salivating."

Blair had been informed that the State Attorney's Office was coming to ask him some questions and would be waiting for them in a conference room. Hague was ushered down three hallways that required special clearance to access, and finally led into a well-furnished conference room with a large table. At the head sat a plump, gray-haired man with bushy gray eyebrows and hanging jowls, dressed in an off-the-rack business suit. Only forty-eight, he looked older, the way heavy drinkers often add years to their appearance. Still, he was so normal-looking he could easily have disappeared into a crowd of retired CPAs.

Hague introduced himself to Henry Johnson Blair, and gave him background on Billig's case and the telephone calls in question.

"I've never heard of her," Blair told Hague evenly. "You have to understand, our cell phones are cloned all the time. Anybody could have made those calls."

When Phipps arrived with copies of the tapes, they were shown into another room, where they played them for one of Blair's agents, Walter Wilkowski.

Wilkowski, a brown-haired man with a thick New York accent, had worked under Blair since January of 1992, and obviously held him in high regard.

Phipps, dressed in his standard gray suit and corporate tie, looked stoic and a bit sad that this situation was playing out in this way. No lawman liked to bust another lawman. He pressed the play button of a cassette recorder. Out came the southern voice they had all come to know so well: "I am going to be your trainer. Do you still have your period . . ."

Hague felt bad for Wilkowski. "Tears welled up in his eyes. The content of the tapes was disgusting, and he obviously thought it was Blair."

Phipps turned off the tape and rose from the chair. "I guess we better confront him."

Calvar and Hernes arrived, then accompanied Hague, Phipps, and the Customs Internal Affairs agents to the back room, where Blair was waiting. Phipps leaned back in his chair, looking unassuming and harmless.

Following procedure, Phipps explained that they were investigating harassing calls made to Susan Billig which had been traced to the cell phone assigned to Henry Blair. The FBI agent leaned forward, asking, "Do you know anything about the calls?"

Blair maintained that he did not.

"Are you aware that some of these conversations were taped?" Phipps asked, smacking the recorder down in front of the Customs agent.

Hague was focused on Blair, and remembers "his face became red and blotchy."

Phipps pushed the button. Hal Johnson's voice emanated from the speaker.

"I . . . I . . . made the calls," Blair admitted with effort.

Hague, Phipps, and the detectives looked at each other with surprise as the information registered.

Phipps continued in a steady voice, "At this time, I have to advise you of your rights . . ." He kept cards in his wallet, in English and Spanish, to read the Miranda rights. Blair obviously knew them by heart, nodding a feeble yes to each section. At the end he signed a Miranda waiver and said he would answer their questions.

Sitting slumped in his chair, speaking sometimes with eyes closed, and apparently knowing what constituted Florida's new laws for aggravated stalking, he admitted to making the calls for a few weeks. When played further tapes, he finally acknowledged that he had made the calls for at least eighteen months, the dates as outlined on the cell phone bills, but claimed he had looked up Sue Billig's number after seeing the case profiled on *Unsolved Mysteries*, and that he knew nothing about Amy's actual disappearance. He might seem to know so much about the case, but "was just manipulating the facts," as he had learned to do as an undercover cop.

"But why?" Phipps asked. "Why would you do this?"

Blair shook his head. "I don't know why. It's an obsessive-compulsive thing, I guess. It's a mystery, and all mysteries intrigue me." He said the local section of the *Miami Herald* was his "porn," and that he would call "to get my mind off pressures. I guess I should have drank instead. It would have been a lot better for me. I just fucked up."

"Haven't you been calling for at least seventeen years?" Phipps pressed. "Didn't you ask her why she

hadn't come to the Burdines, just like she hadn't come
to Fort Pierce?" Which had occurred in 1979. Only the
person known as Hal Johnson could know about that
incident.

Blair was too canny to admit that amount of time. "I
said a lot of bullshit," he answered. Then he tried to
blame the situation on Sue Billig. "She has a tendency
to twist things around." Still, he maintained he was
"not violent at all," and made the calls when "the pressure would mount." And "I would go out and get
drunk . . . I would call and then it would subside." He
would have sought psychiatric counseling, but thought
it "might end his career."

In the end he was adamant that he had never physically seen, touched, or come near anyone in the Billig
family. He looked up with no remorse and said the obscene conversations "were just a bunch of crank calls,
is what it boils down to in my mind."

On March 5, 1974, the day Amy vanished, Henry
Johnson Blair had just married Cynthia Anderson, now
a hospital nursing administrator, and honeymooned in
San Francisco. The couple returned to Miami two days
before Amy disappeared. In the following weeks, a no-
tation in Sue's notebooks reads that a "Mrs. Blair"
called and said her husband had seen Amy walking
down the road in North Miami. Was that a mere coincidence of names? Investigators wanted to find out.

Henry Blair was born in 1947 in New Orleans, the
middle of three kids. His father was a career Coast
Guard official, his mother a housewife, and they
moved around the country following his father's sta-

tions, until the family settled in Miami in 1964. Hank
attended Coral Gables High School, and later Miami-
Dade Community College, while working at a local
Sears changing tires. He was a D-plus student who ex-
celled only in judo before attending the University of
South Florida in Tampa as a history major. There, he
did well only in behavioral psychology. He joined the
U.S. Customs after he graduated in 1970, and with the
exception of occasional temporary duty assignments,
had remained stationed in Miami ever since. He became a sky marshal in 1973 and graduated to group supervisor of a smuggling investigations team, where he
was credited with significant narcotics seizures over
the years and was awarded a medal by King Juan Carlos of Spain in 1995 for recovering a stolen national
treasure: a painting by Peter Paul Reubens.

At the time of his arrest, Blair's two daughters were
twenty and seventeen, the latter the same age that Amy
was when she disappeared.

After decades of torment, Sue made sure she was at
Blair's bond hearing so she could confront him face-
to-face. Sue couldn't believe it. "He was such a
wimpy-looking, pathetic, plump little man," she says.
"How could this little twit, who had to lean against his
wife for support, be so cruel?"

While many wives might have found this crime
grounds for divorce, Blair's wife, Cynthia, and their
daughters, sat tearfully behind him, squeezing his
shoulders and weeping on his collar while he tried to
explain his actions as a psychological problem called
"paraphilia," a branch of scatalogia, which he said
prompted him to make the obscene telephone calls.

The case made international news at the time, appearing in all the major newspapers and magazines. Barbara Walters was the only person to score an interview with Cynthia Blair, an attractive but hard-tempered, middle-aged woman with short-cropped, blond hair. The wife serenely responded to the famous newswoman's questions, saying that her husband had taken a lie detector test, and she believed that he had nothing to do with Amy's disappearance.

During a later interview, Blair would tell lawyers he could easily beat a polygraph test.

Mrs. Blair continued: "It was a total shock, everyone said it just can't be true, but that he just isn't this man . . . He told me the truth, from the time he was arrested. He said he felt this awful shame, but that there were dark pictures in his mind, like dark videos, and when the pressure would build and build and build, he would have to escape into some mystery type of scenario, and he had the compulsion to make phone calls to people."

"To people?" Walters asked incredulously.

"I asked him if he ever called anyone else, and he said, 'Yes, I've called other people, but they told me in the first conversation I was a crackpot and hung up.' "

Walters questioned why Mrs. Blair had consented to the interview.

"The only reason I'm doing this interview is because it has occurred to me over the last couple of days that maybe God sent us this experience so that we could help other people. If we can reach one person who's having those black thoughts and convince them to get help before their lives go into disaster, or if the wife can patch together a puzzle quicker than I was able to, with what I only realized in retrospect, it would have saved a lot of people a lot of suffering."

"Can your marriage survive this?" Walters wanted to know.

"Absolutely," came the answer. "I have told him he's sick and that people cannot be judged by those who love them because of an illness once they know it, if they choose to comply with treatment—and that whatever it takes, for how long it takes, I will stand beside him. I love him very deeply."

Blair came to his arraignment armed with a psychiatric evaluation written by a Jackson Memorial Hospital psychiatrist who described the agent as anxious, depressed, and suicidal. "He has trouble sleeping and experiences crying spells." The subject was an alcoholic whose ailments included hypertension, glaucoma, thyroid problems, and impotency. During his appraisal, Blair was guarded and tearful, prompting the doctor to call him an "emotionally disturbed individual who has difficulty in interpersonal relationships. . . . There is also an indication of obsessive compulsive behavior. He is most likely an individual unable to cope with the stress of his environment, and is unable to communicate effectively."

Blair claimed he never threatened Billig and characterized his calls as conversational, saying, the two often "chatted" on the phone.

Sue scoffed incredulously when she heard that remark in court. "Yeah, right. He thinks we were just chatting about all the cruel, sexual things he claimed he was doing to my daughter!"

Hague and his trial partner, Howard Rosen, were incensed. Hague says, "Blair was a manipulative little whiner who didn't want to take responsibility for what he had done."

The judge, Alex Ferrer, a former police officer and prosecutor, scorned Blair's argument and levied a $75,000 bond on the Customs agent. Blair was going to trial.

The most the telephone stalker could be charged with under Florida law was three counts of aggravated stalking. But that could put him behind bars for a total of fifteen years. Trouble was, it was a new law with few precedents. What actually constituted stalking under the law?

20

The stalking law *seems* straightforward when read in black and white:

Florida Statute 784.048

(3) Any person who willfully, maliciously, and repeatedly follows or harasses another person, and makes a credible threat with the intent to place that person in reasonable fear of death or bodily injury, commits the offense of aggravated stalking, a felony of the third degree . . .

But to a criminal defense attorney, even the simple spaces between words are gaping loopholes, because terms such as "credible threat" and "reasonable fear of death" are highly subjective. All you needed was one juror to question whether such actions as "cutting out" Amy's tongue constituted a threat that Susan should also have to fear, or whether Johnson's admonition to "watch out" was simply a warning of concern.

For Susan, the next few months were a whirlwind of exhausting depositions by Hank Blair's lawyers,

William Norris and Fritz Mann, who interrogated her
mercilessly about how long she could prove Blair, as
Hal Johnson, had been calling her. Just how many calls
had she written down immediately? How many entries
in her diary reflected the exact wording of Blair's
calls? How many had been taped? When had the calls
actually started?

Norris wore large bottle-thick eyeglasses, had dark
graying hair, and was thin, prim, and officious. He
paced in quick strides and spoke moving his eyebrows
up and down, using a connotation in his voice, as if always questioning Sue's veracity. She pictured him as a
sort of Frank Burns, Hawkeye's nemesis in *M.A.S.H.*
Mann was tall, wide-shouldered, methodical, and
even-voiced, but, she thought, an equally dangerous
litigator.

The pair was an intimidating and experienced legal
team who picked at the smallest details of her notes
and even accused her of writing in a series of incriminating calls by Blair into her notebook since the time
of the agent's arrest.

A December deposition lasted hours. Sue's head
pounded with a migraine caused not only by the brutal
questioning, but simply by having to relive the excruci-
ating memories. Norris grilled the witness and questioned the journals line by line: Why was this note
written on a slant in the margin? Why was this word
crossed out? Why did the police case number appear
on this date and not on that date? Who did she speak to
about the telephone calls and when? Where was a particular scrap of paper she claimed to have written a
note on?

Norris became increasingly argumentative, and asked why police investigator Jack Calvar told a *Miami Herald* reporter: " 'She's tiny, just about five feet tall'—referring to you—'but she'll blow your head off. I think she wants . . . Blair's head—understandably.' My concern is if you do want the defendant's head, what, outside of these two tapes and journal which you kept, is there that would give us some idea of what you were saying about these calls at the time?"

Sue responded that these were Jack Calvar's words, not hers, but "isn't it understandable that I should be very angry at this man, okay? That's what he's portraying to you."

"So your feeling is one of anger?"

"No. I'm angry that—let's see, is the word *angry*? I don't think I'm angry, I'm questioning *why*?"

"Nothing wrong with anger . . ." Norris prompted, possibly trying to obtain an uncontrolled outburst.

Sue bit her tongue and took a breath before replying. "I'm questioning why this man—did he have an agenda? Why did he keep on calling me? Those are my feelings, okay? It was very painful and it was very cruel and very unnecessary. It was punishment to me; every call was cruel and unusual punishment, and I suffered every time he called me."

By the time Norris finished his questioning, Sue's head felt as if it was being split open with an anvil. It would be good practice for the coming trial.

The *Herald*'s Meg Laughlin wrote a powerful story for the newspaper's *Tropic* magazine—now defunct—detailing the case against Blair. It provoked a deluge of commiserating letters, including one from Patrick Sessions, the father of Tiffany Sessions, a University of Florida student who disappeared while jogging in Gainesville in 1989. After years of searching for his own daughter, he was sadly one of the most qualified of people to offer his opinion about the case.

After reading Meg Laughlin's Dec. 17 article on Sue Billig and her tormentor, my reaction was the same as every other father who read this article. Please give me 15 minutes in a dark alley with Hank Blair.

As Tiffany Sessions' father, I have had more than my share of crank phone calls, nasty letters and extortion attempts. But none of them come close to the hell that Susan Billig has endured over the last 20 years. There are not words strong enough to describe the despicable behavior from the kind of slime who would prey on the tragedy of a mother's love for a missing child for his own sick thrills. The only emotion stranger than this disgusting behavior is the strength that Sue Billig has shown throughout this ordeal. Until you have listened to someone describe the abuse of your child, you cannot imagine the heartbreak that Sue has endured for the 20 years. It proves an incredibly strong love and devotion for her daughter and a willingness to do anything to find her.

I only hope that the prosecutors and the judge who try this case understand the seriousness of this behavior and punish the guilty one accordingly. Unfortunately, those of us who would love to have the opportunity to appropriately punish him will probably never get the chance to make his life as miserable as he has made Sue Billig's.

Patrick Sessions
Jensen Beach

Fearing for Sue's health, the judge and prosecutors made sure that the trial came up quickly. Jury selection started on February 25, but proved hard to empanel after all the media attention, including coverage of a preliminary hearing where Blair had admitted to dialing many victims over the years, and told the court that "the *Miami Herald*'s local section was my soft porn." After that comment, several *Herald* reporters joked that they were porn writers for a while.

At the time, all of Miami was in an uproar. On February 24, two civilian planes flown by the Brothers to the Rescue, a Cuban-American group that searched for rafters fleeing their homeland, were shot down by Cuban MiGs. It was an international incident that would not be equaled again until six-year-old Elián Gonzales set foot in Miami on Thanksgiving 1999.

The preponderance of fifty juror candidates who managed to make it to the court that day said they had been so offended by what they knew about Blair that they couldn't be impartial. But, eventually, the requisite six jurors and two alternates were found.

* * *

The Miami-Dade Justice Building is testament to the ugliest of governmental architecture: a squat-looking, nine-story, 1960s–era concrete building, with long, narrow windows and a facade of laced concrete in front. It had not aged well, and was undergoing extensive renovation that had taken years. Escalators and elevators broke down constantly, and the feeble air-conditioning was as reliable as the Miami-Dade bus system.

There were constant bomb threats that emptied the building during contentious trials or when, many Miamians suspect, some devious criminal attorney actually phoned in the threat to delay a trial because they were running late. It is also probably the only court in America that must employ a "Santeria patrol," which gathers up daily offerings of dead chickens and other ritualistic paraphernalia left by followers of the Afro-Cuban religion to influence trials. Judges have even had to dodge white powder, which is supposed to drive away evil spirits, thrown at them by defendants' family members. Only Miami, it seems, has a problem with possessed judges.

On February 29, there had been a month-long drought, and three hundred acres of the Florida Everglades State Park were on fire. Sawgrass smoke filled the air, closed down highways, put airplane traffic on alert, burned your eyes and sent asthmatics to the hospital.

But inside the courtroom, the outside world was put on hold. Here, in this room of varnished wood paneling, high ceilings, and three rows of upholstered chairs that could seat fewer than a hundred people, a person's life was about to change, and it didn't matter what was happening outside. The gravity of the situation seemed accentuated by the stream of sunlight that bathed the judge from behind with an ethereal aura.

The judge for this trial was Alex Ferrer, an athletic Cuban-American in his late thirties, with short-cropped, jet-black hair and a square jaw. Ferrer had little idea that half the female clerks and court workers had crushes on him. He had the laid-back, yet authoritarian manner of a man completely comfortable in his courtroom, and had been given high ratings by Miami's legal community. His decisions were considered logical, reasoned, and unbiased, and he always went beyond the call of duty to award a fair trial. Despite the judge's previous jobs as a police detective and a prosecutor, Blair couldn't have prayed for a better courtroom.

Ferrer addressed the jurors with extreme courtesy and explained what they were about to hear:

"The best idea about what an opening statement is, to me, is like the picture on the box of a [jigsaw] puzzle. You can imagine how difficult it would be to build the puzzle if you had no idea what the picture was going to look like when you finished. So with that in mind, the attorneys are going to give you what they think the pictures are going to look like. That way when you hear the testimony coming in, in bits and pieces, it may not come in the same chronological order, you'll still know what it's intended to prove, what the final picture is expected to look like. Whether it will look like that or not will be your decision because this is not evidence."

Prosecutor Howard Rosen started his opening statement. He was about five-ten, thin, with a low-key attitude, soft voice, and balding pate. His unassuming looks had fooled many an astute defense attorney, however, as he had a winning record and was head of the Miami-Date State Attorney's anticorruption unit.

Rosen pulled up a large pad, propped it on an easel, and began to detail the case, starting with Amy's last family breakfast on March 5, 1974, and her subsequent disappearance. "Let's jump ahead now, two decades to October 12, 1995. Her mother, Susan Billig, seventy years old—on the night of October twelfth, she was in a dark parking lot at Burdines with an FBI agent and a Coral Gables police officer, screaming into the night 'Come out! Come out, you coward!' What brought her from that beautiful spring morning to that night of October 12, 1995? What went on in her life in those intervening twenty-one years, seven months, and seven days—or 7,891 days?" He wrote the number 7,891 in large black letters on the pad.

He described Sue's arduous search through the years, and continued: "There was one constant while all this was going on, one constant in Susan's life, and that constant was a stalker—a telephone stalker—by the name of Johnson. These calls from Johnson started coming really early-on after Amy's disappearance. Horrible calls, threatening calls in the middle of the night . . . The caller told Susan, 'I have your daughter, we're torturing her, you're next, watch out. We've cut out her tongue. . . . ' " Rosen detailed all the terrifying telephone calls that Susan had endured through the years and explained why she never changed her telephone number—because it was the only link that Amy might still have to her former life.

Blair sat at the defense table with his hands clasped together, steepled up to his flaccid jowls. His eyes darted to the prosecutor or the jury, but mostly stared directly ahead, one eye twitching. His wife, her elderly parents, and his two daughters sat behind him, sometimes whispering together, but all exhibiting the stern faces of people who couldn't believe their family member was being tried for making such a small mistake.

Rosen steadily put the case together, explaining how the cell phone number was traced to Blair, telling about the agent's powerful confession, and continued with how the cell phone records would prove the Customs agent had called Billig at least fifty times in the last five years alone.

In his only dramatic act, Rosen walked over to Blair and pointed at the frowning culprit. "So, folks, it was this man *right here*—Henry 'Hank' Johnson Blair— who was the man who Mrs. Billig was at Burdines looking for that night, 7,891 long, torturous nights after her daughter disappeared. It is *that man* who is the aggravated stalker, and you are going to find guilty after hearing the evidence in this case."

Defense attorney William Norris rose and walked

painfully over to the dais, as if struggling to comprehend what he had just heard, and rested his arms on the podium. "Ladies and gentleman, the prosecutor has woven for you a terrifying yarn." He took a dramatic breath and admonished the jury to remember what the judge had said—it wasn't evidence. ". . . the problem is there is other evidence in this case that you're going to hear that call into question much of this universe that the prosecutor has woven for you in telling this yarn, and that Susan Billig has told. . . ."

Norris continued to tell them that the tape-recorded telephone conversations would "put the lie to much of what the prosecutor has suggested that Susan Billig is going to say to you from the stand. I'm not saying this woman doesn't believe it, I'm not saying this woman doesn't have some of it written down. But those telephone conversations show that it's not true . . ."

Norris told them that the conversations would prove a different version of events. "My client, Henry Johnson Blair—'Hank' Blair—is accused of doing some very vile things. And indeed he has done some things which are terrible. Hank Blair has done some bad things, but he's not a bad man, I submit to you. You're going to hear that he's had a twenty-five-year career in federal law enforcement. That he's married. You're going to get a chance to meet his wife on the witness stand. He has two daughters. His family continues to support him. I'm not asking you to support him in this case. I'm not asking you to find that he's a good man, even though he did terrible things. Because a trial, although it's many things in many contexts, it's not a popularity contest, okay? I'm not asking you to find

that Hank is a great guy. I'm not asking you to decide
that you'd like to take him home to dinner or that
you're going to *give him your telephone number*.
[Here, journalists in the room almost cracked up.] And
I'm not asking you to think that Sue Billig, a woman
who is clearly tormented, and has been tormented for
over twenty years by the loss of her daughter, is anything other than the person who is entitled to your pro-
found sympathy . . ."

Then: "The point is that this case is not about making telephone calls. This case is about the contents of
the communications that go on in the telephone calls
that Hank Johnson made to Susan Billig. . . ."

As expected, the lawyer questioned the words "credible threat," saying that, in the wording of the law, "the
threat must be against the life of, or a threat to cause
bodily injury to, a person." So was there ever a credible
threat against the life of Susan Billig? "I think you'll
find that there has not been!" he declared.

He went on to tell about Blair's Customs career: The
agent was "engaged in the war on drugs. . . ." He dealt
with the stress "with booze . . ." and "made obscene
telephone calls, though he fought valiantly against it."
But when a victim told him not to call back, he would
hang up and never call them again. Billig, he insisted,
was a "different kettle of fish" who welcomed the calls.

He downplayed all of the early calls. The only important calls were the recent ones that had been
recorded, he said, but the threats couldn't be "credible," because Hank Blair had never said "I" will do this
to you, but that the "*Arabs*" would. He said that the
legislature had written a law requiring a "credible

threat" and "a credible threat is absent from this case."
He took his seat.

Now it was time for the prosecution to bring on their witnesses. Of course, Sue would be first to take the stand.

21

Sue took the stand, wearing a dark jacket over a white silk blouse. Her hair was dyed a dark brunette, matching her simple onyx earrings. This was the first time she had ever testified in court, and she'd been worrying about it for days. She hadn't slept, hadn't eaten, and was fighting one her of powerful migraines. By the time she appeared in front of the jury, she was wiped out, completely enervated, and wanted to get out of the court as soon as possible. To top it all off, the air-conditioning was on the blink, and it was stuffy and hot inside the courtroom. She spoke in low, quiet tones and looked sweet, demure, and nervous.

To establish why Sue did not have notes of Blair's earliest calls, Andy Hague asked her to explain about the confusion surrounding Amy's disappearance in 1974. The prosecutor wanted the jury to understand just how important the leads generated through the telephone were, so that when Blair had begun calling, Sue hadn't told him to go to hell right there and then.

Hague asked about the content of the calls.

Sue sighed and told the jury, "They all kind of

sounded the same, like an ongoing story, like a bad soap opera. He would pick up from where he left off on a previous message."

"Please tell the jury what the caller would say back in the seventies."

Sue spoke slowly, pausing between each sentence, remembering the terrible hurt that had accompanied the telephone calls. "That he—or 'they'—had Amy, that she was their slave, that he was training her, that he was making her a valuable commodity. Things like that. Kind of disgusting . . ."

"Was there any pattern when this 'Hank' or 'Hal Johnson' would call?"

"When he called—he would call consecutively for a couple of days, and then he wouldn't call for a couple of months. Then he'd call again and start over again. He knew so much about me, that's what frightened me."

Hague asked her to explain how Johnson had compelled her to travel up to Fort Pierce in 1979 on his misinformation. Over a period of a couple of hours, Hague made her relive the entire story of her life: the Tulsa and Seattle trips—the cancer. It was very difficult for her, but she knew how important it would be for the jury to hear everything from her own lips, so they would truly understand how all-consuming her passion was to find Amy.

Back to the telephone calls. Hague asked if there was a distinct pattern.

"No," Sue said with difficulty. "It was like a story. He would keep on calling me, and say things like 'I have your daughter and she's in a slave trade,' a livestock auction; and that he had trained her, and that they had seen me, and now they wanted me, and now he was going to be my trainer, and I was going to be a slave."

To counter the defense's argument that Sue was making up calls that hadn't occurred, Hague asked if she had written down every telephone call. She responded that she hadn't because:

"He would call at three, four in the morning. He called me when my husband was dying beside me—I was sick. . . ." Later in her testimony she recalled the time immediately after Ned's death. "After two weeks, he called and knew my husband was dead. He seemed to know a lot of things about me. I had the alarm system updated, installed a chain on the door, slept with my windows closed. I was frightened for my life."

They went through the Burdines episode and Johnson's recorded calls.

Why did that frighten her?

"The fact that he said he wanted *me* now, and I presumed that all the terrible things through the years that he said about Amy he was going to do to me."

"And the portion about wanting a couple generations of nipples to play with?"

"Well, that really frightened me."

"And did there come a time when you told him not to call anymore?"

"That's the one where he said they wanted me now. 'They've seen you and they want to work out a trade. . . . ' I told him that if he had nothing real, meaning something important regarding Amy, I didn't want him to call me or bother me again. Except for a hair sample or a picture, which I had been begging him for always . . ."

She identified her notebook, which was entered into evidence.

With prompting from the prosecutor, Sue explained to the jury, "The thought that someone was doing this to my child made me physically sick, I was throwing up all over the place, I was just beginning not to be able to handle it anymore. The talk had gotten to a point where it was like violent. As he spoke to me, the calls became progressively more violent, and more personally against me again. . . . For instance, if he's saying he did these things to Amy, and that he wanted me now, I presumed that he was going to do all the things he said he had done to Amy to *me*, because he said 'they want you now.' I offered to trade myself for Amy, and he said, 'No, they want you both.' "

All this time, Blair sat twiddling his fingers, occasionally glancing at Sue, but mostly staring forward or up at the ceiling. His daughters and in-laws sat behind him as if condoning everything he had done.

"Did you enjoy talking to Hank Johnson?" Hague had to ask.

"No!" Sue exclaimed in horror.

Hague drew a diagram of all the calls on the large pad propped up on the easel. It showed the continuing pattern of harassment.

Finally, Hague played the actual tapes for the jury, allowing the court to hear Blair's even voice emanate out of the speakers. This was the conversation recorded right after Sue, Agent Phipps, and Detective Hernes returned from Burdines when the defendant had failed to show.

It started mid-conversation with Sue's exasperated voice, "Why is it too dangerous? I don't understand you. You told me to meet you! I got up out of bed. I don't understand you. Don't you realize how important this is to me?"

Blair: "It is important. That's why I keep calling. . . ."

As the tapes were played, Blair sat with hands clasped at his chin, fingers touching his nose, eyes closed. His girls sat behind him with straight, utterly unmoved faces, listening to this disgusting conversation perpetrated by their father. Sue, reliving the moment, had difficulty holding back the tears, but she did not want to break down in court.

After a brief exchange of questions, Hague played more of the tape—a section where Blair said he wanted Sue and would be her sexual trainer. Tears swelled in her eyes and a bailiff had to bring her a handkerchief. She wasn't the only one, however. At one point a female member of the jury also began to cry.

Hague knew the defense would question why Sue's voice sounded so strong during these taped conversations, if she was indeed scared for her life, so he pre-empted that by asking, "How did you portray yourself?"

"Well, I wanted to act like I was strong," Sue said. "You don't show the enemy that you're weak. At this point I thought he was my enemy. I felt that if I fell apart, I wouldn't be able to put it together again."

Hague completed his examination two wrap-up questions later, then said, "No more questions, Your Honor."

Bill Norris stood at the lectern, his first question launching an assault on Sue. "In recent days have you talked to the prosecutors about the elements of the offense of an aggravated stalking?" He paced back and forth.

"Can you be more clear?" she asked him.

He faced her directly. "Did the prosecutors tell you that there had to be a credible threat against your life?" He was apparently trying to make the situation look like Sue had fabricated her fear in order to make the charges stick.

Sue shook her head. "They didn't tell me. I looked it up."

He tried to pin her down, asking if she had ever told the judge that she was in fear. His questions were worded so snidely that Hague objected and requested a sidebar discussion with the judge. The sidebar lasted several heated minutes before a marginally more subdued Norris continued his questioning.

"Your recognition about a threat to your life or a threat to bodily injury is an element of the offense charged."

"I understand that."

"When did you come to that understanding?"

"I don't know when—"

"Well, was it yesterday?" Norris prodded.

"No."

"Was it last week?" the lawyer wanted to know.

"It was probably the time that the police people or the phone people told me about the stalking law."

"It *probably* was?"

"I don't know for certain, no. I didn't know that that was what all this was about."

"You don't know that's when you decided that that was an element of the stalking law?"

Sue was quickly becoming aggravated. "I didn't *decide* anything."

"Well, did Hank Blair ever threaten to *kill you*?"

"Not in those words, no. But he threatened to do to me what he said he had done to my daughter, and cutting out her tongue and treating her like a slave—"

"Did he ever tell you—" Norris interrupted.

"Am I allowed to finish, sir?"

Hague objected to the interruption, and Judge Ferrer admonished Norris to allow the witness to finish her response.

Sue continued, "What I perceive as a threat is when someone tells me they've done all these monstrous things to my child, cutting out her tongue, putting her into a slavery thing, selling her to people, and then he says to me that they want to do the same things to me, and that he is going to train me, and that I am going to be his slave. Yes! I do perceive that as a threat to me."

"That's *your* perception of a threat. You define it that way?" Norris asked.

"That's *my* perception," Sue replied, and added, "I'm not a lawyer," as if indicating that Norris was obviously far too devious to define that sort of conduct as a threat.

Norris asked several questions to ascertain if Blair's

statement that he had cut out Amy's tongue was not actually voice-recorded, only written down in her notebook.

His voice became accusatory. ". . . Are there *any* conversations at *any* time where *anyone* except *you*, Susan Billig, have heard what Hank Blair said to you?"

Sue was incredulous. "Are you presuming I'm lying to you?"

"Yes!" Norris quipped.

"Well, the presumption is wrong. I don't lie."

"Good," Norris snapped. "Answer my question. Where—"

"I just did answer you."

After a bit of give and take, Sue said, "I swore to tell the truth."

"Well, let's talk about swearing to tell the truth for a moment," Norris said.

"Yeah, let's," Sue said, letting irony drip from her words.

"This is a very difficult thing for you, isn't it?

"Yes."

"Tremendously emotional?"

"Yes."

"And you're almost seventy-one years old?"

"Yes."

Norris asked whether, in that case, her faculties were good enough that "we have to accept as gospel everything you've said?"

"You don't have to accept anything I say. I'm telling you what I say is the truth."

Norris took that as an opportunity to pick apart a small statement in her journal about the Fort Pierce trip in 1979. She had written down that Blair as Hal Johnson had given her a bogus telephone number to call. On the stand she said Blair had given her only an address and not a telephone number.

Norris gleefully showed her the telephone number written in her notebooks from fifteen years earlier and concluded that her memory obviously could not be relied on to be accurate.

Besides that, the main thrust of Norris's argument was that since "Johnson" had never followed through with the meetings that he had set up with the Billigs at their Grove art gallery, or in Fort Pierce, or at the Taurus, or later at Burdines, didn't she think everything else he told her about what had occurred to Amy must be a lie?

Sue didn't agree at all. It was a quantum leap of logic at best, but Norris pressed on with his point for several questions until prosecutors objected with an "Asked and answered!"

With that, Norris concluded. His main weapon would be Blair himself, and he obviously didn't want to give the witness too much stage time.

After Sue's testimony there was a short recess in which Blair stood up and exchanged smiling pleasantries with his two daughters as if nothing strange was happening around them. The family group looked so at ease, no one just entering the courtroom would have suspected that they had just finished listening to the emotional testimony of the father's long-suffering victim.

When the trial resumed, Hague was granted a short redirect in which the prosecutor allowed his frustration with the defense to tinge his words. "Mrs. Billig, can you estimate the *number* of phone calls you received from Hank Johnson over the years?"

She shook her head. "No, I can't figure it out," she answered quietly.

"Did you tell this jury the truth when you said that Johnson said he had cut Amy's tongue out?"

"Yes, I did, sir."

"Did you tell this jury the truth when you said he said he wanted a mother-daughter team?"

"Yes."

"Is it fair to say that the only other person who would know what came in those phone calls was the person on the end of those phone calls? Mr. Johnson, correct?"

"Yes, sir."

Hague had made his point. "No further questions, Your Honor."

It was now six P.M. Sue had sat so long in the witness chair, she could barely get up, and had to limp out of the courtroom.

Sue, being the prosecution's main witness, wasn't allowed in the courtroom from that point on. Lawyers invoke "the Rule," which keeps witnesses who haven't yet taken the chair out of the courtroom so they can't modify what they're going to say. Sue could read about the case in the morning's paper and hear about it from friends, but the only time she would be able to look Blair accusingly in the eye was during her own testimony. She wouldn't even be allowed to remain in the courtroom when her tormentor took the stand, to hear his excuses in person, in case she needed to be recalled later. It was very frustrating for her to sit at home and paint her nails and clean the house while such an important part of her life went on without her.

After Sue, the prosecution's other witnesses were mainly just supporting the case. Executives from AT&T Wireless testified that under several layers of bogus companies the cell phone number with a particular serial code was assigned to Customs. Customs officials in turn had to verify that that cell phone belonged to Henry Johnson Blair.

Customs agent Walter Wilkowski testified with difficulty (since Hank was his friend) that Blair always knew what he was doing, and that while he had occasionally seen his boss drink, he had never seen Blair get drunk. Prosecutors wanted this on the record to blunt the defense's later argument that Blair made the calls because he was an alcoholic with psychological problems.

FBI agent Harold Phipps was called in to tell the jury how scared Susan had been during the calls, how long he had been hearing about them, and how the calls had been taped after the Burdines incident. He had since been transferred to Atlanta, and flew down for the trial dressed in his customary light gray suit and striped tie. He was comfortable and low-key in the courtroom, exuding a paternal aura, rather than that of a secret agent.

He told the court that each time Sue called him after she heard from "Johnson," that "she was pretty hysterical. . . . She was becoming frightened, and as time went on became even more frightened. . . . It was her feeling that he was lurking outside her home. She felt that he knew where she lived. After her husband died, the calls became more frequent. . . ."

When Blair finally confessed, Phipps said, "I was stunned. I was startled. I said, I guess I have to advise you of your rights.' " He sighed, and told the jury that arresting another law enforcement officer was one of the most distasteful things he had ever done.

Norris cross-examined the agent and asked if he had ever been in the room at two in the morning when Sue received a telephone call.

"No," the agent answered gravely.

"Did you ever hear him threaten her?" Norris questioned.

"No," Phipps answered.

"That's all," the lawyer said, making his point that everything Sue was saying was hearsay.

Prosecutors rested their case. The next day, the defense would let Hank Blair tell his side of the story.

22

The following morning, instead of beginning their defense, one of Blair's lawyers, Fritz Mann, delivered a surprising request, asking for a mistrial because a female juror had cried during Sue's testimony. This was, in some court observers' opinions, plainly a nervous reaction to Sue's powerful testimony of the previous day. The lawyers, rattled, were trying a desperate gambit.

The judge sat back in his chair and admonished the lawyer, "I am aware of absolutely no authority for questioning the jury because they are moved by some of the evidence! I don't think that there's ever a requirement to be selected for a jury and be expected to be completely unemotional or have no reaction to evidence. Jurors frequently sit there and show emotion, whether it be tears or open crying during trials. If the evidence moves them that way, then that's what it does."

Howard Rosen offered the State's view. "The analogy that I'll draw is the situation in a homicide case, where a jury may see grotesque photos that shake them up, but that doesn't mean they can't be fair and impartial in the case. It doesn't mean they form an opinion about the entirety of the case. It just means that particular thing that they are seeing at that moment affects them in one way. These people are human beings, not androids."

The judge said, "I agree with the State. Under the situation that you're describing, where a juror cannot display any emotion, is viewed as a suggestion that the juror should be disqualified in some way, shape or form . . . the most horrendous defendants, the ones in history charged with the most egregious acts, would be constantly absolved of responsibility because no jury could sit there stone-faced and listen to the evidence. I don't know of any legal authority that says that is a requirement. If you're aware of any, I'd like to hear of it."

The judge refused to declare a mistrial, but agreed that he would question the jury about whether they had heard or read news reports about the case that may have biased them. But he certainly wasn't going to question them about their emotional status.

Their daring gambit turned down, there was nothing else for the defense to do but bring on Blair. While the defendant cannot be required to take the stand—and a jury is always told by the judge that failure to testify is not an admission of guilt—the defense had some things they wanted the jury to hear from Henry Johnson Blair's own lips.

Blair took the stand wearing a charcoal suit, a white

shirt with a tight collar that made his neck cellulite bulge, and a burgundy tie with little snowflake-style designs. His speech was very "good ol' boy" style, using simple words, but—without being in the league of, let's say, Hannibal Lechter—he seemed to be hiding a higher intelligence than his speech pattern would suggest. He leaned back and frowned between questions, with his right eye twitching uncontrollably behind his eyeglasses.

A line of questioning laid a base that the defendant's upbringing, following his father from base to base, had kept him from making friends and set him apart as an outsider. He then went on to tell about every position he had ever held during his career as a Customs officer: from sky marshal to undercover officer and finally the supervisor of his marine-narcotics group unit. Who could be afraid of this valiant guy?

Finally, Blair admitted to making many telephone calls to Susan Billig. As before, he said he got her name from the *Miami Herald*, and blamed his actions on the pressure of drug interdiction work and his alcohol abuse. He tried to stop himself from making the calls, but the compulsion always came back. "As I got older, the problems became worse," he said. Eventually, he began to doubt his sanity, and even contemplated suicide, twice sticking his automatic pistol in his mouth, a hairbreadth from pulling the trigger. He referred to his arrest as an "intervention."

"I always considered myself a person of strong will," he said. "I could stay awake long periods of time. I could endure pain, stuff like this, driving boats at night in heavy seas. And basically I would try to will myself not to make these calls. But as I said, it's almost something that you don't have any control over, and it keeps coming back again and again and again. The thought process just reoccurs and reoccurs, it's stuck like a video, stuck, stuck, it runs again and again and runs by you, and you feel like knocking your head against the wall after a while."

One question brought this response: "I feel like I'm a pilot in a nosedive, and I'm trying to pull back on the lever to get it up, and I'm trying to restrain myself not do that. There's like a logical part of my brain that says, 'what are you doing . . . what are you doing?' Don't do this, you know?"

Sometimes he could restrain himself, but not always. "After the calls, there was always a feeling of shame. It's horrible, it's like getting burned, you're trying to rush away from it, get it out of your mind, and trying not to let it overpower you. And when you're with people and you get these thoughts, you wonder if they realize what I'm thinking here." He spoke in a frenzy, gesticulating with his hands, smiling crookedly and seeming to enjoy the clandestine memory. "I may look like I'm normal, and they talk to me like I'm normal . . ." He trailed off.

He said that he started using the cell phone because "it was a subconscious way to end security measures."

Most important, the defense wanted the jury to hear him declare that he never had any intention of harming Sue Billig. Now he was using the drug Zoloft, was feeling quite a bit better, and could control his compulsion and understand what had made him act so maliciously. He said Sue had twisted things in her mind, and that just by coincidence the calls that had been recorded were "the outer limits, the ultimate of the worst" things that he had ever said.

He said he had spoken to Billigs about Fort Pierce in 1979, but had never actually told her to go up there, and "certainly never would I say I would meet you there, you know?"

Blair accused Sue Billig of being an enabler. He only became so outrageous, painting the scenario of Amy's tongue having been cut out, for instance, in order to get Sue to hang up on him and stop taking his calls. "Her obsession [to find Amy] was melting into my obsession. I was trying to get her to say, 'You're crazy, get out of my life, get lost. . . . ' " When his other victims hung up, he said, he always felt a "sense of relief."

A few wrap-up questions later, Norris finished his questioning on a low note.

Hague popped out of his chair like a horse from the gate to begin his cross-examination. He was impatient, aggressive, spoke quickly, and was obviously disgusted with Blair's testimony.

The prosecutor shot out some rapid-fire questions about how many times Blair had met with his attorneys to plan his testimony.

"Seven or eight times," Blair admitted.

Through questioning, Hague sought to establish that Blair was basically doing no more than improvising from a script laid out by the defense. Hague probably

couldn't believe that the defense wasn't objecting—
there's nothing legally or morally wrong with meeting
with your council—but as long as they didn't, he kept
going.

"Now we first met on October twenty-seventh,
1995, is that correct?" Hague wanted to know.

"Correct."

"And that was at the Customs office?"

"Correct."

Now the defense objected to the former "script" line
of questioning, and asked that those questions be
struck from the record. After a sidebar, it was agreed,
and the prosecution leaped forward again.

Hague painted a picture of their first meeting and established that Blair lived within a few blocks of the
Arvida Middle School and Crossings Village Shopping
Center, where some of the pay phone calls had been
traced.

"When we first started talking, Agent Phipps wasn't
there yet, was he?" Hague asked.

Blair's eye started to twitch spastically. "No."

"When I first spoke to you, before the FBI agent got
there, you didn't know that any of your calls had been
recorded on tape, did you?"

The defense blasted the court with objections about
that line of questioning.

"Overruled."

"When I asked you if you knew Susan Billig, you
said you did not, is that correct?"

"That's correct," Blair answered.

"Now, after Special Agent Phipps arrived, he introduced himself and brought out a small tape recorder and laid out the investigation for you, didn't he?"

"I don't know if he laid it out. . . ."

"Agent Phipps told you that he had you on tape and asked if you wanted to listen to the tape, didn't he?"

"Yes."

"And you declined, and he asked you if you knew who made the phone calls, and you said 'Yes'?"

"Essentially, correct."

"Isn't it a fact, Mr. Blair, that when you first told Special Agent Phipps that you made the phone calls, you admitted to doing it for the last two or three weeks, initially?"

Blair thought about it for a minute, seemed to realize how bad he was about to look, and leaned forward to the microphone. "Let me say this. The two or three week part is a blur, I don't know if I said it or not."

"Isn't it true that later on in the interview you said you'd made the calls for five, six, or seven months? Isn't that correct?"

Blair leaned forward again. "Counselor, there's a point where I remember saying something, but again, I was in total, total shock. And I'm not trying to dance around your question, but I don't recall that part, all right?"

"You don't remember whether you said it was five, six, seven weeks, then you changed it to five, six, seven months?"

Blair didn't remember.

"Do you recall when you admitted making the calls for a year and a half, two years?"

Here, Blair nodded. "I remember that, yes."

"That wasn't the truth, Mr. Blair, was it?"

"Yeah, it was the truth, I had called the last eighteen months, certainly."

"But it wasn't the whole truth. Because in actuality, you'd been calling a whole lot longer than that? Isn't that true?"

"Yes, I had been calling longer than eighteen months."

"So you were minimizing your involvement, weren't you?"

Blair leaned forward, nodded and sighed. "Was I minimizing my involvement?" he asked thoughtfully. "Again, let me say this. I was in total shock. I admitted making the calls. I remember saying eighteen months. Did I have a desire to trick you at the time or anything? No, I don't think that's accurate."

"So when you told me originally that you didn't know anything about Mrs. Billig . . . you didn't have any desire to throw me off then?"

There came a long period of give and take, with Blair admitting again to making the phone calls as far back as 1979, the first time his pseudonym of "Hal Johnson" appeared in Billig's notebooks, but wouldn't admit to any earlier calls than that. He admitted to calling from pay phones and from his cell phone. A lot of material from previous testimony was regurgitated without any real point except to get certain facts on the record. Hague let Blair ramble on a bit, while the lawyer studied his notes.

Then Hague went into the content of the phone

calls, and made Blair explain the ploys that he had used to keep her from hanging up on him, such as how he kept dangling a carrot in front of her by promising to reveal more facts.

At one point Blair said that "technically" he really knew very little about the Billig case.

"But you knew enough to dangle hope in front of Mrs. Billig, didn't you?"

"Well, let me say that I never had a preconceived notion that I was dangling hope in front of somebody. . . ."

"You knew that Mrs. Billig was looking for her daughter?"

"Yes."

"You knew that she was turning over every rock in search of her daughter?"

"No, I didn't know that."

"But you knew that she wanted to find her daughter."

"I knew that she was missing and that it was a mystery, and that she was interested in pursuing it."

Blair would begin sentences, cut himself off and start on another tack. He peppered his dialogue with "you know" and "like this," would repeat phrases a few times before continuing. Finally he accused Billig of "just altering things in her mind, too," and of misreporting things in her diaries, though he did admit to calling her at least a hundred times. But again he accused Sue Billig of wanting to hear from him because she was obsessed with the search and didn't "want it to end."

He said he really wanted to be caught, and even once

sported a beard, which he shaved off after he started using the cell phone to call her. "I was just tired of hiding. I figured sooner or later . . ." he would be apprehended.

Hague countered that this statement was ridiculous because the cell phone was registered to a dummy corporation, which offered complete anonymity. Blair said it never fooled the Colombian drug dealers, who had great counter security measures. "We were hoping it would work, but you were about the only person it defeated."

During one heated exchange, Blair insisted, "There was no preconceived notion of intent to harm or harass. And certainly there was *never* an intent to threaten!"

"You learned about that being an element of the crime since you were arrested, didn't you?" Hague queried.

Blair leaned back, looking exasperated. "The answer most clearly in my mind—I never conceived that anyone could think that I was threatening their life. I was overcome with shame, I was in shock, and this and that, but as I said during my arrest, I thought I was making these phone calls to alleviate the pressure of these two diseases. I never had any mal thought of any kind." He continued to insist it was "a way to get rid of these demons in my head," thereby placing the blame on something besides himself.

Blair maintained that he had painted himself as "a fringe person" in the stories he had invented about Amy.

Hague jumped on that statement. "On the tape you say 'I'm' the one who trained her, didn't you?"

"Yes," Blair conceded.

"So you didn't always use the third person, did you?"

Blair pounded on the witness stand. "That was the one exclusion right there. That's what I said before, almost all the time, that was the sole exclusive exclusion at that time!"

"So the one time they got you on tape," Hague scoffed, "that was the sole time in sixteen years that you did not use the third person?"

"That's absolutely correct, counselor," Blair said evenly. During later questioning on the topic, Blair tried to bolster this argument by saying that Sue Billig had reported conversations about the slave trade in 1993 that had really happened shortly before his arrest in 1995. "If she wrote them down in 1993," he admonished, "she must be clairvoyant."

Questions designed to show that Blair knew what he was doing all the time continued to rattle the defendant, making him raise his voice as he insisted on his "fringe, third party" position, and that pressures and alcohol drove him to make the calls.

Then Hague asked, "Your feeling was that this was a game, isn't that true?"

Blair looked away, rubbing his chin thoughtfully, looking a bit like Rodin's Thinker. "You know, I guess everything's a game, narcotics is a game, an obscene game. . . ." He waved his hands and clutched his head. "Other people said the logical thing, 'Drop dead, asshole.' But she talked and talked and talked, you know."

"How many other people that you talked to had a missing daughter or a child who had never been found?"

Blair rested his head on his knuckles and thought for a moment. "None, I guess."

"And in your characterization that this was a game, did you ever tell Mrs. Billig this was a game?"

The defendant leaned back, looking satisfied. "No. But I kept throwing out things—I never said anything in seventeen years that turned out to be true. It reaches a point where in my mind I think there's almost an implied consent. She'd say things: 'I don't mean to hurt you, I don't want anything from you. Call me back. . . . ' She'd just chat along." Blair didn't realize he'd just admitted to an extra year of abuse.

"She was looking for information about her daughter, wasn't she?"

"Perhaps you're right. . . ." Blair answered. Then, a couple of questions later, "You know, I think that's the primary thing, but I don't think it's the only thing. Like I told you before, there comes a point where she's just wrapped up in the obsession to the point that, you know, the obsession is ruling, you know."

"She should have just kissed off the search for her daughter and forgotten about it?"

"You're putting words in my mouth, counselor."

"I'm not trying to put words in your mouth. I'm trying to understand what you're saying. You're saying she should have given up the search for her daughter?"

"I never said that, and never implied that, but that's the second or third time you're trying to put it into my mouth, counselor."

"You never told Mrs. Billig that, 'Hey look, I'm just playing a game, that I really don't have any information about your daughter, but just play along, so we can chitchat,' did you?"

They argued until Blair answered, "There comes a point that I say things that are obviously not true, she says 'Meet me, meet me, meet me,' until it comes to a point that I say 'Sure we'll meet.' She says 'Show up here on a certain day,' and I never show up. And there comes a point over a period of years she's got to say there's nothing here. She is as big an obsessive as I am. We're just two obsessives bouncing off each other, you know. We should both be locked up, probably!"

Hague's voice quieted. "Are you saying Mrs. Billig should be locked up for searching for her daughter?"

"No, I'm not saying that. There again you want to twist the rules, counselor. What I'm saying is this: Mrs. Billig, over the years, has become obsessed, and I know something about being obsessed myself."

"You told Mrs. Billig that her daughter Amy was in white slavery. . . . You told Mrs. Billig that Amy's tongue had been cut out, didn't you?"

Blair insisted that he had come up with these visions only in the last conversations so that Sue would tell him to "Drop dead, get out of here. Preposterous!"

"She had no way of knowing whether there was reality to that statement or not, did she?"

"Well, if you want my opinion, she knew deep in her heart that I was full of bullshit! And she was playing the game for its own sake because it kept her busy, you know?"

"You told Mrs. Billig that *they* wanted a mother-daughter team, didn't you?"

"Yep."

"And that *they* had Amy, and now *they* wanted *her*?"

Blair put his face down and rubbed his forehead. "Yep."

"You said they had seen her and they wanted a couple of generations of nipples to play with?"

Blair conceded that he had said something like that.

"You never said, 'I'm full of bull, ignore me,' did you?"

"I never said those words, you're right. I tried to say it indirectly, I guess."

There was a long exchange focusing on other matters, where Hague asked a couple of questions which elicited long, rambling answers from Blair about Customs procedure, and how Blair dealt undercover with Latin American smugglers. Lawyers often rely on tactics like this to get the witness off guard and talkative before jumping back in with another question on topic.

Now Hague resumed questions on Blair's conduct. "Over the years, you didn't think it was malicious to tell the mother of a missing girl that her daughter was being used as a sex slave?"

"Answer, no . . . As I advanced in these twin diseases, did I have any actual knowledge that I was hurting her, that I could actually say consciously, 'Hank ol' boy you're hurting this woman'? No, I never came to that final thing. I didn't rationalize it, because I wasn't capable of rationalizing in this direct area." His hands gesticulated like a wounded bird trying to make a get-away, fluttering crazily this way and that.

"But you were capable of rationalizing for all your work decisions and phone calls surrounding the calls to Mrs. Billig?"

Again Blair argued that he could change back and forth instantly, be logical one moment for his job but completely out of control the next minute to converse with Sue Billig.

"So you were able to step out of your alcoholic state to handle work calls, but step back into it again for the purposes of making calls to Mrs. Billig?"

"No," Blair said, contradicting his statement of moments earlier. He insisted that he would never have physically harmed Billig.

Hague asked, "You would just call her for sixteen years, tell her that her daughter was being used as a sex slave, that her tongue has been cut out, that she is being sold overseas, and that they wanted a mother and daughter team, but that's as far as you would go?"

Blair was rattled. "I'm trying to answer. Maybe if you stopped bounding around and slugging on me, maybe I could, you know?"

Finally, Hague read back statements from Blair's earlier deposition where he had admitted to telling Billig to "Watch out!" But Blair said he "meant that in a good sense." It was advice for her to be wary.

"I wasn't trying to warn her or threaten her. It wasn't even a conceived thought right there."

"You just wanted to tantalize her about what had

happened to her daughter and what was going to happen to her?"

"Not at all, counselor! You're just twisting and putting words in my mouth there!"

Judge Ferrer had listened to enough. "Are there any further questions?"

"No, Your Honor. No further questions," Hague replied, and sat down at the prosecutors' table.

23

Cynthia Blair, wearing a woman's business jacket over a button-down white blouse, took the stand next, and came across as an astounded wife. "The only calls that I knew that my husband was making were family calls. Over the last three to four years I began to suspect that something was happening because my husband seemed to withdraw. I used to ask him frequently if he was having an affair."

Howard Rosen questioned Mrs. Blair for the prosecution, asking if she had ever seen her husband as drunk as he claimed to be during the telephone calls.

Cynthia shook her head, and replied in hard staccato words—like a parent trying to admonish an unruly child at a store. "I've never seen him falling down drunk, Mr. Rosen. No, *I have not*."

"Well, he was always able to function as a parent, right?"

"He wasn't there a lot of the time, *Mr. Rosen*." Spoken with impatience.

"But you never saw more than one or two beer cans?"

Cynthia answered that she herself had once been addicted to prescription drugs and so should have recognized the symptoms. "I thought about alcoholics like my father, and he was a mean drunk. I never saw any of that in my husband."

The week-long trial progressed to final arguments on a particularly auspicious day—a day that Hague made sure the jury noticed. . . .

"Twenty-two years ago today, March fifth, 1974, a seventeen-year-old girl named Amy Billig walked out of her home in Coconut Grove, and she has never been seen or heard from since. For the last seventeen years, by his own admission, *that man*"—he pointed—"has been calling the mother of Amy Billig—Susan Billig—and dashing her hopes and dreams of finding her daughter, and preying on her disappointment and heartache over her lost daughter. Yesterday, the defendant took the stand and told you that he wanted you to believe his actions weren't intentional. *Give me a break*, ladies and gentleman. You heard the evidence!"

He reiterated all of Sue's experiences searching for Amy over the years. He characterized Blair's calls as harassing and tormenting, and reminded the jury how the defendant had tried to minimize his role, and how he had blamed Sue Billig for accepting the calls.

"He was like a vulture that circles the pack looking for a wounded animal. He saw Mrs. Billig as that vulnerable individual that he could prey upon, and he did prey upon her. For years and years and *years*. We're not talking about a couple of months. We're talking about *years*. When Amy disappeared, President Nixon

was still in the White House. That was six presidents
ago . . . 1974. And by his own admission he has been
calling since 1979. . . . The defendant's calls were
cruel, they gave her false hope, which were then
dashed, and then he hung the carrot out again. . . . Over
the years [the calls] became more and more frequent,
and they became more and more violent about what
had happened to Amy. And then they became threatening to Mrs. Billig, telling her what would happen to
her, describing what had been done to Amy, and that
the same thing would happen to Mrs. Billig. . . ."

Hague explained that the jury did not have to consider the calls in a vacuum and could consider "what
was reasonable for [Mrs. Billig] to believe under the
circumstances; and the nature and the context of what
was being said by *that man* for those decades."

He reiterated many of the telephone calls, especially
the ones that were taped. "He picked her out because
her daughter was truly missing, and he was able to torment her with specific information. Mrs. Billig had no
way to know whether he was making it up or telling
the truth. The defendant said he read the newspaper to
get the information. He didn't get that information by
reading the sports page and calling the person who
won the five-hundred-meter dash or whatever it was
and call them. He picked on somebody who had gone
through a personal tragedy, so he could gain whatever
satisfaction he gained from those conversations."
Hague was emotional and angry, smacking his fist into
his hand.

He continued: "The defendant could have no other
intent than a malicious one. And it's ludicrous to sug-

gest otherwise. Listen to the defense's counsel as they
give you their closing arguments. See what creative explanation they give you as to why this is not aggravated
stalking. But again, ladies and gentlemen, use your
common sense, and I submit to you that at the end of
the case you will go into that room and find that this
defendant is guilty, not of misdemeanor stalking, but
of the charges of which he is charged in the indictment,
and that is aggravated stalking. You have taken an oath
to follow the law, and that law will take you to the con-
clusion that this defendant is guilty as charged. Thank
you."

Bill Norris took the podium and outlined his argument,
speaking in conversational tones, telling the jury that
there was no question that Sue was obsessed with finding her daughter, and asked "whether this is a healthy
obsession of a mother who simply wants to find her
daughter? Or whether this is an unhealthy obsession
driven by guilt of her own irresponsibility of letting her
daughter hitchhike through a town that was occupied
by a biker gang? Because what it is that drives [Sue]
Billig, what her particular obsession is and has been, is
going to affect what she hears and is going to affect
what she tells you."

Jury members looked doubtful, but Norris forged
onward: "You've also gotten to know in this trial to a
surprising, or unusually high degree, you've gotten to
know the defendant, Henry Johnson Blair. You've
learned that Hank Blair is very much a modern American centurion. He is a warrior who has spent his adult
life protecting our borders to make this country safe."

He painted Blair's career as that of a hero who gained greater and greater responsibility until finally "this warrior was struck down. And the irony is that he was not struck down by a Colombian narcoterrorist bullet, but he was struck down by the stress of his job, of his occupation, filtered through his own abuse of alcohol, and filtered through a psychological problem that he didn't understand, that all he could understand, all that he could see of it, led him to believe that he was going crazy. And his struggle with this perceived insanity, with his psychological problem, led him to contemplate to the point of actually putting his service weapon into his mouth on two occasions—led him to contemplate suicide."

He admitted sympathetically that the case was tragic, from Amy's disappearance through Hank Johnson's calls, but declared, "[Sue's] obsession to find Amy, and Hank Blair's sickness, fed off of each other. She could not let him go because she was obsessed that maybe he had information. And he could not force her to make him go away, which is what he wanted, because of her obsession, so his sickness continued. . . ."

He told the jury that the prosecution had not established "credible threat" against Susan Billig. In order to convict Blair of aggravated stalking, the jury had to believe beyond any reasonable doubt every word that Billig had told them. Norris got bold, saying that as far as the taped conversations were concerned, they should listen to them carefully and "if you find on those two tapes, on either one of them, that this man here, Henry Johnson Blair, threatened the life of Susan Billig, threatened bodily harm to Susan Billig, then come right back out—come right back out and tell the judge that he is guilty. . . ."

Norris highlighted Blair's argument that he played his role as an outsider to the terrible things that had happened to Amy, and also stressed parts of Sue's previous testimony where she had difficulty remembering facts to answer his questions. He said Sue was "very facile with her answers, but very cagey with her facts," and questioned her version of the many conversations. He insisted that the evidence did not support aggravated stalking and accused Sue of making up "something that points the finger at Hank Blair."

He continued, "And ladies and gentleman, that's not good enough in this country, no matter what you think of how despicable, how sick, how wrong-headed, how unforgivable what the defendant may have done in this case, and no matter how you may feel about Susan Billig and the heart-wrenching agony that she's been through because she let her seventeen-year-old daughter hitchhike through a town full of bikers, that's not proof beyond reasonable and to the exclusion of a reasonable doubt. . . ."

He told the jury to listen to the tapes and convict his client if Blair had threatened Billig. "But if the only peg you have to hang a hat on is Susan Billig's testimony, then do the right thing and acknowledge if you try to hang your hat on that peg, it's going to hit the floor, because that peg isn't enough to hang your hat up in the air—and come back with *not guilty* on the aggravated stalking counts—all three of them."

The judge would also instruct the jury that they could convict Blair of a "lesser included offense," a misdemeanor stalking count, so Norris argued that his client should not be found guilty on those counts, either.

He summed up his argument: "You know that Hank Blair's family has been supportive of him, notwithstanding what he's accused of, and I ask you in this case to let him return tonight with his family to his life, what's left of it after the crash of this tragedy in his life, and go home and get on with the rest of his life and continue dealing with the psychological problems and the alcohol problems that he has. . . . I thank you."

Norris took his seat, and Hague replaced him at the podium again. The prosecution always gets the last word.

The prosecutor told the jury that they could never go back in time to discover what happened to Amy, but they could "address what has happened in seventeen years by the admission of the defendant to Mrs. Billig and the phone calls she received from *that defendant*!" He jabbed an accusing finger at Blair and continued, "They get up here, and from what I understand, they wrap him in the flag and say he's a centurion, an American centurion protecting our borders!"

Here, his voice modulated: "He's been making phone calls to Mrs. Billig for almost as many years as he's been with Customs. Basically it was a plea for pity, feel sorry for him. He got up and took the stand and gave you that self-diagnosed psychobabble and tells you, 'Hey, if I'm guilty, I've got these problems.' His wife said she never saw him out of control. His coworker who worked very close with him said he never saw him out of control. He didn't drink too much! And [Blair] was very pleased that they 'never questioned my judgment, they never said he's intoxicated, he made a bad decision.' "

Hague produced the visual aid showing how Blair was cognizant enough to take calls from work between the supposed drunken calls to Mrs. Billig. "The defense told you, 'Don't believe Mrs. Billig, she got up here basically and *lied!*' Said that to *her face* and continued to make her a victim by calling her a liar on the stand! What is her motive to lie? If she truly had a motive to lie, wouldn't she get up here and say, 'He told me he was going to slit my throat! He told me he would shoot me with a gun. He told me they were going to skin my hide.' She got up there and told you what was said. . . . The defense told you. 'Don't believe her, she's the only witness.' " He wagged his finger. "He did concede the fact that what Mrs. Billig did describe constituted aggravated stalking. Credible threats . . ."

Hague told the jury that this was a crime that had been committed between two people on opposite ends of the phone. It wasn't the type of crime that has witnesses. He reminded the jury that the defendant had admitted that he told Billig that he said "they" had cut out Amy's tongue, wanted the mother-daughter team, and other threats. "How can the defense go back and tell you it didn't happen, when their own client is telling you that it did!" After reiterating some prior testimony, Hague made the point, "In order to buy the defense's theory there was no credible threat," the jury had to believe "that being abducted into white slavery for the purposes of forced sex is not bodily injury!"

Hague was theatrical without going over the top, modulating his voice, sometimes to a whisper. Perhaps he had listened to some tapes of the famous defense lawyer Gerry Spence, who is a master of his voice. It helped that Hague obviously believed the defendant needed to pay for his crimes. "Yesterday, the defendant, again on the stand, said, 'Gee, you know,' back to his psychobabble again . . . 'she played into it all, maybe the two of us should be locked up!' " Hague was incredulous at the quoted statement. "What crime did Mrs. Billig commit? Answering the telephone in hopes of finding her missing daughter? Hoping to solve the riddle that had been gnawing at her brain for twenty-two years? Hoping against hope that this evil person has the answer? *She* didn't commit a crime, yet she has been locked up for all these years. Afraid to go out of her house, not knowing where her daughter is, being tormented time and time again from the phone calls from this defendant."

He sighed, took a moment to compose himself, then argued that Blair's telephone calls had to constitute a credible threat and a crime. "Defending one's country does not give him the right to put Mrs. Billig through hell. And that's what he did. How dare he [Bill Norris] try to say during his closing argument that because [Blair] was an American centurion, this protector of our shores, that that gives [Blair] the right to do what he did!"

Hague told the jury that the judge would instruct them that Blair's argument of insanity and alcoholism, and "the devil made me do it," should not be taken into account. "What's next?" he continued, sitting in the witness chair and mimicking the defendant. "Don't find me guilty because it's a bad hair day? Too much caffeine, can't find me guilty!" His speech dripped with disgust.

After several more minutes, Hague told the jury that after they reviewed all the testimony, they had to "remember the facts, remember the threats, remember the background. There is only one verdict for you to return on those items, and that is that this defendant is guilty on aggravated stalking on all three counts. There can be no other lawful verdict. I thank you for your kind attention." He swung away and picked up his files.

"Thank you, Mr. Hague," Judge Ferrer said.

After a break, the judge gave the normal jury instructions: that they should basically look at the evidence, make a determination on conflicting evidence, elect a foreperson, and the many other technicalities. The two alternate jurors were dismissed before deliberations began. Six would go into the room to decide the fate of Henry Johnson Blair, who slouched at the defense table twiddling his thumbs.

24

If Hague and Rosen felt confident of their prosecution
and a quick decision of guilt, it was the defense whose
hopes escalated with questions from the jury room.
They wanted a transcript of Blair's testimony (which
they were entitled to have read back to them in court,
but which they couldn't read themselves, as the testimony hadn't been translated into text yet); they wanted
a definition of the words "willful and malicious," as
they are used in the statute (a definition which didn't
exist); and they wanted the easel and flip charts created
by the attorneys during the trial (which, by law, they
weren't allowed). The judge and lawyers looked up the
legal terms of "willful and malicious," agreed to them
in court after a lengthy debate, and sent them back to
the jury.

The jury deliberated for five and a half hours the first
day, and well into the afternoon on the second day,
when the judge received a note:

*We have agreed on the verdict on two of the three
counts, but we cannot agree on the third count.*

How should we complete the verdict sheet based on this?

Nerves were high in the courtroom. The judge asked the lawyers whether he should issue an Allen charge, which would instruct the jury that they could indeed come to a verdict on two charges, but they must try one more time to come to a verdict on the third. Since each of the charges was so similar, this didn't look good for the prosecution.

The judge called the jury back into the courtroom and instructed them to write down their verdicts on the first two charges, then go back into the jury room and individually discuss the merits or weakness of the evidence on the third count. If they still couldn't agree on a verdict, the judge told them he would declare a mistrial on that one particular charge. Not long afterward, the jury sent a note to the judge that they were ready to declare the verdict, minus the third count in question.

Sue Billig, of course, was allowed to be in court for the verdict. She sat with an old friend, Michael Samuels, a Coconut Grove lawyer who would shortly be elected a judge himself. Various reporters and visitors also attended.

The defendant and William Norris remained in their seats as the clerk, a young, slim, African-American woman with orange hair, lots of gold jewelry, and long fingernails, read the form in a toneless voice. ". . . we the jury find that the defendant is guilty of stalking as a lesser included offense of count One. The defendant is guilty as a lesser included defense of count Two, on this sixth day of March in Miami-Dade County Florida. . . ."

Mrs. Blair and her seventeen-year-old daughter, sitting directly behind the defendant, fell into each other's arms, the young girl weeping. Blair and Norris sat stone-faced, though Blair's thumbs did stop twiddling for a moment. Hague put his head down and rubbed his forehead. It may not have been the favored verdict for the prosecution, but it wasn't the verdict the defense hoped for, either.

Sue sat in shock, her stomach in knots, in disbelief at the verdict. The sounds of the courtroom took on a homogenous roar. "What does that mean?" she whispered to Samuels.

The white-haired lawyer squeezed her hand. "The lesser counts are misdemeanor charges. One year max on each," he told her. "They can still retry him on the third count, though."

She stood up in a daze. Blair, too, stood, never once letting his eyes fall on Sue. His daughter threw her arms around his neck and hugged him close. He kissed her teary cheek, telling her everything would be okay, then kissed his wife on the lips.

The bailiff fingerprinted Blair. He took off his tie, his wedding ring and watch, gave them to his wife, hugged her again, wiped the tears gently from his daughter's cheek, and was taken into custody.

As Cynthia and her daughter made their way down the hall outside the courtroom, television cameras assaulted them. The seventeen-year-old screamed, "We've suffered enough! Can't you guys leave us alone? God!"

A female African-American jury member told reporters that she had not felt that the calls were life threatening, but that "I just didn't want him to go free and nothing happen to him, because I believe he should've paid for what he did to this lady."

Two weeks later the court resumed for sentencing. Blair stood in front of Judge Ferrer in an orange jumpsuit, looking humbler than the last time he had appeared in court. The judge declared that Blair would be incarcerated for 364 days on each misdemeanor count, for a total of just under two years. He pleaded guilty on the third count, which Susan Billig agreed to, for which he received five years probation and counseling.

The judge brought Billig up and asked if this sentence was okay with her. "I mean, I'm only interested in accepting this plea if it's okay with you," he said.

Sue, ever the one to turn the other cheek, said, "Absolutely, that's the way I feel. I don't want to hurt anyone any more than they have to be. . . ." Outside the courtroom she told reporters, "The family is ruined, and I feel very sorry for them. I feel I can sleep through the night now, and my son doesn't have to circle my house with a weapon anymore."

Sue waved the cameras away and walked over to where Cynthia and her daughter were standing away from reporters. As the click of her heels echoed in the hall, she knew she probably wasn't welcome. But she, of all people, knew what it was like to have a family in turmoil, and felt that she had to apologize to Mrs. Blair, to let her know woman-to-woman that no malice was intended. Cynthia, wearing a beige linen suit, was broad-shouldered and six inches taller than Billig, but

Sue had confronted massive bikers without fear, and felt none now.

"I just want you to know I don't want to hurt you, I don't hate you, I have nothing against you. . . ."

Cynthia took her hand from her pocket and patted Sue's arm. She declined to speak to reporters at the time, but later told Court TV she had "absolutely no malice toward her [Billig]. I hope she understood that I just don't think that people are disposable and we just couldn't desert him."

Sue, on the other hand, felt hurt that during the entire proceeding Blair never once apologized, and had tried to blame her for his decade long obsession. "He acted like the whole thing was a game. He destroyed my life, but acted like the whole thing wasn't serious to him."

Blair did his time in a fairly comfortable prison. He had his own room, about one-third the size of a room in a Holiday Inn, with clean, white concrete block walls, a single cot, a television, a stainless steel toilet, and, most important, a window, where he posted snapshots of his family. He was attacked and beaten by another inmate, and thereafter was confined to his room for twenty-three hours a day.

A year through his incarceration, Court TV interviewed Blair in prison. The prisoner looked haggard and had lost a lot of weight, including the fat jowls. When the reporter asked him why he had never apologized to Sue, he turned to the camera and said, "For the record, Mrs. Billig, I am sorry. I mean, I don't know what else to tell you. It's meaningless to you. But I'm sorry, there was never any intent to hurt you."

"Is that enough?" the reporter asked.

"Well, it's not enough, but what is enough?" He held out his hands. "I mean you want me to cry out the ears?"

Blair's lack of repentance would come back to bite him in the rear. Sue had entertained no further action at the time, and had never seen Blair testify on the stand. But when she heard what her tormentor had said on the stand, how he had blamed her for his illness, she decided to seek a civil judgment.

At a deposition taken October 8, 1997, just short of two years after his arrest, and after he had been in jail for eighteen months, Blair, despite what he had told Court TV, obviously felt little remorse, if any.

He disagreed with most of Sue Billig's testimony, saying, "You know, I have a lot of empathy for Mrs. Billig, but the way I look at it, her presentation is in two categories, over a period of time her sense of reality in memory is not as good as she thinks it is; and a lot of calls, a lot of people, a lot of problems, have mixed together and she is looking for somebody, something, to blame it on, and focus on; and, therefore, I was convenient, partially guilty. So she molded her story, her approach, to fit the moment."

He continued, "And then the other part of it is her own lies. She made it up because it was better for her. The only thing I can think of is she, over a period of time—she has this quest, this desire, and in order—in her own way, she's a very astute woman, very practical woman, she's learned to become a constant actress, she plays to the moment.

"She's learned how to kick the State Attorney's Office in the ass, how to get the *Miami Herald* to write an article, how to get all the news tabloids, magazines, shows . . . She has her names and she calls them up, she plays it.

"She's had to drum up this interest and so, I mean, I think suddenly—maybe not so suddenly—she has learned to couch everything for her benefit, for the drama, for the coverage, for the money she might have made, or for the coverage of everything else, she needed to have a sensational story, so she changed the facts, you know."

The lawyer asked if Blair considered himself at least "partially guilty."

"Well," Blair said, "to me it would be easiest to ask in the adverse: what I'm not guilty of, you know. I never, ever threatened her. I don't threaten anybody. I never met her daughter. I never kidnapped her daughter. In fact, you know, you might say the use of the phone is sort of like a cowardliness, a long distance. A confrontation is not what I wanted. Meeting her or anybody else is not what I wanted. . . ."

Blair said he viewed the calls as shameful, but never realized they could be considered a felony. The most, he said, "I figured I might lose my job." Asked to play amateur psychologist on himself, he said he might have subconsciously wanted to lose his job. "The job was everything to me," he said, "but it was destroying me. It was destroying my family. . . ."

"Did you ever think about what effects your telephone calls were having on her?" the attorney asked.

After all the time he had spent in jail, Blair characterized the calls in an interesting way. "To a certain extent, but you have to understand she was unique. She's the only one that perpetuated the game, so to speak, and she never seemed distressed. Like my lawyer at the time, Bill Norris, he listened to one of those tapes. He said, 'My God, the tenor of the tape, the intensity—she's breaking you!' It's almost like she was in a sense taking charge. You know what I mean?

"It's like, you know, somehow I'm sure the State Attorney's [office] got ahold of my personal college records, and my only A I made was in judo, and in judo I was a passive judo. I would go out and the person attacks, attacks, and eventually my body naturally felt the move and I would throw them and I was very good at it.

"It's the same with her," he said. "A lot of times I felt she was actually dominating the conversation and what-not, you know. 'Oh, no, no, no, I want to be sure that you understand that I want you to call back at eight in the morning,' you know? 'I have an appointment to get my hair done at eight-thirty. I don't want you calling at 8:25. I want you to call at eight sharp.'

"You understand? It's like—I mean, she was not in the role of a submissive. She gave as good as she got in our little judo stance, I would say." A couple of questions later, he continued, "I felt that she did not feel intimidated and, in fact, it was almost a contest, you know, she was playing chess, playing cards, maneuvering, so to speak. She was good."

Blair insisted that he was always polite, that he never suggested they meet anywhere, and that Billig "put words in my mouth, altered what I said," to suit her needs. Shortly later he characterized Sue as "tough

as nails. She's tougher than I am. She's very—I wish
there was a nicer way to use the word—manipulant.
She's very manipulant naturally." He said she would
have made a good undercover agent.

Did he ever fear getting caught?

". . . I had this toward the end. It was the end of the
last year, I would wait almost for that tap on the shoulder. It's almost like intuitively I knew that this was disregarding every professional ethic in the world. It was
almost disregarding instinct, you know.

"When you do that, you're on the edge of destruc-
tion. It's a matter of time before the odds would come
against you. In that sense, deep down I was waiting for
it, but consciously saying, 'Am I going to get caught?'
No, it's like a dichotomy."

During this deposition he admitted that he had
called many other women over the years and amazingly, "a certain percentage that wanted to meet and
have an affair—that was a by-product." But he said he
wasn't after that.

Even though Blair must have suspected that he
would stand to pay out a large judgment should he lose
a civil trial, his statements seemed to show little true
remorse. When asked again what he felt about Mrs.
Billig, the former agent stated, "I feel ashamed of it. I
think that, you know, I'll bear the scars and cross of it
for the rest of my life. I feel within the confines of what
I did, I have admitted. It doesn't make that right in that
I have admitted to it, and I'm sincerely sorry for that,
and I know this sounds . . . but I'm willing to pay the
piper.

"I'm willing to admit to what I did and I'll always

have to bear the scar, but I do not want to be tarnished with something I didn't do. To me, it's important people know the type of crime I was involved in and the type I will not be involved in. I couldn't have killed the sheriff 'cause I was busy robbing the bank.

"To me it's important for people to know what I did do, which was harassing. She was participating. She could have ended it like everybody else did, and for what I did to her, I'm extremely sorry."

"Did you ever tell her that?"

"No. At my sentencing I was going to say, 'Your Honor, I'd like to have a moment to speak,' and then her friends started saying this guy is a low scumbag, slimy lizard. I said, well, I might as well say nothing.

"It was my intention to tell Mrs. Billig, for what it's worth, I'm sincerely sorry for what I did, and I'll always bear the scars of it, but nobody gives a shit but me about that, but I admitted to what I did. That to me is a step toward perhaps returning to a normal life, you know. But I also feel that beyond that, she's not totally guiltless.

"She played the game, she participated, she concurred, whatever. I think the woman—she's obsessive, too, that's my personal opinion, for what it's worth."

But the most telling thing Blair said was during the middle of the heated deposition: "It even occurred to me she's not as innocent as she seems. Did she ever take a lie detector polygraph? It occurred to me, metaphorically speaking, she could have buried the kid in the backyard. . . ."

In January 1999, Blair settled Billig's suit against him for $5 million. Unfortunately, efforts to get his home insurance and other carriers to pay were fruitless. Having been forced into early retirement, even Blair's pension was a mere fraction of what it should have been. In the end the former Customs officer was ordered to pay between $6,000 and $7,500 a year.

Sue Billig says, "He never bothered to apologize to me in person, so at least, once a year he's got to sit down and write out a check, and remember it, if only for that moment."

Blair's lawyer, Bill Norris, consented to an interview, but did not return calls to set up an appointment. Blair showed up at Norris's office and picked up his file before moving his family to Tallahassee after he got out of jail. He did not respond to attempts to contact him.

At this point Sue felt as if every strange thing that could happen in her life had already occurred. She would never stop searching for Amy, but she had now followed every conceivable thread to its bitter end and had to at least admit to a truce, if never a defeat. But if she thought her life would finally calm down now, she was mistaken. The epic case was about to become even more convoluted and novelistic.

25

Many reporters and detectives secretly hoped that Blair could be tied to Amy's disappearance, as it would be an amazing end to this long case. And there were some intriguing clues that whet their appetites. When *Miami Herald* reporter Meg Laughlin thumbed through some of Amy's old diary pages, she found a sentence reading, "Hank wants me to go to South America with him. I told him he's crazy."

At the time, Hank Blair was a sky marshal on the South American route, and no one can remember any other friend of Amy's named Hank.

When Amy's camera had been found just weeks after she vanished, the one photograph it contained was of a white pickup truck parked in front of a brick wall. One of Blair's old neighbors said the agent owned such a vehicle at the time. Unfortunately, much of the early evidence in the case had been disposed of in the police property room years earlier, when a bumbling new police chief had attempted to clean house. So the old photograph was no longer available.

One of the many contacts that had diverted the Bil-

ligs over the years was a 1992 sighting by a British detective who contacted a Florida associate to tell her
that a woman named Amy Billig from Coconut Grove
had been offered to him for prostitution in England.
The Brit died suddenly, so could not add much further
information, but his lead prompted a lengthy investigation into British biker gangs, called "Travelers." A documentary crew eventually brought Sue to England to
continue the search for Amy, but were unable to find
any more evidence linking Amy to Britain. Very likely,
this began as some kind of hoax on somebody's part—
either the deceased detective or the "Traveler" who offered him the woman.

The Florida detective, Virginia Snyder, invested a lot
of energy in the case through the early 1990s, however,
and even turned up "Sunshine," the Outlaw biker
woman who had seemed to be on her way to Coconut
Grove so long ago. Sunshine, living in Orlando, was
not Amy.

Detective Jack Calvar, who had been assigned the cold
case just a month or so before Blair's arrest, began
looking back at the old bikers again. While he was handling 11 murder cases at the time, he had come to
know and admire Sue Billig, and really wanted to
bring some closure to the case. "I tell you this lady has
balls! Some of the situations she's put herself into—
well, it's amazing she's alive!" he says.

He tracked down Willow Treeland—the Seattle girl
who Sue had never actually seen herself, and had a police associate there send him a photograph. Treeland

was not Amy, either. One by one the old loose ends were being tied up.

Calvar met with "Geronimo," who told him he wasn't even in Florida at the time of Amy's disappearance. Finally the detective found Paul Branch through his criminal records. The biker had been paroled after serving a second-degree murder charge, and was living in a small town in Virginia. Branch agreed to meet with him.

Calvar flew up to Washington, D.C., rented a Grand Am, and dropped in on Branch on a dreary November day that forced the Miami agent to stop and buy a hat at a strip mall. His nut-colored skin drew stares, and he wondered if the Klan would appear to lynch him. It was a long drive through hilly farmland to where Calvar remembers "Branch was living in a trailer way out in the middle of nowhere. You had to take a dirt road off of a dirt road to get there."

The road was potholed and rocky and threatened to smash the oil pan or break the axle of the car. He navigated through two gates to get to the trailer, which was surrounded by engine blocks, mechanical debris, and a rusted pickup truck on blocks. When he finally parked in the driveway, he found the place guarded by two rottweilers and several large chows.

"The biggest dog I've ever seen, a giant chow, jumped right on the hood of the car and started growling. You know these dogs, they don't bark, they just bite."

Branch let the dogs have their fun for a few minutes before he trundled up to the door, propped himself on a cane, shooed away the dogs and motioned the detective up to the trailer.

Calvar was surprised at what he saw. He had pulled Branch's arrest record and photographs, and was prepared for a giant of a man. Instead, the old biker had layers of fat hanging from his frame, his skin covered with enormous pizzalike lesions. One eye had been amputated completely. "Skin cancer," Branch groused. "Who the fuck woulda told me I was going to get it twenty years ago? All this shit from driving a damned motorcycle!"

They leaned against the rail of the landing outside the trailer where Branch lived with a girlfriend and her two daughters. Calvar glimpsed the inside and saw a bookcase filled with videotapes, ashtrays piled several inches high with cigarette butts, and an unused mop and broom standing against the wall among what he describes as "unsanitary conditions."

Calvar, a former Navy man and a recreational biker who had rubbed elbows with a few one-percenters in his time, kept his attitude very low-key and humble. "I could see he was dying, and you don't get anywhere with these guys acting like a police officer. I just told him what I was doing and asked if he could add any information."

The interview lasted two hours, with Branch giving Calvar a very detailed account of his 1979 trip to Tulsa and getting shot by the rival bikers. He maintained that he had not actually kidnapped Amy off the street himself, but had met her at a biker party where she was being mistreated. He had taken her up to Orlando, where they lived together before he went back to jail. He described how he had given Amy and his bike to Dishrag Harry to keep while he was gone. He easily identified a picture of Amy as the girl in question.

"He was still very hard-core," Calvar says. "His memory was amazing, and he remembered details of things that had happened in 1974. But he wouldn't admit that he had actually picked Amy up off the street. He never said he'd done that."

The mean old biker, Calvar says, seemed mellow and introspective and told him, "I'm not so proud of some of the things I've done in my life, and I'm sure I'll have to pay for it."

Paul might have been sorry for "some things," but he would never admit much of the following, which has been pieced together from sources who wish not to be named.

Branch went to jail in Powhatan Correctional Center in Virginia in the early 1980s on a second-degree manslaughter charge. Facing a fifteen-year sentence, he began "snitching" on former accomplices, where sources say he was probably paid in the realm of $1,000 to $2,500 for each person who was convicted.

The biker's cancer first appeared while he was in jail, where he was operated on. His teeth were removed and the tendons in his eye were cut, which made it impossible to open his eyelid without using his fingers. Eventually, he went blind in that eye. He was soon diagnosed with Hepatitis C, and rheumatoid arthritis in his hip, spine, and legs.

His snitching paid off, however. He was paroled in

1987 after serving one-third of his time, and probably continued working with authorities to bust his former buddies.

He met his girlfriend through another inmate and began a correspondence with her. She agreed to take him in, where he apparently doted on her daughters and "was a good surrogate father" for over ten years. He lived in constant pain, however, and became hooked on Demerol. His illness progressed until he was in extremely bad shape by the time he met with Calvar.

Several months later, when the British documentary producers came looking for Branch, on Calvar's tip, they found only the biker's "old lady." She told them Paul had died two months after Calvar's interview, on New Year's Eve. But she also laid down a bombshell. Branch had made a deathbed declaration she wanted to tell them about. Fearing repercussions from Branch's associates, she claims, she did not agree to let her name or face be shown, though they were. To protect her privacy we'll call her "Tootsie." Whatever the case, her words would make international news.

But were they really true?

The producers flew Sue up to Washington, D.C., then drove to the small Virginia town, where they met Tootsie at a gas station. Sue thought, Oh my, another character! The middle-aged woman had curling neck-length hair, a wide face, wore glasses but no makeup, and a long-sleeve flannel shirt. She looked completely harmless, except that she had a Magnum .357 stuck in her belt.

They drove to Tootsie's trailer, where they set up the cameras in front of a dinner table. Tootsie took Sue's hand and told a story which she characterized as Paul Branch's deathbed confession.

She said Amy and a girlfriend showed up at a Pagan's biker party in Miami, where "the drunker she got, the more drugs she did, the mouthier she got with this fella. And he got upset." She said the biker lost face when Amy "got to running her mouth to this guy. He got very upset and started knocking her around." She stopped, worrying about Sue.

Sue told her to go on, she could take it.

"He started passing her around to these different guys," Tootsie said. "The more she would be with these fellas, the madder she was getting. And the mouthier she was getting, the more she was getting knocked around. Basically, what I was told really killed her was an overdose, she was doing drugs on her own free will before, and it was just a party and everything was fine until she started mouthing off. He didn't tell me directly what happened to her body, but he did make mention many times of how it was so uncivilized in Virginia, because they didn't have anywhere to hide the body, in other words they used the alligators in the swamp. He used to say things like, 'It scares him to think of things like that, that happen to women. Women are such victims and they have no real sense of danger until it's too late.' " Tootsie was implying that Amy's body had been cut up and fed to alligators in the Everglades.

With this image in her mind, Sue finally broke down

and cried. Even the producer reached across the table to pat her arm.

Sue questioned why, if this was true, Branch had contacted her so early in the investigation, and driven all the way to Tulsa, where he was nearly killed looking for Amy.

Tootsie said Paul had just been leading Sue on to get money.

And most amazing, she told Sue that Amy was killed "the first night," the same day she disappeared, which was supposedly "the night of the party" which Paul had attended.

Jack Calvar and others were eager to accept this explanation. It put to rest a mystery begun a quarter century earlier. Dying declarations are considered highly reliable by law enforcement and the courts; as there is no reason for a person to lie when they are going to the grave, so many people unburden their guilt held for a lifetime.

But Tootsie now claims that when the producers brought her into the car, they paid her two hundred dollars, which she says she put toward Branch's funeral. Most news organizations will not pay for an interview because it tends to make people enhance their stories, to make what they say "worth" paying for. And Tootsie is no exception. Now she admits that this information was no dying declaration at all, but gleaned from things Branch told her after Calvar's first interview.

After several letters back and forth, Tootsie wrote Sue that "I just wish I'd of talked to you and not a camera. The part [the producers] played in this was monetary and not in keeping with what I consider real concern for you or your feelings. Or for my safety." She insists that the producers promised that her identity would not be revealed, even though it was. Now she carries her gun at all times.

Further indication of the producers' manipulation was shown at the end of the documentary, where they taped Sue mourning at the family gravestone where Ned is buried and Sue's own name appears. The producers asked Sue to have Amy's name inscribed on the gravestone, reading, "Amy, January 9, 1957–March 5, 1974."

Josh was incensed. "I couldn't believe they made her do that, and then had her go out there in the rain so they could get a final shot."

So basically, Branch's confession was not a dying declaration—it was told second hand, by someone who accepted money for the interview.

Attempts to reach the producers for comment proved unsuccessful. Phone numbers have been changed and were not answered by man or machine. One producer died in September 2000.

More questions come immediately to mind.

How did Amy get sidetracked to this biker party by a girlfriend when she was on her way to meet her father and her friends—alone? How did Paul identify Amy's appendix scar, which had never been reported? A girl dies at a party, after which there is widespread media coverage looking for her, and no one ever picks up a phone to say she's dead and gone, including the so-called girlfriend who brought her there?

If Amy died that same day, what about all the sightings? Casey Lange saw her in the biker bar in Fort Lauderdale. The Majik Market owner identified Amy in Kissimmee. Sue found hair matching Amy's in the brush in the Kissimmee apartment. Why would Paul lead Sue all the way to Tulsa and nearly get himself killed if he knew Amy was already dead? Okay, so he got some free legal representation, and meager travel expenses, but the Pagans had lawyers on the payroll, and it was always easy for bikers like Branch to make money by selling or transporting drugs and guns, or by pimping. And even now, his Miami lawyer Rex Ryland remembers that Paul had a stable of girls. Branch was also an "enforcer" who could earn money by breaking bones or even by killing or snitching. Squeezing a few bucks out of an ever-broker Billig family just wasn't very cost effective. And his last telephone call to Sue, giving her the Seattle tip, was initiated by him out of the blue and earned him nothing.

The party story holds about as much water as your standard sieve.

It was obvious that this story was put together by someone who did not know the details of Susan's adventures. Calvar and several detectives before him had been looking for Pompano Red, Branch's roommate and best friend, for years. When I interviewed Calvar shortly after the Blair trial, he told me, "I heard Red had cancer. He's probably dead."

Half that statement was true. Red survived throat cancer and was living in a modest two-bedroom CBS house in Hollywood when I found him.

The old biker would no longer scare anybody. The meat was wasted from his body, leaving skin and tat-

Greg Aunapu and Susan Billig

toos hanging in leathery folds around his bones. A throat operation made his words sound like someone shoveling gravel. At sixty-five, the bones of his chin, nose, and cheeks bulge against his skin like an aged Popeye. During our conversation, he drank cup after cup of instant coffee, mixing it with tepid water from the tap, and paced from room to room, sometimes disappearing for several minutes at a time, then reappearing again to talk after his temper simmered down. He cleaned the counter almost obsessively, maybe a holdover from his life as a U.S. Marine before his biker career. Despite his appearance, his mind was keen, and his manner educated, even though he tried to talk like a biker.

"Paul was the meanest son of a bitch alive," he said. "He'd just as soon kill you as look at you." He described an event in a bar where a fellow biker gave Paul a bad look. "Paul just took his gun out, put it to the guy's head, and pow-pow!" He mimicked a gun with his hand. Paul and his friends tried to hide the body in a Dumpster. In the end, Branch went to jail for that particular crime, and Red did time as an accessory.

And Red remembered Amy well. "She was Paul's girl," he said, "no doubt about it." He said he knew people were looking for her at the time. In fact, he admitted, "I drove her to Arlington, Virginia, in my van."

He was hazy about exactly when, as it really meant nothing to him at the time, and these guys did a lot of drinking and drugging. But he had nothing to gain by admitting he transported a kidnapped girl across state lines.

What was she like? Did she say anything? Did she know who she was?

"She was not lucid," Red said. "She was out of it. Drugged up and hardly said a word." Bikers didn't look at women as someone worthy of conversation, either. One thing he insisted on, however. He believed then, and still believed now, that Amy was a runaway, and not a kidnap victim. In Virginia he gave the girls to another biker, who "brought them up to New Jersey."

Finding Red was very important to the story because he was the only one alive who admitted seeing her, speaking with her, and being in such close contact with her, making the identification at a time when the story was still fresh. His account conclusively dispelled any lingering suspicions that Hank Blair's obscene obsession stemmed from a guilty conscience.

Here is the story the way I see it: Paul, just out of jail, with little cash in his pocket and no woman, was cruising through Coconut Grove on that balmy afternoon with his fellow Pagans or even riding with Outlaws, with whom he had a relationship. He picked Amy up off of Main Highway (either by force, or by what she thought was an innocent lift), drugged her with pills, as the bikers were known to do, and spirited her up the highway.

Branch was one of the arguing bikers in the bar where Casey Lange spotted Amy.

Paul hid out in Orlando and may have even called himself Creature at the time, where he may well have helped the Outlaws set up his Pagan brothers for the kidnapping and murders. That's when Amy became the mysterious Majik Market customer who bought vegetable soup and crackers. When Paul had to go back to jail, he sent his bike and girls—Amy and the other one—with Red, to hook up with Harry. Pompano Red couldn't keep them, because he was going back to Homestead.

Amy survived for a time, and was probably in New Jersey when Miami lawyer Martin Blitzstein said he located her there. By then she had probably witnessed too many crimes, had too much knowledge of the bikers' illegal activities, and may have remembered her kidnapping when the drugs wore off, for the gang to let her return to her family. Since the case was so well-publicized, they probably sent her out West into hiding until the heat subsided, as it always did.

But Sue Billig never quit or allowed the story to cool. At some point someone, somewhere, decided that Amy was too much of a liability. She may even have died of an overdose, as no human body can stay drugged for so long without suffering any consequences.

No doubt, the overwhelming majority of the sightings described in the thousands of letters and telephone calls to *Unsolved Mysteries* and other leads were cases of mistaken identity. Every day I see gorgeous young girls walking down the sidewalk, in animated conversation with friends, who I would easily swear were Amy if I were a well-meaning citizen who had only seen her photograph in a news story a day earlier.

But could every letter be a mistake? Even the ones from bikers? Branch's story at the time, which he told many people over and over again and repeated to Calvar years later, combined with Pompano Red's recollections, mesh too well with other known facts.

While Sue now regrets having etched Amy's name into the tombstone, on the British producer's instructions, doing so did have one positive effect. Since Amy's disappearance, the searching mother had never been able to really live her life, or to accept the possibility that Amy no longer walked the earth. The sight of Amy's name written into the marble has provided the closure she needed.

Sue even hosted a memorial at her home, shortly after the documentary was filmed, which was attended by many of Amy's old friends, family friends—now some of Miami's most respected judges, lawyers, journalists, and musicians—something Sue never could have done earlier.

On-the-job reporters were barred from the party, but Sue, ever her warmhearted self—and grateful for how the media had kept the story alive for so long—couldn't bear seeing the camera crews broiling in the sun. She brought the newspeople cold drinks and said a few words into the cameras so they wouldn't have to leave empty-handed.

Far from a sad party, the memorial was cheerful, upbeat and even a triumphant moment for Sue. "I don't know if Amy would have been a star," she says. "It takes more than just talent to make it. But wonderful things were in store for her. She was a person who enjoyed life so much, she was awed by the sheer joy of being alive. I can feel some of that again."

The memorial was also a healing moment for the community. For the past twenty-five years, Amy's vanishing had haunted the streets of Coconut Grove, a mysterious, shadowy presence flitting just below the surface of conscious thought. How many times did drivers ponder her whereabouts whenever they crossed the intersection of Poinciana and Main Highway, where Amy was last seen? How many times did her friends do a double take when a doe-eyed, dark-haired girl crossed their peripheral vision, only to see it wasn't Amy? How often did a stray thought or word bring her image to mind?

Now, Sue can attend her granddaughters' school plays without weeping, and smile and laugh with the little girls who seem to have a bit of Amy's spirit in each of them. Sue has been elected a councilwoman for Coconut Grove, and holds positions on several City of Miami committees.

"I've had this hole in my heart for so long," Sue says. "It's not healed, it's not filled, it never will be. But, to mix metaphors, I feel the page has finally turned. I can get on with my life. I can now feel that Amy isn't out there somewhere praying for me to save her."

Amy certainly didn't live a long life. But you cannot measure a life in years, because each of us is destined to enjoy different amounts of time on Earth. But Amy described herself better than anybody else ever could just a couple of months before she disappeared.

HOW OLD AM I?

Yesterday was my 17th birthday. I have lived in this physical life for 17 years. That's all it means really.

I could say I am ageless, but that's too general.

I feel different ages with each emotion. When I'm really happy, I feel young and gay. I could be 5 or 6 easily and just play. That's my free age where I haven't been conditioned too much yet by society and I can still feel good about being me and not caring what others may say or do. Innocence.

When I'm angry, I feel very tight and strong and frustrated. Like an old man that has had so many troubles and anxieties I don't know what to do any more.

When I'm lonely, I feel thousands of years old. Lost and forgotten.

Disappointed, I am a little girl who just dropped the whole scoop of ice-cream cone into the grating on the sewer.

When in physical pain, I feel young. When children are in pain, it doesn't hurt for long because they are still green and flexible.

Emotional pain makes me feel about 30 when I would have responsibilities and my own life by then. All I have is me anyway, but now I have my family still to fall back on. When I get older I'll have my own life and pain will be a heavier load to carry. Hopefully though, by then I will be more in touch with myself and will be able to deal with my pain better than I can now. Anyway, I'm working on it.

Different situations make me feel different ages, too.

At work, I feel important and older. Responsibility makes me feel older.

With my friends, who are all older than I am, I generally feel older than I really am. But with friends in separate situations I feel different ages. When I'm playing music, my flute and guitar, & singing with others, I feel absolutely ageless. I just float away and maybe I'm a fetus again in my mother's body or in-between past lives.

When I'm on the beach watching sunrise, I feel like I'm being reborn with the new born day.

Or sunset, I'm dying, yet it's a colorful and beautiful death. One to celebrate, not mourn . . .

Age is a strange word. Different ages have different connotations. Of course, any one of the feelings I've written on these pages could change with the wind, but it's just a general outlook, saying that perhaps it's more interesting to be different ages at different times.

Being one age is limiting and boring.

I just want to be.

Amy Billig
January 10, 1974

Compelling True Crime Thrillers

PERFECT MURDER, PERFECT TOWN
THE UNCENSORED STORY OF THE JONBENET MURDER
AND THE GRAND JURY'S SEARCH FOR THE TRUTH
by Lawrence Schiller
0-06-109696-2/ $7.99 US/ $10.99 Can

A CALL FOR JUSTICE
A NEW ENGLAND TOWN'S FIGHT
TO KEEP A STONE COLD KILLER IN JAIL
by Denise Lang
0-380-78077-1/ $6.50 US/ $8.99 Can

SECRETS NEVER LIE
THE DEATH OF SARA TOKARS-
A SOUTHERN TRAGEDY OF MONEY, MURDER,
AND INNOCENCE BETRAYED
by Robin McDonald
0-380-77752-5/ $6.99 US/ $8.99 Can

THE SUMMER WIND
THOMAS CAPANO AND THE MURDER
OF ANNE MARIE FAHEY
by George Anastasia
0-06-103100-3/ $6.99 US/ $9.99 Can

A WARRANT TO KILL
A TRUE STORY OF OBSESSION,
LIES AND A KILLER COP
by Kathryn Casey
0-380-78041-0/ $6.99 US/ $9.99 Can

DEADLY SECRETS
FROM HIGH SCHOOL TO HIGH CRIME-
THE TRUE STORY OF TWO TEEN KILLERS
by Reang Putsata
0-380-80087-X/ $6.99 US/ $9.99 Can

The Best in Biographies

HAVE A NICE DAY!
A Tale of Blood and Sweatsocks
by Mankind
0-06-103101-1/$7.99 US/$10.99 Can

THE ROCK SAYS
by The Rock
0-06-103116-X/$7.99 US/$10.99 Can

JACK AND JACKIE:
Portrait of an American Marriage
by Christopher Andersen
0-380-73031-6/$6.99 US/$8.99 Can

CYBILL DISOBEDIENCE
by Cybill Shepherd and Aimee Lee Ball
0-06-103014-7/ $7.50 US/ $9.99 Can

WALK THIS WAY:
The Autobiography of Aerosmith
by Aerosmith, with Stephen Davis
0-380-79531-0/ $7.99 US/ $9.99 Can

EINSTEIN: THE LIVES AND TIMES
by Ronald W. Clark
0-380-01159-X/$7.99 US/$10.99 Can

IT'S ALWAYS SOMETHING
by Gilda Radner
0-380-81322-X/ $13.00 US/ $19.95 Can

I, TINA *by Tina Turner and Kurt Loder*
0-380-70097-2/ $6.99 US/ $9.99 Can

....